Words Of My Life, Thoughts, Faith

Based on the King James Version of the Bible

Ronald Bruce Huggins
"Huggy"

Copyright © 2016 by Ronald Bruce Huggins

All rights reserved, which includes the right to reproduce this book or portions thereof in any form whatsoever. For information contact **Ronald Bruce Huggins** via email: **ronaldhuggy@gmail.com** or telephone: **313-926-0214.**

Scripture references and interpretations were derived from my reading of the *Dickson New Analytical Study Bible, King James Version,* Copyright 1973, 1971, 1966, 1964, 1950, 1947, 1941, 1938, 1931 by John A. Dickson Publishing Co. Also influenced by the sermons and teachings of a number of ministers from various churches in and around Detroit.

Library of Congress Cataloging-in-Publication Data

Front cover photo taken by Steve Harris

Cover design by Ronald Bruce Huggins

Printed in the United States of America

Written 2011-2016

Acknowledgements - I give much thanks and honor to God and Jesus Christ. Acknowledgements and love also go out to my mother Blanche Huggins, my sons Raymond and Ryan, my grandchildren Jasmine and Aliyah, Regina Thomas, my family, friends and relatives, my many Christian friends at Grace Community Church on W. Chicago in Detroit and Church of God on Joy Road in Detroit, plus some other churches, and to those that continue to encourage, inspire and support my writing or my life in general, then to Brenda Morgan, my special friend.

Introduction - In this book I have addressed and defined many words that have influenced or impacted my life, thoughts, and faith through life stories, personal observances and reflections, current events, historical information, and Bible references and interpretations. I give much thanks to all who read and appreciate my writing. Hopefully, something I have written will be a blessing, inspiration, encouragement, or learning tool for anyone needing a spiritual uplifting or maybe just a clearer understanding of some words as they relate to life and the Bible.

Hug's Words

There are words that make me happy and some make me sad
Some that uplift and inspire me while some just bring me down
There are just so many words that may hurt and some that heal
Proverbs tells of the usage of fitly and pleasantly spoken words
Those sweet words that quench and relieve our souls and bones
Words communicate meaning as we talk to each other and God
While the usage of many indicates one's degree of intelligence
So we should have a clearer understanding of the words we use
My hope is to define all words correctly and use appropriately
Demonstrating the level of my emotional and spiritual maturity
And may my words speak the truth in the name of righteousness

Hug's First Word

I have chosen *testimony* as my first word because, since November of 2010, I have given a few and sang often about God's glory and love, and that of Jesus. Testimonies center on the tests and trials of our lives, which provide the evidence, that we bear witness to. As Titus, *2 Corinthians 8:24*, we should stand before the church and offer that proof of God's love and boast on His behalf. And I certainly had a great reason for doing just that. A testimony is defined as being a statement or declaration spoken or written, or in Christian terms, a spiritual witness given by the Holy Ghost. I have been truly blessed to be a witness and have been speaking and singing before the church. Now I am presenting my declaration in written word.

On the evening of October 20, 2010, I was watching television and had quite a bit on my mind. Suddenly everything turned to darkness on my left side. My first reaction was that the lights had gone out. However, I quickly realized that I become totally blind in my left eye! I was just terrified as I ran to the bathroom to take a look in the mirror at my eyes. As I looked with my right eye, my left appeared to be out of socket and veering way off to the side. And there was no vision at all, just the darkest shiny black color that I had ever seen. I tried to push my eye back in place with no luck, as it throbbed continuously. I knew then that something had gone terribly wrong, even though I was feeling really good health wise, aside from the stress, worries, family concerns, and some emotional issues that had me a little down in spirit.

After a few minutes it hadn't cleared up and I decided that I had to do two things, pray and go to the hospital. At that moment my youngest son, Ryan, walked in and I excitedly told him what was going on. He then drove us to Detroit's Receiving Hospital, as I kept looking at my left hand to see if anything was turning visible. But there was nothing except that eerie darkness. I was so worried that I would be blinded for the rest of my life in my left eye, and certainly worried about the same thing occurring with my right. As we approached the hospital emergency doors, I had been blind in the eye for over an hour. Then something strange and miraculous happened. I still couldn't see my hand but there was a sudden bright flicker of light at the end of where my fingertips should have appeared, with a feeling of peace and calmness consuming me. I sensed God's presence and was certain that things would be okay then.

We pulled up out front and I got out of the car and ran in to the admittance desk. I told the receptionist what had happened and within a matter of minutes they had me on a stretcher heading into a room full of doctors. They quickly began undressing me and connected me up to all kinds of medical equipment, and as they were doing that I started to see shadows and then faces. I looked down and could see my hand again and was overwhelmed with joy! After a number of tests they couldn't tell me exactly what had happened and wanted to hear every detail of how I was feeling before, during and after the blindness. Then I was wheeled off to another room where another doctor would take a look at me. He performed some tests on my eye that revealed nothing wrong initially. But finally he yelled out that he had spotted something far in the back of my eye. So he performed additional tests, along with taking some pictures. He then told me that he would be leaving out for a short time but returning with a few answers.

Ryan, who was at my bedside, was near tears when the doctor returned and told me that he had some good news and some bad news. He started by telling me that I was one very lucky and blessed person. He said that someone upstairs surely had to have been looking out for me, and that if I wasn't attending a church I needed to find one and start. The blindness had been caused by retinal artery occlusion from a stroke. What he saw in the back of my eye was some cholesterol plaque that had attached itself to the nerves. According to him, it could have and should have gone to my brain where it could have possibly caused some more serious problems. However, it detached and went to a place in the back of my eye where the damage would be minimal. So the bad news, he said, was that I might just suffer a little vision loss that could be corrected whenever I went in for new contacts or glasses. I stayed in the hospital for a couple days, while they took some additional tests to make sure that there were not any more dangerous particles floating around in my veins and body that could cause any future strokes.

They found nothing to be overly concerned about, other than that my blood pressure was a little high; something I never had a problem with before. However, a great thing was that, being a diabetic, my blood sugar level was tested many times during my stay but was found to be normal. I just have to take medicine for the blood pressure and cholesterol, along with an aspirin each day and a lot of continued prayer. Plus watch my diet, of course. Then, I'm back to my two to five mile walks. The exercise is supposed to make the medicine work better in increasing the blow flow, and it helps to keep me more relaxed. But, as my doctor said, my thanks should be directed above. I knew that God was with me when I saw the light that instantly settled me down, after the blindness had me really rattled and nervous. A stroke is a serious thing, and I know people who have died or have suffered the more severe consequences of having one. I was truly blessed and couldn't wait to get back to my church and give *my testimony* in word and song, as I am a real witness and greatly blessed to be a living and healthier one physically, mentally and spiritually. My faith, trust, hope, and health are surely with God and Jesus.

I'm A Spiritual Witness

When the lights went out I became a spiritual witness
As I laid there allowing God to take care of His business
They all looked confused when I began to see my hand
But I was at peace knowing who was then in command

The doctor told me that I had been blessed from above
And we both agreed that it was truly out of God's love
Now I can give a testimony and provide real evidence
About how my darkness ended when I felt His presence

I can stand proudly before the Church in word and song
Boasting and giving my thanks before the faithful throng
For even as believers we seek proof that He's always near
So I'm presenting my declarations for all to read and hear

He Saved Me

He saved me when I was lost
He saved me when I was sick
He saved me when I was hungry
And He's saving me today

He saved me when I was angry
He saved me when I was giving up
He saved me when I was lonely
And He's saving me today

Yes the Lord saves
The Lord saves
With His loving arms around me
He's saving me today

I thank the Lord for saving me
For where else would I be?
Certainly not a good place
His love has saved me again

Words Of My Life/Thoughts/Faith

I was inspired to write about the following words. However, there are just so many more that I could have written about as well. God willing, I may do so in a future book.

A - Abiding, Ability, Abundance, Accountability, Adoration, Adultery, Advantage, Age, Altar, Amen, Anger, Armor, Army, Attitude - *pages 13 to 24*

B - Baptism, Belief, Bible, Birds, Birthright, Blackness, Blessings, Blood, Boldness, Boredom, Breath - *pages 24 to 33*

C - Calling, Cast, Changes, Cherish, Children, Choices, Chosen, Christians, Church, Closeness, Clouds, Comfort, Commandments, Commitment, Compassion, Complacency, Condemnation, Confidence, Confusion, Contentment, Control, Courage, Covenant, Creation, Cries, Crime, Criticism, Cross, Crucifixion, Curse - *pages 33 to 58*

D - Darkness, Death, Deception, Decisions, Deeds, Delegation, Deliverance, Depression, Destruction, devil, Direction, Discipline, Disobedience, Distraction, Distress, Diversions, Divorce, Doubts, Dreams, Drugs - *pages 58 to 75*

E - Ears, Earth, Education, Effort, Enthusiasm, Envy, Escape, Evil, Eyes - *pages 75 to 83*

F - Failure, Faith, Faithfulness, Falling, Family, Fear, Fellowship, Fight, Flee, Following, Forgiveness, Forgotten, Freedom, Friends, Fruit, Funerals, Future - *pages 83 to 98*

G - Gifts, Giving, Glory, Gluttony, Goals, God, Goodness, Gospel, Greatness, Greed, Grief, Growth, Guidance, Guilt - *pages 98 to 112*

H - Habits, Hands, Happiness, Hate, Healing, Health, Heart, Heaven, Help, Holidays, Holiness, Home, Honesty, Hope, Huggy, Humility - *pages 112 to 127*

I - Idols, Ignorance, Imperfection, Independence, Injustice, Integrity, Investment - *pages 128 to 136*

J - Jabez, Jesus, Job, Journey, Joy, Justice, Justify - *pages 136 to 144*

K - Keepsakes, Keys, Kindness - *pages 145 to 147*

L - Laughter, Legacy, Life, Light, Listening, Loneliness, Love, Loyalty, Lust - *pages 147 to 158*

M - Majesty, Marriage, Meekness, Mentors, Mercy, Messengers, Mind, Mission, Models, Money, Moodiness, Morals, Moses, Mountains, Mourning, Moving, Multi-Tasking, Murder - *pages 158 to 181*

N - Nature, Nazareth, Noah - *pages 181 to 185*

O - Obedience, Objectivity, Observance, Obsession, Obstruction, Opportunity, Optimism, Ownership - *pages 185 to 193*

P - Pain, Parents, Passion, Patience, Peace, Pity, Plan, Pleasure, Plentiful, Potential, Power, Praise, Prayer, Prejudice, Presence,

Pride, Procrastination, Promises, Protection, Psalms, Punishment, Purpose - *pages 193 to 223*

Q - Questioning - *pages 223 to 224*

R - Rainbows, Reading, Rebellion, Reckoning, Rejection, Relationships, Reliance, Relief, Religion, Remembrance, Repentance, Rescue, Resources, Respect, Rest, Restoration, Resurrection, Revelation, Revenge, Righteousness, Risks, Rivers, Roads, Roles, Rules - *pages 224 to 250*

S - Sacrifice, Salvation, Satisfaction, Seasons, Security, Self-Destruction, Selfishness, Self-Reliance, Separation, Servants, Shelter, Sin, Skies, Sloth, Smiles, Soldiers, Songs, Sorrow, Soul, Spirit, Standing, Storms, Strangers, Strength, Stress, Stroke, Stubborn, Success, Suffering, Suicide, Sun, Supplication, Symbols - **pages 250 to 290**

T - Teaching, Temptation, Terrorism, Tests, Thanksgiving, Theory, Time, Tithes, Transformation, Trust, Truth - **pages 290 to 300**

U - Understanding, Unemployment, Unity - **pages 300 to 305**

V - Victory, Virtue - **pages 305 to 307**

W - Waiting, Walking, Walls, War, Warnings, Wealth, Weariness, Will, Windows, Wisdom, Witnessing, Words, Works, Worship, Wrath, Writing - **pages 307 to 324**

Y - Year, Yoke - **pages 324 to 325**

Abiding - Being *abiding* means that it is everlasting, continuing, persistent, permanent, perpetual, steadfast, constant, or simply lasts for a long time, as an abiding faith. I am abiding in Jesus, and it entails much more than just *doing* Christian things, like going to church, praying, witnessing, doing good deeds, and fighting sin. It is about *being* and I am doing what God is calling me to do, but in His strength. I have an intimate relationship with the Lord that is more important than the things I do or don't do. The more I have abided in Him, the more faithful I have become. I can hear His voice clearer and have more peace in my life as I experience His presence. And Jesus tells us that we will abide in His love if we keep His commandments as He kept His Father's.

In *John 15:4,5, and 8,* Jesus tells us that we must abide in Him as He does in us. He is the vine and we are the branches, and without Him we can't do anything, for a branch can't bear fruit unless it abides in the vine. We bear fruit glorifying God, so abiding in Jesus means that God has to be inside us as we are in Him. Therefore, we can abide in Jesus, and prove to be His disciples, by drawing nearer to God along with experiencing His presence in our lives. Success is derived from the relationship that we have with God and Jesus. And *1 Corinthians 3:14* says that we will be rewarded if what we have built through an abiding faith survives. We may be assigned different tasks but with just one purpose, as *1 Corinthians 3:8* states, to do God's work while being in His will.

Ability - We should always strive to do things to the best of our *ability*, which is the power or capacity of being able to do something physically, mentally, legally, financially, morally and etc. It can be a natural or acquired skill, or a God-given talent, and we all have a Spiritual nature with unique abilities.

Our Christian faith can inspire us to be the best that we can be in all aspects of our lives, and we have been entrusted by God with certain abilities to be used in His service.

Romans 12:6 encourages us to use our abilities (gifts). It states that they are different from person to person according to the grace that is given us, and that we should utilize them in proportion to our faith. So as *12:7* states, if teaching is your thing, then teach. *1 Corinthians 12:4* says that there is a diversity of abilities but all in the same Spirit. As Christians our lives no longer belong to us. We are to take whatever God has given us and use it to the best of our ability to His glory. And God has given ability to all His children.

Abundance - *Abundance* is an extremely plentiful or oversufficient quantity or supply, and in life gives us the ability to have and do many things. God wants us to enjoy the abundance of His creation. However, most of us don't enjoy it nearly as much as we should. As Christians we have the power to attract abundance and prosperity, and manifest everything we want. The first thing is understanding that we have to learn to trust the lives that have been given us, and that any abundance that is not for everyone is a false abundance. God blesses us with abundance to be shared and is sustainable for all.

In *John 10:10,* Jesus says that He came to bring us life and its fullness, but at times we just seem to limit ourselves immensely. *Ephesians 3:20-21* tells how His power is at work in us and that because of Him we are able to accomplish abundantly far more than we could ever ask or imagine. God offers us all an abundance of grace, joy, life ,love, power, and supply. We can look to Him for what we truly desire and believe deeply that we need and deserve, along with being satisfied, as in *Psalm 36:8.*

The life you have right now is mostly the reality of your desires and feelings. View abundance not as a way to life but as a way of life.

Accountability - It has been so very disturbing over the past few years hearing all the news about the corrupt politicians and business people, along with other government and school employees in my city being dragged through the court system for various crimes. I just wonder if they have any conscience, and if they ever cared about anything other than power or greed. The one thing they most seem to have in common is that they will lie in court, under oath in the name of God, and tell even more lies when they are behind bars, or has lost lucrative contracts and well paying positions. Then they try to place the blame on someone or something other than himself or herself. Their problems, they believe, stem mostly from making simple mistakes or from people who were just out to get them. But let's face it! They just need to tell the truth and accept their *accountability*, which is the act of being responsible for one's actions. Especially since the evidence against most has proven them to be guilty of their wrongdoings.

I certainly understand that it is difficult for most to humble our selves and admit to doing things that are illegal or immoral, in court, to other people, and especially before God. The solution is to simply abstain from doing anything that you may have to worry about paying the consequences for later. However, the greater problem is that some people just have the idea that they can get away with most anything, or can always rely on others to stand behind them even if they are caught doing something wrong. *Romans* tells us that we all will stand before God's judgment seat to give an account of ourselves. So you had better confess to your sins and criminal transgressions before it's too

...r God's sentence will far surpass any jail time you could ever spend here on Earth. No lies, lawyers, loyal supporters or any amount of money will be able to save you. God knows all and sees all, and He will hold you accountable no matter how hard you try not to.

Adoration - Love given with deep affection is called *adoration* and means giving homage or worship to someone or something. In life, I see there being *observers* and *worshippers.* Observers simply admire what is taking place in their lives and around them, while experiencing few feelings of true love and devotion. And anyone can go through outward emotions. Worshippers possess an inward love of God and offer their hearts to Him. I am a worshipper and even just hearing songs about God may cause my heart to beat faster, as I think about the glorious future He has for me. Without question, He and Jesus are the only totally adequate sources of my adoration. God is perfection and can fully satisfy our instincts of reverence, and elicit the total homage of our souls.

The revealed precept to the adoration of God was spoken to Moses and reaffirmed, in *Matthew 4:10,* as Jesus told Satan that God should be adored and only He should be served. Adoration is about mind and will too. Our minds have to perceive God's perfection as being infinite and our will allows us to worship His perfection. Then as humans the adoration we feel inside will seek outward expression. We have a need to just let go with some type of physical act to satisfy our spiritual and emotional needs. In *Genesis 17:3,* when Abram fell on his face before God, it was clearly an act of adoration as a great example. And in *Psalm 25:1,* David tells God that it is He who he lifts his soul up to. David sang and danced before God, as we all can do along with showing our adoration in many other ways.

Adultery - Voluntary sexual intercourse between a married person and someone other than his or her lawful spouse is called *adultery*. I read where in a recent study, in the United States, about 10-15% of women and 20-25% of men admitted to having engaged in extramarital sex. Adultery is one of the symptoms that helps cause many divorces. One can lose most everything good in his or her life just on the account of having a single enccounter. The price to pay for adultery can be very steep as it affects the adulterer as well as those around them. Our sefish choices weaken our credibility as followers of Jesus and damage God's reputation as well. Adultery is a sin of temptation and calculating the cost of it beforehand could provide the deterrent needed, for some at least.

Exodus 20:14 lists *adultery* as the seventh of God's Ten Commandments. In *Matthew 5:27,28,* Jesus interprets it to also include adulterous thoughts and emotions, even though the physical act may never occur from them. Then, in *Matthew 5:32,* Jesus considered it to be the only legitimate grounds for divorce. With adultery on the rise in our country, its good for many that *Leviticus 20:10* isn't enforced, where it says that the adulterer and adulteress will surely be put to death for their sin. It wouldn't stop adultery here but the number of people committing it would certainly drop steeply. I read where a woman in a foreign country was scheduled to be stoned to death because of adultery, even though she knew the consequences of being caught before her actions. Sadly that is a problem with human nature and sin. At times, we just don't weigh the potential costs of our sins against the risks that are involved.

Advantage - A person is at an *advantage* when they are in a position or condition of superiority. I had an advantage over some students in school because I studied more. I had an advantage over other runners in track because I trained harder. I had an advantage over other workers on jobs because I was more focused and determined. And I am at an advantage today in my life because I have placed my hope, confidence, trust, love, obedience and faith in God and Jesus.

Job 35:3 tells me that it is an advantage if I don't sin, as the Bible defines the word as being a *profit* or *benefit*. Then according to *Luke 9:23-25*, I must deny myself and follow Jesus or lose my advantage. By giving up my life for Him, I will be in return saving it. But if I try to save my life without Him, I will lose it. Then *2 Corinthians 2:11* warns us that if we allow Satan to outwit us and we are not aware of his schemes, he gains the advantage over us.

Age - At about 10 years old I just couldn't wait to become a teenager. Then after that I was in a rush to reach the age of 21. I wanted to experience all the things that came with growing up to adulthood as quickly as possible. Life was great as I grew in my life and finally realized my faith, but then one day things seemed to start moving at too fast of a pace for me. I am at the age now where I wish that I could just tug on the reigns and begin slowing the horse of my life down. However, with that not being an option, I am viewing age as nothing but a number, as God wants me to. I am not a senior citizen yet but am a person with much experience and knowledge that may be beneficial to my children, grandchildren and others younger or older than myself. They can surely learn a great deal from listening to my stories and asking for my advice. God still has a plan and much work for me to continue doing on His behalf.

Age refers to the length of time that something has lived, and the Bible lists two types of age - a *limited period* and a *period of unlimited duration.* Lifetimes were originally very long but became shorter after Abraham, who died at the age of 175 years. *Joshua 24:29* has Joshua dying at 110 years old, while David died as an old man of 70 according to *2 Samuel 5:4.* The thing is that these men continued to work for God even at their advanced ages. He never gave them the chance to rest, retire, or stand aside for younger replacements. They were instructed to get to work and accomplished a great deal. At my present age and beyond, I am hoping to do some amazing things that I never imagined before, along with learning more about myself and continuing my Christian growth. It is said that Joshua was nearing 100 years of age when God called on him. So I too am planning on doing His work no matter how old I become.

Altar - An *altar* is any structure upon which offerings such as sacrifices and votive (expressing a vow, wish, desire, prayer) offerings are made for religious purposes. In old times the most visible sign of devotion to God was the building of an altar or traveling to one. Today a lot of churches just have a certain area that they consider to be an altar, and anyone can build their own symbolic one by just setting aside a place and time for encounters with God each day. It can even be in the driver's seat of your car, if that is where you pause daily for prayer.

It is said that the first altars were probably built of earth. Then *Genesis 8:20* says that Noah built an altar after he left the ark. The early patriarchs, according to *Genesis 12:7, 35:1,7*, built them wherever they pitched their tents. When Moses was given the law at Sinai, he was directed by God to make two altars - *the altar of burnt offering and the altar of incense.* He was also given specific instructions as to how they would be constructed, with measurements and materials, and where they would be placed, as permanent altars.

Amen - When I end my prayers I say "amen". After I give my thanks to the Lord at the dinner table, I finish by saying "amen". When the pastor at a church says something in a sermon that really hits home to me, I respond by saying "amen". Plus there are many other situations where us Christians utter the word. So I got to thinking about the true meaning of it. We know that it is a word of praise and acknowledgement but what is its origin and definition? For many it just seems to be something that they have just merely been programmed to say.

Deuteronomy states over and over that all the people should say "amen". So the word goes back to *The Old Testament,* where it says that it is a word of steadfastness and firmness where people bind themselves with an oath. Another meaning is just the words "so be it" as you are saying it as an affirmation. In *Revelation,* the Lord is called "the Amen" in being the true and faithful witness. Then in *1 Kings,* when Solomon was appointed ruler over Israel and Judah, Benaiah answered King David by saying "amen" when asking the Lord our God to declare it and be with Solomon to make his throne great.

Anger - Anger is an emotion that is related to one's perception that they have been offended or wronged and a tendency to undo it by retaliation. We all get angry, and the outbursts can be destructive because they may cause us to say hurtful things or result in physical violence. It is especially frustrating for us Christians who hate becoming angry and feeling that we have lost it. I feel guilty no matter what another person might have said or done to provoke me to anger, and may spend a great deal of time afterwards thinking about how the entire situation could have been avoided or handled differently.

The main thing to remember is that anger, in itself, is not a sin. However, it can impel us to sinful behavior. For Christians, who may have just an occasional outburst, we need do no more than turn to our Bibles. *Psalm 4:4* tells us that there is nothing wrong being angry, and that we should deal with it through meditation in our hearts and rest. Then *Proverbs15:1* tells us that a gentle answer will turn away wrath but a harsh one will stir up anger. Just think about the pained or startled expression you left on a person's face when they tried to provoke you but only received a polite response as you simply walked away.

Armor - We all like to be protected against bad things. The Christian is engaged in warfare, and we need God's *full armor* of protective covering to prevent any damages from being inflicted upon us. He both provides and bestows it, and its my responsibility, duty and task to put it on and wear it daily, along with learning how to best use the weapons provided me. I feel safer being well armed for any conflicts I may enter, gather my strength from the Lord, and am prepared to stand against the wiles of the devil and anything that may confront me. We don't have to be bound emotionally, spiritually or physically, and can overcome any obstacles that may prevent us from living more happy, successful and safer lives. Our Christian armor provides us with the ability to defend ourselves and fight back.

Paul gives a detailed description of the Christian's armor in *Ephesians 6:13-17,* but without thorough explanation many conclusions have been drawn. Through my reading, I side with the following:
The Belt of Truth - refers to honesty, integrity, sincerity and truthfulness in life
The Breastplate of Righteousness - the need to guard our heart's affections, values, priorities and desires

The Shoes of Peace - gives us the stability we gain through the personal assurance of our salvation
The Shield of Faith - the truths of God's Word that we are to place our confindence in
The Helmet of Salvation - represents a knowledge of God's Word
The Sword of the Spirit - this also represents God's truth but when used as an offensive weapon, so you have a shield for defense in one hand and a sword in the other to attack

Army - I was watching an old movie, *The Day The Earth Stood Still*. It was about a spaceship that had landed on Earth. An alien had arrived accompanied by a large robot with destructive powers. Their mission was to be a peaceful one but with a warning. Some other planets had created an army of robots to police the universe for trouble. Earth was on their watch list because of its history of wars and conflict. There was a fear that technology would reach the point to where we could begin space travel, and become a threat to all the planets that had found a way to live together in peace. So, the warning was a simple one - either the people of Earth changed their ways or face total elimination in the future. He was greeted only with mistrust, fear and violence though, and was forced to demonstrate his un-earthly powers for all mankind to witness. It was a combination moral and science fiction story, but it got me to thinking about how wonderful it would be if there was no longer a need for military armies on our planet.

An *army* is a large body of people organized and trained for land warfare. The Bible reports that a standing army dates back to the time of Saul. He was thirty years old when he began his reign, and *1 Samuel 13:2* says that he had an army of 3,000 men. Then under David the number was greatly increased. His army, according to *1 Chronicals 27,* consisted of twelve divisions of 24,000 soldiers each. Armies became mobile, in *1 Kings 9:19,* when Solomon started using horsemen and chariots. And of course, later warfare was extended to the waters and then the skies. It is believed that the early armies were supported by public funds but the soldiers probably were not paid. *Numbers 1:3* says every man over the age of twenty was required to be a soldier. Now it's a sad testimonial that armies have been fighting throughout history. There has never been a time period where there has been total peace over our planet, and most likely there will never be. But, we don't have to worry about a force from another planet coming here to stop us. We have the technology now to destroy Earth ourselves.

Attitude - We all may have a certain manner, disposition, feeling, position, etc., with regard to a person or thing that we call an *attitude.* And because of our sinful nature, even as Christians we have those times when we do something contrary to what we know is right. These are the sinful attitudes that when left unchecked can ruin churches, damage relationships, wreck marriages and destroy friendships. Take for example the shady business deal or the cheating husband. The guilty person doesn't really want to obey Jesus because their attitudes are sinful. So they go ahead and do wrongful things anyway, while summoning up all kinds of reasons to justify their behavior. Their focus is just on their hearts and not God's, and they need to repent, which is to change their way of thinking, to develop a godly attitude concerning the sinful acts and desires.

Romans 8:5-8 tells us that people who live with an attitude of sin have their minds set and will act on what their sinful nature desires. They are considered to be hostile to God, as they will not or cannot submit to His law, and their minds are set for death. However, people who live in accordance to the Spirit have their minds set on what the Spirit desires, and for life and peace. The businessman with the crooked attitude will continue to make his shady money-making deals and not worry about suffering the consequences, while the one with the honest attitude will always fight those sinful urges. And the same goes for the husbands who have different attitudes concerning being faithful in their marriages. In *Hebrews 3:12-14,* it is written that we should maintain an attitude of belief and confidence in Jesus, while offering encouragement to each other daily.

Baptism - On January 25, 1981, I was baptized so that I could become a member of Pleasant Hill Missionary Baptist Church of Detroit, Michigan, and believed that the ceremony was also to acknowledge that I was turning myself over to Jesus with the drenching symbolizing the washing away of my sins. The meaning of *baptism* has been the subject of a lot of controversy, with some even saying that it isn't essential to our salvation. Yet, in *Acts* it does say that we should repent and be baptized for the remission of our sins. *Titus 3:5 and Mark 1:4* also state that, and many denominations support that view of baptism. The thing I remember most about mine was that I was a little heavier then and was accidentally dropped instead of being immersed into the water. So, maybe the sprinkling method some churches use would have been better for me at that time.

There has been much debate concerning the meaning, modes, and subjects of baptism, but I will only discuss the timing of it here. The philosophies on when to do it may differ by church. Some say that it can be done later because it's just an outward sign of our inner grace. Others say that you need to 'grow in Jesus' to become good enough first. And then there are some that use baptism as a requirement for being allowed to join their church, as it was in my case. However, it appears that the Bible places believing in Jesus for salvation and baptism together. *Acts 2:41* tells how 3,000 people were baptized on the first day of the Christian church, only after establishing their belief. And verses *38 and 39,* made it clear that all who accepts Jesus, as their savior, will always have to come to Him through baptism.

Belief - *Belief* is the mental act, or habit of placing my trust or confidence in something, as I have done with God and Jesus. I have a conviction and acceptance that they are true and real, and my belief in them is stronger than ever. Plus I hold a strong belief in myself as being a devout Christian. It wasn't always that way as I always believed in God, and Jesus, but wasn't a dedicated follower. When faced with trouble, at times I would just try to ignore my problems or fight my battles alone. Now a true believer, I pray and look to God for His answers.

Belief entails trust, reliance and acceptance, as Jehosaphat did when he spoke to encourage the people of Judah and Jerusalem in *2 Chronicles 20:20.* They were headed into battle against Moab and Ammon, and he told them that they would be successful if they shared a belief in the Lord and His prophets. There hadn't been much hope initially as they were greatly overmatched. However, victory came as God responded to Jehosaphat's prayers of faith. The same thing can happen in our lives no matter what problems we find ourselves up against.

Bible - For many years one on my New Year's resolutions was to read the *Bible,* the sacred book of Christianity, and 2007 was no different. I had attended a church service where they were encouraging the congregation to join them in reading it over the course of the year. They, also, were handing out a reading plan, like many I had tried before. Normally, I would start off full of fire, only to cool down and then finally find the flames completely extinguished. However, this year was going to be different. I was really focused and comprehending what I was reading more than ever. Even the areas that seemed to be a little confusing or repetitous during previous readings were more clearer and inspiring. I was extremely excited and stepped up my reading pace. Finished on August 3, 2007, rather than taking the entire year to do so. Then on August 31, 2007, I completed the reading of a Devotional Bible for men as well.

Reading the Bible doesn't have to be the near impossible task that it appeared to be for me all those previous years. It requires mostly devotion, which implies a serious commitment or choice. You have to give its reading a higher priority and schedule your life around a workable plan. In 2007, I set aside a regular time each night for my Bible reading, and later included mornings. Now I feel a much closer relationship with God and Jesus, and the Bible was written with that specific purpose in mind. It has also brought about changes in my heart and life, as I have become more like the Lord in love, patience, strength, courage, holiness, joy and other ways, along with being able to minister to others. My life will never be completely without struggle, but I am better equipped and confident in my battles because of my bond of faith. God can provide the answers to all my questions and offer me a life of continued hope and peace, beginning with the Bible as His instruction manual.

Birds - Birds have always fascinated me. There appears to be so many of them and I enjoy watching them soar across the sky. They just look so free and, during the troubled times, I wish that I could join them and fly away from everyone and everything. One built a nest in the outdoor patio of my house one summer. I don't know how long it took but it was beautifully constructed out of mud, string, twigs, and straw. It was vacated after some baby birds were born and later able to fly. I watched as the mother pushed them out of the nest and they all flew away. When I saw that they weren't coming back, I removed the nest and gave it one of my sons for his science class.

I read where there are now around 10,000 different spieces of birds over the world. My Bible says that there were as many as 348 spieces found in old Palestine alone. It may also be read that birds were distinguished then as being *clean* and *unclean*, with doves and pigeons offered for sacrifice, and quails and partridges used for food. Male birds are some of the most colorful and display their colors to attract female mates. *Psalm 19:1* tells us that in the heavens we can witness the glory of God and the work of His hands in the skies. He provides signs of His presence through the beauty of nature, and we are able to observe it just by looking up and admiring all the birds in flight.

Birthright - We all have rights, priviledges, or possessions that we are entitled to at birth, like citizenship, freedom, or even the right to a secure and loving home environment. During Bible times, *birthright* referred to the special things that were awarded to the first-born son. He became the priest of the family and received a double portion of his father's wealth, along with inheriting the father's honorable title or royal authority. However, the rest of us have birthrights too, and with the death of Jesus we inherited the birthrights of such things as confidence, courage, hope, belief, faith, and the trust in God as the source of our hope. These birthrights are to be used in accomplishing God's plan for our lives, but it's left up to us to actually use them to our advantage. He won't force us to receive or keep our inheritance. Plus a birthright can be taken away by God or parents as a penalty for any wrongdoings.

Genesis 25:24-34 tells the story of twin brothers, Esau, the first-born, and Jacob. Esau grew up to be a skilled hunter, while Jacob was a quiet man who stayed among the tents. Jacob was cooking some stew one day, as Esau came in from hunting in the country. He was quite hungry and asked his brother for some of the stew. Jacob told him that he would, if Esau sold his birthright to him. Esau swore an oath and received some bread and stew in return for his birthright. So, yes we can sell off our birthrights. Many of us know people who have inherited money or homes, when their parents died, only to lose it all over a short period of time. As Esau we don't always look to the future and give in to our immediate desires and temptations. Before giving in, we should stop and pray first. Even us who are not first-borns have birthrights, as in *Jeremiah 29:11,* the Lord says that He has plans to give us all hope and a future. It's up to us to be patient and not give our futures away as Esau did.

Blackness - One person emailed me criticizing the original title of my first book, *Still A Black Man With The Lord: Huggy's Journey Of Faith.* I was told that religion isn't a racial thing. However, if this fellow writer had read beyond the title, it would have been easy to see that my book was one for all. I've heard the talk that black men stay at home while the wives and children are in church, and must admit that I know of some husbands and fathers who seldom or never attend services. Then there have been some black friends who have told me that the Bible was written for other people, and that it would be better if I concerned myself with our black causes. Even others have laughed behind my back because of the struggles I have faced recently, in spite of me being a good Christian. I could go on but the fact of it all is that I am still a black man with the Lord.

I'm a strong black man who has joined a few battles to support my race, but know whom it is who will ultimately lead us to victory. So, even in my blackness I want God at the forefront. And the battle against evil and the devil isn't a racial thing. We are all in this together. Jesus spent some of his final hours on Earth in prayer that His remaining followers would share a love for each other. There can be unity in my church, along with other churches and church leaders. The Bible speaks of *believers* and *non-beleivers*, not about black and white or other. *John 17:20-23* says that Jesus prayed for all believers and wants us all to be as one as He is with God the Father. His prayer was for complete unity, not the divisions that we continue to see between people all over the world. He loves us all as equals and wants us to share His love in peace and a global fellowship.

Blessings - Far too many people seem to ask for mostly monetary blessings in their prayers. Then others who may have much more wealth than they need continue to pray for more. The thing about monetary wealth is that it can be lost so quickly through bad investments, the loss of a job, health issues and death, and other things. It's best to pray for what you need most, and if you are wealthy pray for the things that will enable you to retain and use it in a godly manner. God listens and acts on the basis of true need, while turning a deaf ear to prayers of greed and selfishness. Mick Jagger of the Rolling Stones sings a song that says basically that you always have a better chance of getting what you need than what you want, and all you have to do is try. For us that means turning to God who blesses effort.

Many months I prayed for the blessing of a job that paid well enough for me to end my financial struggles. After my stroke I included the need for the health and strength to work once I'm blessed with that job, along with being able to continue my religious efforts and other activities. I have never limited my prayers to monetary things but even more so now. *Blessings,* according to the Bible, are divine favors and benefits, and are limitless. I give much thanks for all that are bestowed upon me, as the Bible also says that I should give recognition to God's goodness in a *thankful and adoring manner.* Like David, in *Psalm 103:1*, I praise the Lord with all my soul. Then there is reassurance as in *Psalm 129:8* it states that my blessings will always be in the name of the Lord.

Blood - *Blood* represents life and is regarded as being sacred by God. Under *Old Testament* law, Israel had to offer blood sacrifices in order to become right before God. That involved the slaughtering of animals. The blood would be spread on the altar and the animal's body was cut and burned in sacrifice. *Leviticus 16* desribes in detail how Aaron made a sin offering of a bull, ram, and goat to make atonement for himself and his household. In the *New Testament,* Jesus became the final sacrifice for us all, as His blood sets us right before God. It is a requirement that blood sacrifices be made to facilitate the removal of sin from God's presence. First it was done with animals. Later it was done by the blood of Jesus that was shed to save us from our sins, and for all-time when we place our trust in Him for eternal life.

In *Leviticus 17:11,* God tells us that the life of a creature is in the blood, and we can make atonement for ourselves on the altar through the blood. *The Day Of Atonement, Leviticus 23:29,* was designated by the Lord to be the tenth day of the seventh month. A sacred assembly was to be held and an offering to God was to be made by fire. There was to be no work done on that day, and anyone who did not deny themselves would be cut off from their people. Also, in *Genesis 9:3-4,* God made it forbidden to eat the blood of animals. Then in *Genesis 9:6,* He made it law that death would be the penalty for the shedding of man's blood. If that law was still enforced today, there would certainly be far fewer murderers in the prisons and walking the streets freely. But I'll leave those blood stains on the hands of the lawmakers, lawyers, judges, and society, who God surely takes issue with. He demands that life and the blood remain sacred.

Boldness - *Boldness* is an opposite of being shy, which described me for many years. During my senior year in high school, I was voted "Most Shy Boy" by my graduating class. I hated that title but couldn't think of another boy who was more deserving. Then when I sang my first solo in church I was trembling, had to hold on to the microphone with two hands because it felt so heavy in one. Imagine that - a man who could lift over two hundred pounds struggling with only a couple. Nowadays, I still may have some quiet moments, but will exhibit a boldness by being much more fearless, daring, courageous, and confident. I am most anxious and honored to be called on to sing in honor of God and Jesus, and have even done it several times without being accompanied by musical instruments. This boldness has carried over in to other areas of my life too, as when my working career has required me to give speeches before large groups of people and taking charge over many different projects.

Paul, in *1 Thessalonians 2:2,* told the people that their boldness was in God despite their previous sufferings and insults in Philippi. The Gospel of God would be told in spite of strong opposition. The Bible also tells of Hezekiah who displayed his boldness during a most desperate time. *2 Kings 18-19* tells of the king of Assyria, Sennacherib, sending a written message threatening Jerusalem. The people were told that they faced imminent defeat, and that it was a waste of time listening to Hezekiah. He was said to be misleading them with his talk of the Lord delivering them from harm. However, Hezekiah reacted in boldness rather than fear. He took the letter and walked deliberately up to the temple, where he spread out the letter and asked God to intervene. God answered his prayer through Isaiah the prophet. It was foretold that the pagan king, who had refused to acknowledge that his success had come from God, would have his army decimated and then be sent home where he would be killed. That's exactly what happened.

Boredom - I have experienced some days recently where I have felt so totally bored. During my many years of marriage, I was always kept busy with a wife, children, work, church, and a variety of other things. Now I may find myself alone trying to discover ways to become more active and put some excitement back into my life. It's tough, especially since many old friends have passed away or are have been out of touch for some reason. Then I am not presently involved in a steady dating relationship with a woman, as much as I would like to. The best thing to do when feeling bored is to channel your thoughts toward the more positive activities that you can become involved in. You don't have to resort to any of the many negative things that some people may in seeking excitement, like crime, poor associations, drug or alcohol abuse, adulterous affairs, etc. Being active in the Lord is a much better alternative.

2 Thessalonians 3:6 warns us about idleness. It is written that we should keep away from others who are idle and not living to the teachings of the Lord. Idleness has always brought about boredom for me, so I have always tried to stay as busy as possible. Plus living an active and fruitful life will help you to avoid dealing with those who may tempt you to do things that are out of your character. They won't have your best interests at heart and will only bring you down to their ungodly ways of living. When I am not working, in church, enjoying my grandchildren, doing my exercise walks or other things, I fight hard to resist the temptations from boredom and idleness. My memory serves me well in remembering the times I didn't, only to get in trouble hanging out with the wrong crowd. Now I may read my Bible, do some writing, or chat with my Christian friends on the computer or telephone, and it helps me through it.

Breath - On October 2nd many years ago I inhaled the air of life in my birth. I became a living soul, and God laid out a plan for me to follow over the course of that life He has given me. There have been detours and distractions that have altered my path, as every person, but I always find my way back through God and Jesus. I will always place my hope, trust, and confidence in them until the day that I breathe my last breath here on Earth, only to inhale the breath of a new life in Heaven.

Genesis 2:7 tells us that God formed us from the dust of the ground, and we became living beings when He breathed into our nostrils the breath of life. Yet there are those who curse His name and deny His existence, while living outside of the plan set for them. According to *Isaiah 25:4-5,* the breath of the ruthless is like a storm driving against a wall and will be stilled. For those who revere Him, He gives help for the poor and needy in distress, shelter from our storms, and a shade from the heat.

Calling - A *calling* is when God calls on you to serve Him in one way or another, as He did with me several years ago concerning His music ministry. I heard the laughter when some first heard that I would be joining a choir, and then later singing my own songs solo. It's a good thing that I listened to God and not them. He knew my limitations and weaknesses better than anyone, but also my heart and potential. There was surely much doubt and fear within me. However, I was open to the challenge and answered God's call to minister to others through my singing, along with my writing. People no longer laugh at the thought of me singing, and I feel so honored and blessed when I visit a church and am immediately placed on their program. At times I laugh at myself though, because it's difficult for even me to believe that it's me. Just always be prepared. For like myself, God will call you based upon what He knows you may become, and not on what He knows you already are.

The Bible says that God calls on us all, even before our births, as He gives each person a special purpose in life. Paul, in *Ephesians1:4,* says that God chose us in Him. We just have to set aside our doubts, fears, laziness, etc, and be open to hearing His call. *Jeremiah 1:1-9* tells of the Lord calling him to be a prophet. God had prepared him before his birth to become His voice to God's people. Jeremiah, who was a child when he was called, answered saying that he did not know how to speak. But the Lord told him not to be afraid. Then He placed a hand to Jeremiah's mouth, telling him that His words were now in his. His mission was to testify to the sinful and stubborn people who had been led by false prophets, and to witness their doom. He was persecuted by the people of Anathoth, where he lived, and even by his own kinsmen. So he moved to Jerusalem to escape and have a wider field of activity. For forty years he declared the Word of the Lord faithfully and fearlessly, only to see his nation go from prosperity to its final destruction.

Cast - One definition of *cast* is the throwing of something, like when I turned my life over to the Lord. I had to cast away the *old me* to become the *new me*. I've talked to people who refuse to do the same because they say that being a Christian is no fun, by having to give up some things they enjoy. I try to tell them that the Lord isn't against fun. He wants you to cast away your sinful ways, the things you should be giving up anyway as you mature and grow in life. I have gained much more than I gave up, and enjoy a lot of fun but in a more righteous and safe way.

The rewards for being a Christian are surely worth giving up a few things. *Isaiah 38:17* tells how Hezekiah was kept from from the pit of corruption and destruction by the love of the Lord, as his sins were cast behind him. He was suffering from an illness when the Lord heard his prayers and saw his tears. Hezekiah recovered and had fifteen years added to his life. It's great having a God you can look to during your more uncomfortable times, like when we are feeling anxious. *1 Peter 5:6* says that by humbling ourselves, we can cast our anxiety upon Him because He cares for us.

Change - *Change* is the process of becoming different, and people often turn to religion when they desire and seek change. There is much anxiety in today's world, and the promise that our lives will become more peaceful through spirituality is appealing. So, it's nothing new to hear about released prisoners, recovering drug addicts and alcoholics, and others dealing with all kinds of behavioral issues and other problems turning to the Lord for help. Then there are many who want to change some ungodly characteristics that they may have inherited. Things like greed, abusiveness, quick tempers, unfaithfulness, racism, atheism, and etc. are often influenced by one's family history.

Positive change is a good thing, especially when it is in relation to your spiritual growth. The starting point for change is to change your mind and heart, along with overcoming your stubborness and resistance. No person, or even God, can make you do it. You have to truly want to change when you seek out the Lord for help. And the great thing are the rewards that you may receive by becoming the *new you.* You'll feel much better about yourself and the world around you. *2 Chronicles 15:7* says that if we are strong and not give up our work will be rewarded. All we have to do is set some goals and move on them in changing from our past.

Cherish - I *cherish,* or hold close, many people and things. First there are God and Jesus whom I place the most ultimate of my affections in, as they are the source of all my trust and hope. Then there is the love that I feel and show for my mother, sons, grandchildren, brothers and sisters, relatives, friends, pastors, fellow church members, and others. I also cherish things like my rights, freedom, and faith. However, there may be times when I am feeling down that I forget to just cherish myself.

Ephesians 5:29 says that a man should never hate his body. He should nourish and cherish it, just as the Lord does the church. Since my stroke, I now cherish each day more than ever and am not allowing the negative people or any bad circumstances to worry and upset me as before, along with watching my diet and back exercising. Plus I have returned to the churches where, as it says in *1 Thessalonians 2:7,* they have never been a burden to me, but always gentle like a mother cherishing her children.

Children - A few years ago I had dropped my car off for repairs one morning and was waiting on the street for a bus to take me to work. Suddenly I heard all these violent and profane racial comments being shouted out at me. I turned around and there was a day care school with children playing outside, except for one. A little white boy, maybe 4 or 5 years old, was standing by the fence voicing loudly out to me all the things he had heard his father say about black people. I turned away and thought about going inside the building to complain. However, when I looked back a woman was dragging him away by an ear, something I thought was forbidden in these times where disciplining even the worst behaving children seems to be frowned upon. But it didn't bother me at all in this instance.

On my way to work I felt sorry for the boy. It was obvious that he was living in a house where there was no God, just an atmosphere of hate. A goal of parenting is to raise happy, healthy, well-adjusted kids, along with teaching respect for others. But I could tell that this child was well on the way to growing up with social issues, and most likely a few others. *Ephesians 6:1-4,* says that children should obey their parents, but in the Lord. And fathers should not provoke their children to wrath, but bring them up in the training and instruction of the Lord. Then *Proverbs 22:6* says that a father should train a child in the right way they should go, and they will not turn away from it when older. Hopefully, the father of the boy I saw has since found the Lord and is now training him in the right ways.

Choices - In life we often have to make *choices,* which are a preference or selection of something. The choices may involve deciding upon which college to attend, whom to marry, where to live, how to dress, choosing a career, whether to buy that new car or a new house... We just have to beware of the temptations that may turn us away from God, even if only over the shortest periods of time. The things that you do and the material things you own are just temporary substitutes for God's love, the only thing you can ever have that can last forever. The purchase of that new car isn't a bad thing if God has blessed you to be able to really afford it. If not, it could very well end up on the repossession lot. The best choices are made in devotion to Him.

Wise people make wise choices. I like where God says, in *Proverbs 8:10-11,* that we should choose His instruction instead of silver, His knowledge rather than gold, and that wisdom is more precious than rubies, in that nothing you desire can ever compare with wisdom. *Proverbs 10:22* goes on to say that the blessing of the Lord brings wealth without worry. So, He will bless you with that new car or other things and add no trouble with it. However, it will be frowned upon if the pursuit of any wealth is your top priority in life. *Deuteronomy 30:19* says that life and death have been set before me, as are blessings and curses. I am looking to make choices that will give me the better life, and God is life.

Chosen - Beginning when I was about 14 or 15, many of my friends and myself always wanted to play playground football with the older guys in the neighborhood. However, I was often one of the few who was actually chosen to play. That was because I was usually the fastest player on the field, regardless of age. I wasn't as big and strong as most of them, but once I had the ball and was running in the open field it was a difficult task to catch and tackle me. People have often chosen me for other things too but the greatest thing possible is to be called and chosen by God. I'll never reject His mercy and have chosen to live a Christian life that will make me worthy and acceptable for Heaven.

The Lord often uses the expression "For many are called, but few are chosen", as with *Matthew 22:14*. The Jews had been called but most of the nation was wicked and their lives showed that they were not chosen to salvation. Then with *Isaiah 45:22* the Gentiles were invited to be saved, with few showing themselves to be real Christians. In *Matthew 22,* Jesus tells the *parable of the marriage of the king's son* in describing the kingdom of Heaven. In the end a man, who had been called to attend, was bound and thrown out into the darkness for not wearing a wedding garment to the wedding. It will be the same for those in church now who prove to be without their wedding garments, showing that they were not truly the chosen of God. They'll be cast away from Heaven, just as the man was from the wedding, to where there will be *weeping and gnashing of teeth.*

Christians - Us followers of Jesus Christ are called *Christians.* According to *Acts 11:26,* the name was given first to the disciples at Antioch in Syria around 43 A.D. *Disciples* are the followers of teachers and are called *believers* in *Acts 5:14*. The *World Christian Encyclopedia* says that there are now over 30,000 Christian organizations in the world, with about 1,200 in North America, and names ranging from the *Amish* to *The Way*. Their denominations are sorted into 15 families, according to their historical roots, and the examples include the *Adventist, Baptist, Lutheran, Pentecostal,* and *Presbyterian*. The *Christian Churches Together,* an ecumenical movement, offers a broader classification of only five families that are the *Evangelical/Pentecostal, Historic Protestant and Racial/Ethnic, Eastern Orthodox,* and *Roman Catholic.* Then they may be further sorted by segments, branches, political wings, theological beliefs, and other ways.

2 Corinthians 6, says that as Christians we can commend ourselves for our endurance in troubles, hardships and distresses, and also for things like purity, understanding, patience, kindness, love, truthful speech and righteousness. We are Christians through glory and dishonor, bad and good reports, and even when we are genuine but regarded as imposters. In death we live on, in sorrow we are always rejoicing, and we can have nothing and still possess everything. However, we should not allow ourselves to be associated with unbelievers because we have nothing in common with them. *Galatians 5:1* says that Jesus set us free for freedom and Christians never again have to be yoked by any kind of slavery. *Ephesians 4* tells us that our unity is in Him and we should be humble, gentle, patient, and bear with one another in love and peace. In spite of all the organizations, we only have one body and one Spirit. And as it says in *Philippians 2,* we should always imitate the Lord's humility.

Church - When I was a youngster, it was during a time when going to church was mandatory for most of the kids in my neighborhood. But, it was still fun and I spent a lot of time there during my early and then later school years. Church was the place for us guys to meet the girls and see our friends. However, I didn't get serious about being in church until actually joining one after my marriage. It became really important for me to finally devote myself and be there for the right reasons.

The church has three missions. They are Devinely commissioned to teach and make disciples of all people, baptizing them in the name of the Father, and of the Son, and of the Holy Ghost *(Matthew 28:19).* They impart spiritual enlightenment as we are taught the ways of the Lord and to walk in His paths *(Isaiah 2:3).* Then they are to witness for the Lord and receive His power all over the Earth *(Acts 1:8).* A *church* is an assembly of saints engaged in those missions, and I am there now for real Christian worship and fellowship.

Closeness - There are times that I really feel alone and miss the closeness of others. I miss being in a home with a wife and children. I miss being able to hang out with all the friends I used to. On this cold and snowy day of winter in January 2011, I miss being outside enjoying conversations with the neighbors and watching the birds fly over. Everyone and everything just seem to be so distant at times, and I feel like I'm missing out on the closeness of life.

When I am feeling a little out of it, I try to think of the pleasant things that make me smile and about God. *Closeness* may be defined as being a condition of being friends, chumminess, companionship, comradeship, familiarity, fellowship, intimacy, etc. I have all that and more with God as the Holy Spirit is my constant companion. *Exodus 40:38* offers a reminder of God's closeness and how He remains with us, as it tells how He was over the house of Israel day and night during their travels. So I am never really alone. I feel His closeness greatly on this day, along with that of His son, Jesus.

Clouds - One year some time ago, I was involved in three car accidents, none of which were any fault of mine, and including one that was a hit and run. Then there were all kinds of other crazy things happening in my life. I got to the point where I woke up every morning only anticipating another day of trouble. It just felt like there were these dark clouds always over my head, ready to drench me in a downpour of continued problems, uncertainty, worry, and hopelessness. Then I finally woke up one morning remembering that all I had to do was look to God for my direction and peace of mind. It had been my choice to continue being discouraged and living in fear. When I decided to turn back to Him, and my church, the clouds of faith began to roll in and take over again. There are still some battles needed to be won but I am no longer trying to fight them alone.

One definition of *clouds* in the Bible is *gloom*, which I knew very well. However, not all clouds are bad as one miraculous cloud is told of. *Exodus 13:21-22* details how a pillar of clouds symbolized the Lord's presence as Moses led the people of Israel. During the day these clouds guided them on their way, and they turned into a pillar of fire at night to give them light. Therefore, they were able to travel by day or night. *Nehemiah 9:19-21* says that the Lord did it out of His great compassion and never abandoned them in the desert. He sustained them for 40 years and they lacked nothing. The clouds guided them while the Spirit instructed them, and they always had food and water, while their clothes and shoes never wore out. He is now leading me back in the right direction and had never left me alone. I was forcing those dark clouds to remain over me, but He was still providing what was needed for my survival too.

Comfort - We all have those times when we need some comfort and relaxtion, especially when things aren't going too well or after an unusually tough day. Some may take a scenic drive or a short vacation. Others may go to the gym, golf course, movie theater or a bar after work, as even others just relax in the comfort of their homes reading a book or watching television. A thing that I enjoy doing for comfort is heading out to Belle Isle in Detroit to do some walking. The exercise and the beautiful views of the water surrounding the island are most relaxing for me. When needing comfort from the stress and unpleasantness of our daily lives though, all we have to do is look to God for our strength and insight. However, we often go for that quick escape rather than seeking it through prayer and patience.

There is comfort for God's people and He proclaims it twice in *Isaiah 40:1*. He is the comforter of all people and can change our circumstances and put an end to our sufferings or lessen them. God is the Father of compassion who comforts us in all our troubles, and desires that we comfort others in the comfort we receive from Him. The sufferings of Jesus flow over into our lives, and also through Him does our comfort overflow. When distressed, it is for our comfort and salvation that we be comforted and use our experiences to comfort and encourage others. All of this is written in *2 Corinthians 1:3-7*. During the tough times, God may send a friend with an encouraging word, a meaningful gift, or maybe to give you a nice hug, listen to you, or simply sit with you in silence, and you can do the same for someone you know when they are hurting.

Commandments - *Commandments* are commands or mandates, or orders from authority. God established a set of obligations and responsibilities for us to obey in demonstrating our devotion to Him and the seperation from sin. He chose Israel to be the messengers of His love for us all through His convenant. A list of ten commandments was given to Moses at Mount Sinai, over 3,000 years ago after the Hebrews were delivered from slavery in Egypt. However, the *Law of Moses* is said to be made up of over 600 rules. Christians still accept the commandments because Jesus tells us that knowing and keeping them enables us to inherit eternal life. Yet most don't have them all memorized, including myself.

The Ten Commandments are listed in *Exodus 20* and are as follows:
    1- *'You shall have no other gods before Me.'*

2- 'You shall not make for yourself a carved image-any likeness of anything that is in heaven above, or that is in the earth beneath, or that is in the water under the earth.'
3- 'You shall not take the name of the LORD your God in vain.'
4- 'Remember the Sabbath day, to keep it holy.'
5- 'Honor your father and your mother.'
6- 'You shall not commit murder.'
7- 'You shall not commit adultery.'
8- 'You shall not steal.'
9- 'You shall not bear false witness against your neighbor.'
10- 'You shall not covet your neighbor's house; you shall not covet your neighbor's wife, nor his male servant, nor his female servant, nor his ox, nor his donkey, nor anything that is your neighbor's.'

Deuteronomy 6 tells us that we should love the Lord our God with all our hearts and that we will be blessed in obeying the Commandments. He also wants them to be posted in our homes and taught to our children.

Commitment - Being successful as a spouse, parent, friend, student, athlete, entertainer, entrepreneur, employee, or even a Christian, requires a great deal of personal *commitment,* which is the act of committing, pledging, or engaging yourself to something. You have to be willing to give it your all. I would have never completed my reading of the Bible or the writing of my first book had I not made a promise of commitment to myself for doing so. As believers in Jesus, we can't be part-time Christians and give Him less than our best. He tells us that if we follow Him, we have to be devoted and take our commitment seriously.

2 Timothy 22:1-2 encourages us to be strong in the grace that is in Jesus, and that things heard before many in witness be entrusted to reliable men who will be committed in teaching others. Christianity isn't always a popular thing and there has to be a strong commitment in living, saying and doing some things even if being offensive to others. In *John 6,* Jesus says that He knew that some of His followers were not believers and there just for the free food and other things. He surely offended many then, with that being said, and when He complained of them seeing some miraculous things and still not believing, along with telling them that only those who came to Him would never be turned away.

Compassion - We are showing *compassion* for others when we have feelings of sympathy and sorrow when they are stricken by misfortune, along with a strong desire to help them alleviate their suffering. That definition must include human kindness, as a compassionate person has love for others and enjoys doing good deeds. God has shown His mercy to us in Jesus and desires us to be active in showing our compassion to others. His definition of *compassion* includes the faith in Him. He has compassion for all who believe and trust in God. All we have to do is believe in His power to perform miracles.

God desires to free us from any suffering and has compassion for those that are lost. He wants us to repent and have a true desire to turn away from sin. It is in belief that we are blessed by His compassionate nature, and *Mark 1:41* confirms His compassion for the faithful through Jesus. *Mark 9* then tells of the healing of a boy with an evil spirit, with Jesus stating in *verse 23* that everything is possible for a believer. *1 John 3:17* advises us that godly people perform compassionate acts. We should show pity and reach out to a person in need if we have the ability to provide any kind of help.

Complacency - Complacent people often like to play it safe and as a result may never reach their full potential in life or as Christians. Promotional opportunities are passed on at work and some become stuck on jobs for years that they really dislike. It's especially a bad thing when a person suffers a lack of spiritual growth from it, like the individual who is content and satisfied with just occupying a seat in church every Sunday morning. They may faithfully attend service but never offer their talents or participate in anything much more. Life and Christianity are adventures. The excitement and fulfillment of both are lost when you are not ambitious or open to change. You have to be advantageous because the windows of opportunity may only get smaller with each passing day.

In the Bible unbelievers are viewed more favorably than the complacent Christian. *Revelation 3:15-16* states that the Lord knows our works and desires us to be either cold or hot to the Gospel. Unbelievers are considered to be *cold,* while the true Disciple is *hot.* Those in the middle are *lukewarm.* They are clearly members of the Church but are complacent and fail to bring about the works of the Spirit required to walk in the ways of the Lord. He really looks down upon these kinds of Christians and says that He will spit them from His mouth. Also, *Luke 12:47-48* says that the lukewarm believer will be beaten with the stripes of greater judgment than the unbeliever, because more is expected from those who are given more.

Condemnation - In criminal law, *condemnation* is a final judgment for a person found guilty in a criminal case and the punishment that is imposed. Usually that person may spend some time in a jail or prison until their sentence is up. They are then considered to have paid their debt to society and released into the streets, where some just go back to doing the things that had them facing condemnation in the first place. However, it is always hoped that a far greater number are rehabilitated and take on more honest and fulfilling lives when they are returned to freedom. Another thing is that we all face an ultimate judgment which could result in our condemnation, regardless of any guilt or innocence based upon the rules and laws of man.

Condemnation, in the Bible, is the sentence of God against sin. It's a universal punishment caused by the offence of Adam in the *Garden of Eden (Genesis 3),* and final judgment is far greater than a jail or prison sentence as it's for eternity. Unlike crime, all people sin. However, God offers leniency where the courts won't. *Roman's 6:23* says that the judgment for sin is death, but the gift of God is eternal life through Jesus. We have to first have a belief in Jesus and then confess our sins to Him. *John 3:18* tells us that believers are not condemned, while non-believers are already condemned. God demands that there is a belief in the name of His only begotten Son. The failure to do so is a sinful act punishable by condemnation.

Confidence - One day a friend of mine, who had become a pastor, came over to the house and was reading a plaque on the wall that had an inspirational poem on it that I had written. He was fairly new in his calling, full of fire, and all knowing even over such a short period of time. The poem was one of my first efforts, and my spirit and confidence were shattered when he criticized my writing saying that the words weren't of the Lord. However, I wasn't going to just stop based on his evaluation. I continued to write while learning and growing in my faith, which made me more knowledgeable and confident. Plus my real confidence is in God whom I was learning from and building a closer relationship with. True *confidence* is placing your full trust, belief in His power, and reliability in Him.

I now have the confidence in my ability to succeed in anything more than ever. As in *Ephesians 3:12-13,* I don't have to allow the words of others, or any distractions or sufferings, to discourage me because I can approach God with freedom and confidence. Also, *Psalm 3:3* tells me that it is the Lord who bestows glory upon me and lifts my head up. It's a good thing that I didn't allow the words of my friend discourage me. About a year later, he came back to the house and read the same poem, not realizing it was the one he had previously read. However, this time he had nothing but praise and even asked if he could use my words in one of his sermons, saying that there were straight from the Lord. Obviously he had learned and grown too. It was quite a confidence booster, but I already had plenty.

Confusion - Today's world is a *Ball Of Confusion,* just as *The Temptations* used to sing. There just seems to be so many people who appear to be totally lost, whether they realize it or not. A lot of them are going through some tougher times than they have ever experienced before, and it has them in a position where they just don't know which to turn or who to look to for help. Then there are those who really need to wake up to reality, like the kid who actually believes that his best option for success in life is becoming a drug dealer, because that's where the fast money is and it's easier than working a real job. So what we see in our world is much confusion, with many living in desperation and fear, others who have just accepted their fate and have given up, and then some only headed for their own self-destruction at the expense of others.

Job 10:15 presents a good example of a confused person. In that Scripture passage, Job describes himself as being full of shame and drowning in affliction, in not knowing his innocence or guilt. *Acts 19:29* tells of an entire city filled with confusion, and *19:32* goes on to describe an assembly in confusion, with some shouting one thing and some another, with most not even knowing why they were there. A Bible definition for *confusion* is *shame* and *tumult,* and *James 3:16* says that confusion and every evil practice can result from envy and strife. Therefore a confused person may commit some shameful acts, which are out of the ordinary for them, in attempting to alleviate their pain or the jealousy felt towards those who are not suffering as they are. However, a great thing is that God offers His help to any of us who need to refocus and seek direction. According to *Psalm 32:8,* He will instruct and teach people in the way they should go, as well as counsel and watch over them.

Contentment - Even when doing well, I just never feel satisfied, as I believe that there is so much more that can be learned or accomplished. I have desires for wealth, as most, especially when finacially burdened, but the contentment will come in not how much I am able to acquire but in how I am best able to use it. Plus there are other kinds of wealth that can be shared, like knowledge, compassion, and a giving spirit. A person believing that just monetary wealth is the key to their happiness and satisfaction may only find themselves living lives of greed and temptation, along with turning away from God. I can be content with the basic neccessities of life in having food to eat, good health, and a secure roof over my head. However, I'm determined to come as close as possible to reaching my full potential in life, and realize that being content with my present status may leave me far short of that success. God desires much more from me and my true satisfaction will come through Him.

God is pleased when we are satisfied and live the way He instructs us. However, the lack of contentment may be used as a learning tool or punishment. Joshua questions, in *Joshua 7:7*, why his people had been led across the Jordan, supposedly to enjoy a better life, only to be delivered into the hands of the Amorites and face destruction. He goes on to say that they could have been content in just remaining where they were. But it had been done to teach them a lesson. *Joshua 7:10-12* tells how God responded to Joshua in detailing how Israel had sinned and violated the covenant He had commanded them to keep. They had made themselves liable for their destruction through their stealing, lying and other wrongful actions. He'd never be with them again unless Joshua destroyed anything among them that was devoted to destruction. So the key to true contentment is first to be right with God. Obviously Joshua's people weren't content in spite of all that had been given to them, and they paid the price. Just remember that whenever you are not satisfied in your life and try to win a personal battle, or achieve something, while not living for God.

Control - We all want to be in *control*, which is just another way of saying that we want things to go our way on our terms. I, for example, prefer being as self-sufficient as possible; not relying on anyone for anything, along with being able to do whatever I want, go wherever I want, and whenever I want. However, it only takes a couple of events to remind me that I will never have the control over my life that I would like. It is vividly remembered the shock experienced when hearing my first long-term job was being lost because of a company closing, especially since I was the controller and saw the handwriting on the wall but was caught by surprise nonetheless. Then there was the time my car was repossessed when I could no longer afford making the payments because of a work layoff. Control?

As I laid in the hospital recovering from my stroke, it was quite evident to me who was in charge. God is in control whether it's that unexpected layoff or an illness. We may think that we can handle most anything that life throws at us, but that belief is just a false sense of security. I knew that the present situation was something well beyond my control, and had placed my faith and the outcome fully in God's hand, just as I have relinquished control to Him in overcoming some other problems. *Job 38* gives a great example of being in control as God spoke to him. First God challenges Job for speaking without knowledge and then demands answers to His questions, saying that he will surely answer. Next He convinces Job of his ignorance while telling of all His great works in creating everything to His exact specifications. In *verse 38* it's evident that God even has His clouds numbered from a question asked of Job. That's control!

Courage - I get my courage from God whom I can trust for my protection and be given the strength and empowerment to do many things and accept challenge without fear. *Courage* is the state of my mind or spirit that enables me to face difficulty, danger, pain and other situations without fear. *1 Corinthians 16:13* tells me to stand firm in faith and be a man of courage, while *verse 14* tells me to do it in love. Then *2 Timothy 1:7* tells me that I can be courageous because God provides me with the spirit of power, love and a sound mind, while having no fear. In confidence I have no worries about what any man can do to me because the Lord is my helper and the source of my courage (*Hebrews 13:6*).

In *Nehemiah* it is told how he had inspected the walls of Jerusalem and determined that they needed to be rebuilt. There were other rebuilding and repair projects going on to in the area by others too. However, there was opposition to Nehemiah's project by Sanballat, a Horonite, who mocked the Jews questioning their purpose for doing it. Nehemiah prayed and continued the work, with even having to arm his laborers because they faced danger. Sanballat used paid prophecies to terrify Nehemiah and discredit him but that failed, and five times his enemies tried to lure him out of the city, where he would be killed. However, he was not fooled and, in the face of great terror, continued his work without fear. Through prayer he found the strength and the *courage* to have the work finished.

Covenant - A *covenant* is an agreement or promise. So, it can be said that when you sign any legal document for the purchase of a home, car, or terms for anything else, that is considered as being a *covenant* in Bible terms. That would include verbal agreements and handshakes of good faith as well. Over the years I have been been involved in many agreements. However, the one that I made with God is the most important. It's one thing to default on a few credit obligations, but certainly a much more serious matter when you break your covenant with God.

The Bible cites many examples of God honoring His covenants with us but often we break ours with Him. He promised His favor to Adam and Eve, in *Genesis,* for their obedience but that didn't stop them from sinning. He also promised, according to *Genesis,* that Noah would survive the great deluge and that there would never be another flood of that magnitude, in return for his faith and obedience. I just wonder what the world would be like today if Noah had reneged on his promises to God? We should surely keep our convenants with God just as He has kept His with us, and with Jesus as our *Mediator (Hebrews 8).*

Creation - I am a true believer that God is the Creator of all things, and it is so difficult to imagine and comprehend the magnificence of it all. He created the entire universe and everything that exists in it. I just read in amazement whenever a new spieces of life, or an uncharted planet or galaxy, has been discovered. It just confirms to me that God is still at work. That's why I am a believer that other life may be in existence outside of our world, for in believing in God you can always have a belief beyond anything that could ever be imagined. Life itself, as we know it, is an impossibility because everything has to have a beginning, but He has made anything possible.

Genesis opens with the doctrine that *God is the author of creation;* making real all that which did not previously exist. He created the *heavens and the earth, all forms of life,* and *the elements.* An account is given in *Genesis 1-2* as to how He did it all in six days and rested on the seventh. For man's creation, my Bible says that the first chapters of *Genesis* and *John* should be read together:
In the beginning God -
  In the beginning was the word.
Created the heavens and the earth.
  All things were created by him.
And God said, let there be light.
  That was the true Light.
Let us make man in our image.
  And the Word was made flesh.
I certainly believe that I am a living being today by the glory and majesty of God's Work.

Cries - There is this old Shirley Temple movie that brings me to tears every time every time I watch it. She portrays a little girl in search of her father, a soldier who is missing and thought to have died in the Civil War, if memory serves me right. After visiting a few hospitals, she finally finds him and in the ending scene runs to him as he cries out her name, *Sarah,* from a hospital bed, where he laid recovering from a head wound. I don't know why. Maybe it's because I lost my father to death when I was young, but that scene always makes me cry, no matter how hard I try not to. No one knows it but me though, because if I'm watching the movie with others, I make an excuse to leave the room at just the right time.

Crying isn't a bad thing but my macho side doesn't want me to reveal my sensitive side to others at times. However, nowadays I find myself crying more than ever as I have grown as a Christian. I have always been a very caring person but seem to really take things to heart now. And when I hear the cries of others I may be driven to act, as in *Exodus 22:22-23,* where God gives a warning that He will be angered and take action when He hears the cries of a woman or ophan being taken advantage of. My problem is that I have my own concerns and people seldom seem to hear my cries. But even if I grow weary calling out for help, I can just do as David, in *Psalm 69:3,* and wait on God. For as in *verses 1-2,* I can ask Him to save me from all that troubles me.

Crime - As a young teenager, without a father, there were some tough times. One day my mother had given me some money to go to the drug store for her. As I picked up a few items, a crazy idea came to me. Being a very fast runner, I thought that I could just bolt from the store before anyone noticed or be long gone before the police arrived. Then a voice in my head told me that I could get away with it and only be enticed to commit more criminal acts, or be caught and have to suffer the consequences. So, I decided against the theft, and that marked the beginning and end of my criminal career. However, I understood too though that we all commit crime according to the Law of God.

The Bible defines *crime* as being *sin, vice,* and *iniquity,* and *Ezekiel 7:23-27* tells of how the land where Ezekiel lived was full of crime and the city full of violence, and how God was to punish them severely for not heeding His warnings through the prophets. He was going to send wicked nations there to unlease a reign of terror all over them, and they would seek peace but find none. Their king would mourn and the people would tremble in fear as He judged them. They were to be dealt with according to their conduct and judged by their own standards. In that way they would know that He was truly the Lord. Sounds like they were going to pay quite a price for their crimes, just as God will make us pay for ours, even today.

Criticism - I believe in constructive criticism. If I am criticized for doing something wrong and it's said in truth, I will surely listen to acknowledge my mistakes and then make efforts to correct myself. I'm never defensive when someone is only out to help when telling me something that's for my own good. However, it's another matter when I hear things that are totally unfounded; the criticizer who, maybe out of jealousy, hate or ignorance, says things to degrade, control, or just plain anger me. Years ago, a person I respected criticized me for wearing sunglasses a lot. He accused me of being on drugs, ignorant of the fact they were worn because of a lazy left eye that was very sensitive to the sun. I just let it go but it bothered me that his criticism was never voiced to me personally, and I really felt sorry when he discovered that his own son was actually the one with a drug problem.

Criticism is an expression of disapproval towards something a person has done. If it is justified you can learn from it. If it is unfounded, unfair or ignorant you can disclaim or disregard it. I pretty much just laughed it off upon first hearing of my drug addiction, while according to Bible accounts, Job chose to defend himself against one critic. Eliphaz the Temanite criticizes Job, in *Job 22,* with the accusations, that in spite of being a man of substance, he had given no water to the weary or food to the hungry, among other things. In *Job 23,* Job proclaimed his innocence, and desired to stand before God to state his case. He said that his mouth was full of arguments and God would press no charges against him, if He would listen. That was a great example of dealing with a critic out to get you but, as stated in the beginning, not all criticism is bad. My example is one where a choir director offered advice for improving a song I had written, and was worried that the criticism would offend me. However, I was open to suggestion and the result was an inspirational song that surely touched many more people than the original would have, when I sang it.

Cross - I wear a gold chain around my neck with a gold cross attached to it, along with a gold cross in my ear. They are in recognition and pride of who I am; a Christian. And while they may be on display for others, they are often reminders to myself whenever people or circumstances bring out the devil in me.

Boastful people may often be looked down upon but boasting is viewed positively in *Galatians 6:14.* Paul said that he would never boast except in regards to the cross of Jesus Christ, our Lord, for it signifies and glorifies the atoning work of our Savior.

Crucifixion - *Crucifixion* was a form of capital punishment often used in ancient times, where a person was bound to a cross while alive. Alexander the Great was said to have once crucified one thousand Tyrians, and Antiochus Epiphanes crucified Jews who wouldn't renounce their religion. In the past other methods of capital punishment were also used, like stoning, hanging, firing squads, and the chopping off of heads. With the exeption of stoning, where it could take one stone or many to kill, the other methods gave the victim a quick death. In crucifixion the victim was nailed to a cross and bled slowly to a most agonizing death.

Just thinking about how Jesus suffered such a terrible death makes me shake all over, as I think crucifixion had to be the most cruel way of ever executing a person, especially for one who was so innocent of any wrondoings. *John 19:31-33* tells how some victims would have their legs broken to make them die faster. They were often given a potion to lessen the pain too. *Matthew 27:34* says that Jesus was given a mixture of vinegar (wine) and gall (a bitter liquid from the liver) to drink, which He refused. Gall also signifies *a venemous attitude toward that which is good,* as in *Acts 8:23,* so it's no wonder why Jesus wouldn't drink, along with other reasons, while dying for us.

Curse - When I think of the word *curse* it brings about two meanings to mind; the usage of profanity or when people believe that a person or an outside force has willed it for some bad things to happen to them. However, here I will just talk about profanity, as I was riding up front in our church bus one day and couldn't believe some of the language coming out back from one of the young girls. It was certainly addressed, during a church service, by our pastor after I informed him about what I had heard. Now children using profanity are banned from riding the bus, and are only allowed back on if they promise to watch their language.

I never curse unless someone really pushes me over the limit, and have been asked by some children and teenagers why they don't hear me using profanity like many adults. I tell them that it's just not a nice thing to use that kind of language. However, you can watch programs for younger people on television, these days, where profanity may often be heard. With that, and hearing it at home, on the streets, and in school, it's not surprising that many grow up believing it's ok to curse, even to the point of disrepecting others. I have even heard parents being cursed at by their own children, which the Bible certainly frowns upon. *Leviticus 20:9* said that any person cursing their mother or father would be put to death. They need to read that.

Darkness - As I laid there in the hospital bed recovering from my stroke, I was thinking about that gloomy darkness experienced during my hour or so of blindness, and it made me think even further about how we are all born blind and in darkness; only a spiritual darkness. Only when we grow up with the belief and acceptance of Jesus Christ as our Savior, are we able to bask in the light of God's love. I witnessed that light and felt His presence as my sight was being restored, upon the flickerings of light at my fingertips signaling the end of one of my most darkest episodes. Had I not allowed the Lord to take charge over me many years ago, who knows what the outcome would have been. The doctor said that someone from up above was surely looking down on me in a good way that evening, and there was no question in my mind as to whom it was.

In ancient times there were many stubborn and rebellious people living sinful and disobedient lives. A savior was needed to deliver them out from their spiritual darkness and separation from God, and Jesus would become the one to bring the light to a dark world. Through Him there would never again be a need for people to worry, fret or fear, as they received the light of God's love. *Acts 26* tells how Paul spoke before King Agrippa to defend himself against the accusations of Jews who wanted him dead. He told of the conversion from the days of his youth as a Pharisee *(separated from God)* to being appointed as a servant of Jesus, who had promised that He would rescue him from his own people and the Gentiles. Paul would be sent to open their eyes and turn them from darkness to light, and from Satan to God. The people would then receive forgiveness for their sins and a place among those with the Lord.

Death - After a certain age we all come to know what death is but there is also death among the living, as many people today are living lives of hopelessness, fear, confusion and without God. I like the expression *dead man walking*, which can mean that a man is on his way to death or is already dead but doesn't know it. Either way it describes a life with no future. However, unless you are in prison and on the way to the electric chair, there is always a chance to revive your life through God and Jesus.

The first thing is getting your life in order as God instructed Hezekiah to do before adding 15 years to his life *(2 Kings 20)*. Hezekiah had been ill and at the point of death, but this example is a great one for the non-believers and part-time believers as well, who aren't yet facing imminent death. Any person who is not right with God could have their lives shortened rather than lengthened by Him. *Proverbs 24:20* says that an evil man has no future and that the *candle* lighting his life will only be put out. *Proverbs 11:7* says that all hope for an evil man ends in death.

Deception - The act of deceiving or being deceived is called *deception.* Some synonyms of the word are cheating, crookedness, cunning, deceit, dishonesty, double-dealing, fakery, fraud and trickery, while some antonyms are forthrightness, good faith, ingenousness and sincerity. I try hard to live a life that is an antonym of deception, however possessing qualities like a caring and giving nature may only leave you open to being taken advantage of through the deceit of enemies, friends and others alike, as I have a few times. My younger brother calls that being a *Sucker Bob,* and it is true that, in deception, some will say or do anything to get your money or receive favors, and may have no intention of ever honoring any promises made to you. Deception can be used against you too, by others and even yourself, especially in sinful ways.

The Bible cites many cases of different kinds of deception, like when it's used against you, on yourself, or to trick you. *Jeremiah 38,* tells how Jeremiah had been thrown into a dungeon when some princes, wanting him dead, lied and deceived their king into believing that Jeremiah was only out to hurt the people there rather than helping them. Then King David used deception in convincing himself that he could have an adulterous affair with Bathsheba. It continued as he schemed and told lies trying to cover up what he had done, and finally devised a plan that had her husband, Uriah, killed *(2 Samuel 11).* A final example is Jacob using trickery in disguising himself so that his father Isaac, with failing eyesight, would believe he was his brother Esau *(Genesis 27).*

Decisions - Over the course of my life, I have had to make many decisions big and small, as life is one of constant decision-making. We make them every day and have to make sure that they are the best choices, especially in our relationship with God. My most important decision came when I decided that it was time to officially turn my life over to the Lord. I was a believer, but out of stubborness and having a busy life-style, hadn't wanted to commit myself to being a full-time Christian. It surely was time for me to become more serious because this decision concerned the quality and success of my life then, along with my future and place in eternity.

Turning to the Lord our God means prosperity. If you love Him, walk in His ways, and obey His commands, decrees and laws, you will be blessed and live and increase (*Deuteronomy 30:15-16*). God is our life and may give us many years just as He had sworn to give Abraham, Isaac and Jacob (*Deuteronomy 30:20*). When his people were shaming themselves before their enemies, Moses made a request for all those who were on the Lord's side to come to him, and all the sons of Levi did (*Exodus 32:26*). As with me, it was the best decision that they could have ever made.

Deeds - The acts that we commit and work that we do are *deeds* and, in true faith, God wants us to be active workers. I pride myself in having a caring and generous heart, and know that He wants me to walk in faith rather than just talk as some do. Therefore, I have always had a giving nature and have done many good deeds for others and in doing what God asks. He blesses us when we have pure hearts and act accordingly.

James 2:26 tells us that a body without spirit is dead, as is faith without works. In *verse 18,* James says that he would show his faith through the things he did. Faith has to be accompanied by action. If we see one in need we should make every effort to help them if able, otherwise our faith is dead and we can't be saved (*verses 14-17*). When we listen to God and do what He says, we will be blessed for our deeds (*James 1:25*).

Delegation - Over my working career, I have held mostly managerial positions that required *delegation,* the assigning of authority and responsibility to subordinates under my direction and supervision to carry out specific activities. In the business world, it may save time and money, along with helping to build skills and motivate others. In delegating work the manager remains responsible for the outcome of the work that is passed over to others. Therefore, I have had to always be good at it because poor delegation can cause a lot of frustration, confusion and failed assignments. Plus, I admit to placing a little too much upon myself at times, especially when I wasn't confident that some under me were capable of successfully doing some things.

Moses decided to use delegation after his father-in-law, Jethro, convinced him that his workload was too heavy to handle alone and would only wear him out. So, he chose able men out of Israel and made them heads and rulers over the people. They took care of the small matters, while the difficult ones were handled by Moses (*Exodus 18:17-26*). The greatest examples of delegation, however, were by Jesus. First He called on twelve disciples to work for Him, and gave them the power and authority to cast out unclean spirits and heal sickness and disease (*Matthew 10:1*). Then He appointed seventy-two workers who, two by two, would first visit every city and place that He was to later arrive in (*Luke 10:1*).

Deliverance - The rescue from bondage or danger is called *deliverance*. Jesus is my deliverer as I believe that He is the Son of God who died for me and rose again. When I confess to Him, He will renounce all the influences of Satan in my life. He knows all the demons that oppress me, harrass me, entice me, and enslave me. I faithfully believe that I am saved by the blood of Jesus, and through His blood I am justified as if I have never sinned. Through His blood, I am also sanctified and able to build a closer relationship with God. There is redemption from the hand of the devil and God will rescue me from peril. Jesus says that there shall be deliverance when we call upon the name of the Lord.

In the *Old Testament* of the Bible, deliverance was when God rescued those in the midst of trouble and danger. He rescued people from their enemies (*1 Samuel 17:37*), the wicked (*Psalm 7:2*), famine and death (*Psalm 33:19*), the grave (*Hosea 13:14*), and the greatest example was when He delivered the people of Israel out of Egypt (*Exodus 3:8*). In the *New Testament*, believers are offered deliverance from sin, evil, death and judgment (*Galatians 1:4*). However, all deliverance is only through Jesus Christ, who was delivered up for us and born again for us (*Romans 4:25*). Only He can rescue us from the "wrath to come" (*1 Thessalonians 1:10*).

Depression - I must admit to having my bouts of *depression*, which may be described as feeling sad, unhappy, miserable, or just plain down in the dumps. I just expect so much of myself and can start feeling really depressed when things aren't going as I would like. When that happens I try concentrating on things that make me feel happy and that help to ease my mind, like my walks at the park where I often talk to the Lord. My trust is in God and Jesus, as I am a true believer that they will never place upon me more than it's humanly possible for me to handle. In faith, I know that the storms of my life will always subside eventually if my burdens are placed before them. However, at times I feel that there is much defeat in even allowing people or circumstances to drive me to a state of depression in the first place. My faith is my strength. I just have to call on it more.

A great thing to read when feeling depressed and in need of some encouragement is something like *Deuteronomy 31*. Joshua wasn't depressed but, before he was to take over the leadership of the people of Israel, Moses wanted to voice some words of encouragement to him. In *verses 7-8,* Moses tells Joshua to be strong and courageous, and that the Lord would go before him and be with him. God would never leave or forsake him, and there was no reason to be afraid or discouraged. The words encourage me too as my depression is usually accompanied by feelings of loneliness. I feel that it's me alone against the world, with none to talk to or look to for any kind of help. However, as Joshua, I know that the Lord will go before me and be with me through anything that confronts me. We all may need an occasional confidence booster and have to look no further than to Him for that.

Destruction - On this day in Egypt, February 8, 2011, talks continue concerning the political demonstrations that have caused destruction and death there. Hundreds of thousands of people have participated in the chaos where it is believed that at least 300 people have died so far, with a countless number of other people being injured. They are calling for their president, Hosni Mubrak, to resign, ending his 30-year reign as an authoritarian ruler. There is division in Egypt, as most want a democracy where governing power is derived from the people, by consensus, through fair elections. In authoritarian rule, political power is concentrated in a leader or leaders, who are typically not elected by the people, and may possess exclusive, unaccountable, and arbitrary power. From my understanding, the Egyptian army has yet to decide whether to remain with their president or side with those demanding change.

I've read where there are 734 occurrences of destruction written in the Bible, and the division of people was a cause in many cases, as it presently is in Egypt. *Mark 3:24* says that having division in a kingdom will only lead to *destruction*. I see no problems with demonstrations for a reasonable cause, as long as they are peaceful. However, if they cause fighting with one another, the Egyptians must take care in making sure that they do not cause the *destruction* of one to another (*Galatians 5:15*). Then they have to look at the consequences of the demonstrations if they only lead to even more violence. *Luke 9:25* asks the question of what profit will a man gain if he gets the world but undergoes the loss or *destruction* of himself. The majority of people are favoring democracy and are willing to fight for it. Hopefully, the price in obtaining it won't be at too high of a cost, and I'm optimistic that there will be a new transition of power soon that will be good for all.

devil - The *devil* is the supreme spirit of evil and the tempter of us all. My dictionary says that the word is often capitalized, but I don't think he deserves that honor. He is the ruler of hell and is only out to take you there with him. He will use temptation and lies in attempting to lure you into his trap, which only results in broken promises and shattered lives. I've known a few people who seemed to be living with the devil in them and who have tried to entice me to join them in their wicked ways. Then there have been others who may have just worked my nerves in trying to bring out the devil in me. That's how the devil works.

He will come at you directly, and when that fails he will call upon the many that he has enlisted to do his dirty work for him.

God represents truth, while the devil is a liar. As a matter of fact, as according to *John 8:44,* he is a murderer and a liar, along with being the enemy of God and the divine order (*Matthew 13:38,39).* The devil is very aggressive in the recruitment of his followers and will come at us in every way possible, with the many tricks he has up his sleeves. However, *Ephesians 4:27* and *6:11-16* tell us that we can resist the devil and even run him away from us. Something that I didn't know for many years was that it is generally believed that the sin that caused the devil's fall from God's grace was *pride,* and that is supported by *1 Timothy 3:6.* We must be most mindful of that, as many people have a lot of pride, which may cause an unwillingness in some to admit any wrongdoings, even before God. That only plays into the hands of the devil.

Direction - There are times when we all could use some direction, especially when faced with those difficult soul searching situations that test our faith. Aside from Jesus, none other was born into this world as a perfect human, and no person, no matter how great, successful, talented, brilliant or wise, has ever been able to do it all without at least a little help from others. The thing that is most important is to always include God in our decision-making. Our intelligence, skills, bravery, expertise or experience may fail us, but He won't. So it's best to pray first before we attempt to do anything of importance or get out of that troubling situation. Jumping into action without prayer may only lead one in the wrong direction.

When Jerusalem needed rebuilding, as it layed in ruins, Nehemiah first prayed to God before seeking the help of others in carrying out his strategy. *Nehemiah 1:1-11* tells how he confessed to the sins of himself and the people of Israel. He asked that God would listen to him and be granted favor as he planned to reconstruct their nation, starting with the rebuilding of a positive relationship with God. During these most difficult days of the present, where so many lives have been destroyed through unemployment or other unfortunate circumstances, people must look to God first as Nehemiah did. He will forgive the guilt of sins, and provide direction in the rebuilding of lives, when those in need are obedient and pray for His blessings.

Discipline - Instructing a person to follow a particular code of conduct is *discipline,* and it often regulated through punishment. It is an enforcement of order that is used as a learning tool. My parents used discipline on me when I disobeyed or misbehaved, just as I used it on my children. God will discipline us too. The Bible presents numerous examples where people were punished for being disobedient and ignoring His warnings of the consequences that would be faced for not following His codes of conduct. The great thing is that He forgives us, through love, and will give us chances to make things right with Him.

Job 36:9-12 tells about God's discipline. When a person commits sinful acts, He will first let that person know about it, and then make them listen to His disciplinary instructions, commanding them to repent for their sins. If the person obeys and serves God, they will spend the rest of their days in prosperity and have years on contentment. If the person doesn't listen and obey, they will only face a death without knowledge, which says that they failed to learning anything through discipline. Discipline is called *chastisement* in the Bible, meaning that there has to be correction in punishment.

Disobedience - When people behave in a manner that is totally opposite than what they know is right it is called *disobedience,* and it appears to me that we are breeding a culture of disobedience these days. Or maybe the definition should be changed because so many aren't being taught appropriately or being disciplined as strictly as in previous times? I have just seen so many youngsters exhibiting rebellious, disrespectful, uncaring, non-intelligent, and even criminal behavior, in their homes, in church, in school, and most any other places. On February 10, 2011, a story appeared on the front page of my local newsoaper where a teacher told of being taunted, threatened and physically assaulted by her students. However, even worst was that the story was actually one about *grade-fixing,* where a struggling school may alter their academic records to show improvement. This teacher had handed out 94 grades of D's and F's, only to have them changed to C's without her consent. That means that there were bad students who were actually rewarded in the receiving of a better grade, when they deserved no more than being disciplined for their real grades, which were really poor and unacceptable, and the mistreatment of that teacher.

Disobedience all started with Adam and Eve, who knew exactly what God's instructions were but acted in violation of them nonetheless. Today, poor home training and teaching may cause one to grow up with a disobedient nature. With Adam and Eve it was the enticing of another to do wrong *(Genesis 3),* kind of like the peer pressure that many face today. There was a tree bearing fruit in the middle of the Garden of Eden that God had instructed them not to eat from. A serpent approached Eve and talked her into questioning Him. He then deceived her into believing that she could eat from the tree if she wanted to. When she ate the fruit and had Adam join her, they received a punishment that would extend to all mankind. Sin had invaded their seemingly perfect paradise, and we have to try to keep it out of our lives as best as possible. We have to be fully educated in knowing what is *right* or *wrong* with God, along with not allowing ourselves to become vulnerable to the temptations of the devil by ourselves or the encouragement of others. It must be remembered too that God will not erase the consequences of our bad decisions and behavior, or inadequate learning and teaching, as it appears some schools may do. Plus some parents should be more disciplinary and never try to simply ignore or attempt to justify any child's disobedience.

Distraction - When we don't give God and Jesus our full undivided attention it is at times caused by *distraction,* where our focus is not on what we should be doing - our tasks, goals, purpose, etc. In today's world there are just so many things that we may allow to distract us and turn us away from doing our Bible reading, taking time out for prayer, or attending church services. Distraction is a major cause of procrastination, as some just put their faith on the backburners until it becomes more convenient for them; like the man who says that he will start back going to church on Sunday after the pro football season is over, because service and games times often coincide with each other.

1 Corinthians 7:32-35 discusses marriage and distraction. God wants us to be free from concerns that are not of Him, however it is written that an un-married man is concerned about the Lord's affairs and how he can please the Lord, while a married man is concerned about the world and pleasing his wife. So, the married man's interests are divided. It is desired that we all live the right way in undivided devotion and attention to the Lord. However there is now quite a difference from biblical times to the present, where today many un-married men are concerned mostly about only what pleases them and what the world has to offer. The same goes for the married men who aren't concerned with either pleasing the Lord or their wives.

Distress - Being out of work caused me much *distress*, in pain, suffering, agony, grief, sorrow and misery, as the unpaid bills began to mount and all the stress resulting from it was taking a toll on me mentally, physically, emotionally and spiritually. So, I needed to find some relief while continuing my job search and trying to keep in a positive frame of mind. My writing and refocusing on my faith helped me greatly in doing just that. I know that God is always at work for me during my times of distress, just as He will be for you if you call on Him. He will hear your cries for help when you are dealing with unemployment, financial worries, troubled relationships, life and death situations, or whatever else that may be the source of your distress.

The Bible gives two definitions for distress. One is *pain* and *grief*. The second is *to trouble*. When we are in distress we can can call out to God as David did in *Psalm 25:7*. He asked for God not to remember the sins of his youth and his rebellious ways, but to remember him out of His love. God loves us and even during our most distressful times we have nothing to fear because He is with us, just as David declared in *Psalm 23:4*. He walked *through the valley of the shadow of death* in confidence, knowing that God was with him. Then *2 Corinthians 4:8* tells us that we can be troubled from every direction but not in distress, along with being struck down but not destroyed, as it says in *verse 9*. It's the Lord who can help us to endure through any of our daily troubles or persecutions.

Diversions - To help keep our minds off our jobs or any kind of stress, we all have things that we enjoy doing, like a Saturday night at the movies or out dancing, attending a concert or sporting event, a day of shopping, enjoying a hobby... There are just so many things that we can do in finding pleasure, relaxation and maybe even a little peace of mind. However, we have to beware of the more destructive diversions like excessive gambling, adultery, drug and alcohol abuse and etc, along with understanding that what we may consider to be productive diversions still only offer a temporary rescue from the harsh realities of our daily lives. Diversions may fill the empty spaces inside of us from time to time, but can also entrap us to the point that the pursuit of pleasure consumes and controls us. It's only God that can totally fill our voids and give true meaning to our lives.

Ecclesiastes tells of King Solomon who was able to indulge in every passion, with wisdom, riches, and abundant pleasures at his command. He built many great things that delighted him, but also sought pleasure through things like alcohol use, obtaining servants to work for him, having singers to perform for him, and keeping many women around to satisfy his sexual desires. Yet, even with his worldly influence, tremendous wealth and many achievements, his pursuits of pleasure only brought about more disappointment than happiness. He said that upon looking back on all his work and labor there had been no profit as the pleasures were meaningless *(2:11)*. He understood the vanity of his seeking pleasure and that only a man who pleased God would be rewarded with the wisdom, knowledge and happiness that he had sought *(2:26)*. Solomon had been seeking to please only himself and not God, as many of us often become guilty of, and it is true that we are only headed for a big letdown when we make pleasure our god.

Divorce - My divorce was especially hard on me because I truly believed that my marriage would surely end only by death. Much to my surprise the marriage ended suddenly, after many years, while I remained very much in love. I'm still not exactly sure what happened but realize that there is a reason for everything, even beyond explanation. I had tried to be the very best husband that I could possibly be, but evidently had some shortcomings that derailed me from my goal of a lifetime of happiness with one woman. However, I pride myself in the fact that I gave it my all whenever possible. I was a husband who always treated his wife with the utmost of love and respect.

God is certainly against the divorce of a man and woman He has joined together in matrimony, as it says in *Mark.* Throughout the Scriptures husbands and wives may read about the help He offers when they commit themselves to being together for life. *Matthew* tells us that fornication is the grounds for divorce. Also that a man who marries another woman after divorcing his wife, for reasons other than being unfaithful, has committed adultery. God wants all marriages to work. As a husband, He wanted me to listen to the concerns of my wife and commit myself to her needs, along with always looking for ways to bring her happiness. I tried hard but obviously just failed a bit. Yet, I rejoice because infidelity or any kind of abusive behavior was never an issue.

Doubts - No matter how great, powerful, influential, successful, intelligent, wealthy, talented, confident or self-assured we are, doubt is something that we all have experienced and may continue doing so. I never doubted myself when I was running track. I was always confident of being able to compete at a high level when training right and being mentally prepared and focused on winning races. However, when it came to becoming a Christian, there were doubts concerning my worthiness and whether I was really ready to commit myself. Then during the bad times, as many of us do, I've had doubts about my self, my future, my faith and other things, though never blaming any of my troubles on God as some may. He is the solution and never the problem. We should be prayerful and never allow our doubts to drive us away from Him, along with understanding that we can be doubters even during the best of times too.

Being uncertain or lacking faith is called *doubt* according to the Bible, and *Deuteronomy 28:66* says that it can have you living in constant suspense and fear both day and night, and never being sure of anything in your life. In *Matthew 21:21-22,* Jesus tells us to have faith and not doubt. We will receive what we ask for in our prayers, if we truly believe in Him. Then in *1 Timothy 2:8,* He tells us to pray, while lifting up holy hands, and without any anger, disputes or doubts. *Verse 2:4* also tells us that there is only one God and one mediator between Himself and us - Jesus. Therefore, we can pray and place our faith in either without having any doubts. And *Mark 11:22-23* tells us that faith can be the solution to any of our problems, if we pray without having any doubts in our hearts. It's a good thing to remember also that even in certainty we still need God and Jesus in sustaining it.

Dreams - I at times have dreams about the happier days of my past in my sleep at night, with vivid images, ideas, emotions and memories going through my mind. Then there are my daydreams that may include things like becoming involved in a meaningful relationship with a woman or going on a nice long trip to just get away from every one and every thing. And finally I have the big dreams concerning my life and future that God encourages me to have. Even though things haven't been going as well as I would like lately, I am not placing any limits on my dreams or lowering my goals or expectations.

In the Bible much significance is attached to *dreams,* which may simply be called *sleeping visions*. However, *Ecclesiastes 5* could be viewed in terms of the dreams we have whether sleep or awake. It says that dreams may come through our many cares, as I presently have. We must be in awe of God though, otherwise all of our dreams are meaningless, as well as our words. *2 Thessalonians 1:11-12* goes on to assure me that through prayer, if I am worthy of His calling, God may fulfill all my desires, along with acting in recognition of my dreams. The name of Jesus will be glorified in me as I will be in Him.

Drugs - Recently a man became really angry and accused me of being a liar when I told him that I had never seen real *crack* before. But I was serious, also knowing very little about the other recreational and prescription drugs that people get hooked on. I'd just seen the fake stuff they show on television and at the movies. I have seen how it *has* or *is* destroying many lives though, and I know a few people who have been in and out of drug programs with no long-term positive results. They seem to only just drift back to it sooner or later. Then there are others I suspect of using one drug or another who will probably be on that same roller coaster ride before long. The one thing they all appear to have in common is *denial.* And the first step to overcoming their drug addiction is realizing and confessing that it is a problem that is far too big for them to handle alone or through the many programs that may only provide temporary treatment but no real cure.

Drug abusers are like the wine drinkers in the Bible that were condmned for their drunkeness. *Hosea 4:11* says that wine takes away the heart, and it's the same for people with a serious drug addiction. They will steal even from their own mothers to get money to purchase their drugs, and think nothing of it. Then as the drunkards, it only leads to misery and grief as they run after it from morning until late at night, until it takes over them *(Isaiah 5:11)*. Eventually they are only to be excluded from Christian fellowship and from Heaven *(1 Corinthians 5:11, 6:10)*, and their lives turning to poverty *(Proverbs 23:21)*. Drug addiction is a very serious problem and is spreading all over amongst people from all walks of life. It's like Epharim, in the Bible, where even the priests and prophets became drunkards *(Isaiah 28:1-7)*. However, all is not lost, as there is help in the Lord. He can be a person's strength every morning and provide the salvation for any kind of distress *(Isaiah 3:2)*.

Ears - When I suffered the temporary blindness from my stroke, I thought about what it would be like if I ever lost the use of my ears too. We just take so much for granted, and even in having ears many can still be totally deaf at times. Some only hear what they want to hear and others simply may refuse to, especially when it concerns God. There are just so many people in today's world who are spiritually deaf and won't open their ears to any words of reason. When needing to be lifted, they often only hear the words of those who will only keep them down or drop them further. The suffering are often vulnerable to being preyed upon by those who will tell them exactly what they want to hear, whether any of their words are based on truth or not. But God's Words always speak only the truth to those who will lend an open ear. He may not always tell you what you want to hear but will always tell you what you need to hear and what's best for you in truth and out of love.

Zechariah 7 tells of the Lord (God) speaking to Zechariah, who was to pass His message along to the people. However, they totally closed their ears in refusing to listen to anything Zechariah said. That made the Lord very angry. Therefore, when it came time for the people to call on Him, He did the same as they had done. He refused to listen and scattered them among the many nations, where they became strangers. The pleasant land they had occupied was left desolate. So it's easy to see that the penalties for closing our ears to Words of the Lord can be quite severe. *Psalm 135:17* also speaks of people having ears but not not hearing. We all may need some help in hearing from time to time, and *Proverbs 23:12* tells us to open our ears to words of knowledge. Then in *Matthew 11,* Jesus says that He is truthful and wants all who have ears be allowed to hear Him. But some don't want that, so we must also watch out for those who, through false words or any other means, will try to keep ears closed to the truthful Words of the Lord.

Earth - I read where the Earth as we know it may not be recognizable by the year 2050. The global population will have reached nine billion, up from seven billion in 2010. Therefore, there will be even more people competing for even far fewer resources, and it is estimated that more food will have to be produced over the next 40 years than was produced over the past 8,000. Then look at all the damage man has done to the planet in just over the past 100 years, with air and water pollution, damaging the ozone layer and causing global warming, the extinction of many animals, increasing crime and poverty, new diseases, and etc., along with technology that one day could cause our total destruction in a world war.

According to *Psalm 104:5,* God set the Earth on its foundations and it can never be moved. However, man now has the intelligence and capability of doing the impossible and crossing boundaries that *Psalm 104:9* says we would never be able to. *Isaiah 11:9* tells of the Earth being full of the knowledge of God and of man not being able to hurt or destroy anything in His holy mountain. That mountain is no longer a safe haven though as we continue to find ways to misuse our knowledge. We are tearing down more mountains than we are building up and the pillars that *1 Samuel 2:8* says God erected to support the Earth are showing cracks as they never have before. Future generations will surely have to be concerned about feeding an overpopulated planet and correcting our mistakes.

Education - The best education comes when you have good teachers teaching students that are committed to learning; a combination seriously lacking in public schools today with graduation rates at their lowest ever. I had great study habits and, when applying myself, always learned a lot and did well in school, even being a Dean's List student in college. However, as a student of Christianity, like many, I never did very well. I learned from my church pastors through their sermons but seldom studied the Word. My present pastor is always trying to build up the attendance for night bible study classes and has had little success. I've participated a few times and, beyond some of the ministerial staff, there were never many other people there. Most seem content with opening their Bible on Sundays at the pastor's instruction, along with maybe reading a couple of their favorite Scriptures at home when they need to be uplifted.

Uneducated children, not knowing anything, should hear and learn to fear the Lord our God (*Deuteronomy 31:13*), as the fear of the Lord is the beginning of knowledge (*Proverbs 1:7*). I would say too that those words are applicable to any adults that don't know or fear the Lord. Also, there are no limits to education and the wise man will always hear and continue learning *(Proverbs 1:5)*. The fools, however, will only despise wisdom and any instruction given them *(Proverbs 1:7)*. We should all understand that whatever was written in the past was written to educate us, and that our hope is through patience and the encouragement of the Scriptures *(Romans 15:4)*. There also may come times when we are called upon to educate ourselves. *Matthew 9:13* tells how Jesus answered a question some Pharisees had asked and then told them to go out and learn the meaning of His answer.

Effort - Succeeding at anything requires a great deal of *effort;* hard work. The writing and self-publishing of my first book was just that, especially with having no previous experience. I learned a lot and the knowledge I acquired will be very helpful to me in completing my second book. Plus, this time I started off by drafting a plan, and proper planning is important for the success of any project, just as those detailed in the Bible.

I was looking at some photographs of a kitchen I remodeled in my first house many years ago. It made me think about how God called on people to do work for Him who, as myself, had no experience to rely on. He gave specific instructions and Noah was able to build an arc to His exact specifications *(Genesis 6)*. If you are willing to put forth a little effort, you may be surprised at some of the things you may accomplish too.

Enthusiasm - Displaying an intense enjoyment, interest, or approval of something is called *enthusiasm*. However, the original uses of the word were confined to religious inspiration or emotions, as an *enthusiast* was defined as being a person possessed by a god. When we dance and shout during our church services we are being much like the 4th century Euchites of Syria. They were a religious group that became known as the *Enthusiasts* because of their intense religious displays and belief that man was inspired by the Holy Spirit through prayer, contemplation, and using self-denial as a means of attaining a high spiritual state.

Socrates, the ancient Greek philosopher, taught that a form of enthusiasm was the inspiration received from poets, like myself, and throughout the *Psalms,* King David is seen as *David the Poet* and the *Sweet Singer of Israel*. He poured out his heart in enthusiasm to God, on his knees, dancing, singing and shouting in repentance and thanksgiving, while asking for God's assurance, strength, deliverance and instruction. King Solomon also spoke of enthusiasm according to *Proverbs 2:2-3*. He said that in seeking God's wisdom, we must be sincere in our hearts, along with crying out for knowledge and lifting up our voices for understanding.

Envy - Hating another person for what they have is called *envy* (jealousy), and it's a sin that family, friends, and enemies alike may be guilty of in being envious of another. The love of their own good causes them to believe that they should have more, even if it means that another person will have less because of them. Envious people often rejoice in the failure or suffering of others and think that they, and not you, should have the better education, job, marriage, home, car, or etc. They may not be very giving either and can be very deceiving in their selfishness; like the person, claiming to be looking out for you, who will call with information concerning a job opening only after knowing that the position has been filled. The fear is that helping you may eventually place you back ahead of them and, during the troubled times, it is often the envious person who will smile in your face and laugh behind your back because they had always wanted to be in a better position than yourself.

Moses is a great example of a person having to deal with envious people. He enjoyed many advantages, in his relationship with God, and some wondered why him and not them. *Numbers 12* tells how he was talked about out of envy, and *1 Peter 2:1* says that we should lay it all aside. The Lord despises it and will punish us just as He did those who were envious of Moses. However, there is a cure for envy called *love*. *1 Corinthians: 4-8* tells us that love is patient and kind, and it is never boastful, proud, self-seeking, rude, easily angered, or envious. Love rejoices in the truth, and is protectful, provides hope, always perseveres, and never fails. Only in love do we succeed and our only concerns should involve our own God-given blessings, rather than comparing ourselves with others. It is the Lord who will lift us up (*James 4:10*), if we humble ourselves, and not at the expense of others. Rather than competing, we should always serve God with what He gives us.

Escape - People, when facing problems, often seek an escape through the idols of pleasure, rather than turning to God for strength and insight. While that football game or family outing may provide some temporary relief and comfort, it's prayer and patience that will provide the more lasting and effective ways of toughing it out. And acting out on some temptations may only result in one having to face more problems than they started off with; like the person who finds their escape at the local bar, only to consume too much alcohol and later cause an automobile accident or be arrested for driving under the influence. The best course of action is in first drawing upon your relationship with God, rather than just seeking a quick fix for those issues of concern. He will guide you through your most troubled times, and you may still be able to take that getaway trip to the Bahamas, but only with His guidance, approval, and blessings.

God wants us to always stand strong, while being careful not to fall *(1 Corinthians 10:12),* and He will provide our escapes when needed. According to *1 Corinthians 10:13,* the only temptations that can seize you are those that are common to man, and God will not allow you to be tempted beyond what a person can bear. He is faithful and will provide a way out when you need an escape from your problems or temptations. *Luke 21:34-36* also tells us to beware of allowing our hearts to be weighed down by the problems of our lives. We should always be on the watch and pray that we will be able to escape from all that may happen, in being accounted as worthy to stand before the *Son of man*. Then there may come times when you just have to escape for your life. In that kind of situation *Genesis 19:17* instructs us to move forward. Looking back or staying in one place may only cause one's destruction. When you have found favor in the Lord, He will make your escape a safe one.

Evil - It is said that King Manasseh of Judah ignored the prophets and entrusted his welfare and that of the people to false gods. He had fortified the cities and their soldiers to be prepared for any attacks from the Assyrians, saying that evil would never come to them. However, he himself had been doing much evil in the eyes of the Lord, who then spoke to him and his people but they paid no attention *(2 Chronicles 33:10).* Upon that the armies of Assyria were brought against the people of Jerusalem. Manasseh was taken prisoner *(2 Chronicles 33:11),* and only after the king sought God's favor and humbled himself was he brought back to Jerusalem and his kingdom *(2 Chronicles 33:12-13).* Manasseh then knew that the Lord was God and, when he prayed, God listened to his pleas. In today's world there are many bad and wicked people practicing their evil ways much to God's displeasure. There is continued war and the daily threat of terrorism by some very violent groups. We need to listen to God and be submissive to His voice. Yet we seem to have learned little from the stories like that of King Manasseh.

There were those who believed that we had become safe from evil ever occurring again on our own soil, like the surprise attacks on Pearl Harbor by Japan on December 7, 1941, because of our technology, power and preparation. As a result, when it was forewarned (or prophesized) about the attacks that were to come on September 11, 2001, some weren't paying close enough attention that could possibly have taken action to help prevent it. Evil struck again as the Al-Qaeda led by Osama bin Laden hijacked our own aircraft to crash into the Twin Towers of the World Trade Center in New York. It was a terrorist act that was meant to inflict mass murder and destruction upon us. Many are still in prayer for the safety of our country from the evil of others. However, is God listening? *2 Chronicles 34:27* says that God favors and hears those that humble themselves before Him, while He has been forsaken here with things like the banning of prayer and Christmas celebrations in many places, and some seeking to even have His name to be removed from our money. It's no wonder that evil has come to us.

Eyes - During my stroke, and already blind in my left eye, I was in great fear of losing the sight in my right as well, and having some most terrifying thoughts about the possibility of a life without my eyes in the eerie darkness that I was witnessing. Then while lying in the hospital bed recovering, with the Lord having restored my vision, I thought about the many people that have the use of their eyes but are walking in blindness. The

Bible says that we walk in faith and not in sight (*2 Corinthians 5:7*), and there are many who may never see or experience the Lord's work firsthand, as I did, because they have little or no faith, or in blindness fail to see or understand what they should.

In *Mark 8,* as the disciples boarded a boat for travel, they had forgotten to take along any bread, having only one loaf that was already there. Jesus questioned them upon hearing their discussion about not having any. They had seen Him feed four thousand people with only seven loaves of bread, with bread left over. Had their hearts been hardened? Did they not remember? Did they have ears and eyes but failed to hear or see? Or had they seen but didn't understand? In faith, even without their eyes, they should have seen that they had more bread than they needed, as they had already witnessed. However, as those without faith, they were blind in relying only on what was in their actual sight before them, and not on Jesus.

Failure - We may view it to be failure when things don't go as we would have liked or planned. However, things may happen that are just beyond our control as a matter of life. Good workers get laid off. Healthy people become ill. Great drivers have car accidents. Loving marriages end in divorce. Business deals fall through. *Failure* is being left wanting, disappointed or feeling defeated, while most of us strive for success, even if it may be self-serving. And some people can be pretty mixed up in distinguishing the difference between failure and success, as imperfect accomplishments are really failures. Take the businessman, for example, that resorted to all kinds of illegal activities in building his business. He may be a success in one way but quite a failure in others.

1 Corinthians 13:8 tells us that love is the only thing that never fails. With love we can't help but exceed, as the kind of love the Bible speaks of includes virtuous things like patience, honesty, trust, forgiveness, and good manners, while having no motives of self-interest. I guess that could simply mean that in being a true success you have to be a *people person,* as the Lord tells us to love one another as He loves us (*John 13:34*). *Deuteronomy 31:6* also tells us that the Lord, our God, will not fail us, and God is love, as *1 John 4:8* states. Then *Job 11:20* warns that the eyes of the wicked will fail when they need an escape, and their lives will be without hope. With godly love we don't have to worry about failure and can enjoy lives of hope and success, even if things may not always go our way.

Faith - *Faith* displays a confident belief in the truth, value, or worthiness of a person, idea, or thing. And that belief may not rest on any logical proof or material evidence, as faith implies a reliance of trust upon future events or outcomes. Therefore, as I continue to have a few problems, God is my faith, and in faith is my belief that He will turn things around for the better. I am a believer and trust in the promises God made through Jesus and the Scriptures by which we are justified or saved. No matter how bad things may ever become, faith provides my hope. *Hebrews 11:1* defines faith as being the assurance of what we hope for with the certainty of things not seen. So while I can't presently see the end of my struggles, I'm confident that I will.

As a Christian man of faith, *James 5:13-16* instructs me to pray when I am in trouble, sing songs of praise when I am happy, and call on the elders of the church to pray over me and anoint me with oil in the name of the Lord when I am sick. The prayers of faith will make me well and my sins will be forgiven, for the prayer of a righteous man is powerful and effective. I realize too that my blessings will only be received through faith. It is impossible to please God without it, and He rewards only those who come to Him with the belief that He exists and diligently seek Him (*Hebrews 11:6*). I maintain that belief and a hope for being blessed in living righteously by faith, just as those were along with a faithful Abraham (*Galatians 3:9,11*).

Faithfulness - There is no faith without *faithfulness,* which the Bible defines as *constancy.* True faith is steadfast and unwavering. However, some claiming to have faith may ignore God when life is good. Only when things turn bad do they return to calling upon Him and acknowledging their faith. Then there are others that may turn away from God when things aren't going well, blaming Him and/or others for their circumstances. Both groups are acting without conscience or faith in behaving like the non-believers considered being sinners, as *Romans 14:23* tells us that anything lacking of faith is sin.

We need to be forever faithful as God is to us, but there will always be a struggle for many to do so because of the certainty of sin in every person. But God never gives up on us as some may with Him. In the Bible, the Israelites constantly sinned and rebelled, while God remained faithful and true to them. The Apostle Paul wrote, in *2 Timothy 2:13,* that God remains faithful even when we are faithless because He can't deny Himself. *Lamentations 3:23-24* tells us that God is great in faithfulness and we are not consumed by our sins because of His mercies. His compassions will not fail us and are renewed every morning. I wish we could all rise up and stop failing Him.

Falling - Any person may be flying high one day and then finding themselves falling fast and out of control the next. At times one's circumstances can be just that unpredictable as the pendulum of life may suddenly swing from good to bad without warning or reason. The thing to remember is that no matter how far a person falls, a strong faith will provide a safety net from them falling further. They may feel overwhelmed for a while but the Lord never is. He can break their fall even if it appears that there is absolutely nothing left for them to hold on to and, better yet, help them to climb back up to a more comfortable position or even beyond where they originally were.

The Lord rescues those that are upright and avoid evil, and their lives are spared in keeping their ways. It's the proud and arrogant people taking from others that may only be destined for destruction or to continue falling, while the humble find good in resolving their issues and having things turned back in their favor, as those that trust in the Lord and handle their matters wisely are blessed. This was all told in *Proverbs 16:17-20*. Then *Jude 24* tells us further that the Lord will keep us from falling if we keep ourselves in His love, build ourselves up in faith, pray in the Holy Spirit, and wait on His mercy.

Family - The *traditional family* consists of a husband and wife (man and woman) and their children, whereas during Biblical times a man's family included a wife or wives and concubines, their children, families of their children, and the servants or slaves. Then in today's world the *single parent family* has become very common because of divorce, adoption, artificial insemination, surrogate motherhood, death, child abuse, child neglect, or abandonment by one of the biological parents. Single parenthood may place hardship on the children because there is one less parent at home to monitor them and give them the attention they need, along with statistics indicating that they are more likely to grow up in poverty than are children from two-parent families. Then it is even tougher for boys because many may not have the regular presence of a man in their lives, if any. I read that in 2006, a single parent, of which 80% were women, headed 12.9 million families in our country.

I was born into a two-parent family but my father died before I was even a teenager. My mother did her best but my transition from child to manhood was a tough one without a father around. Things were just so different back in the days when I was born. As a youngster all of my friends had two parents at home, and I remember the sadness of being in the Boy Scouts and having to miss out on a Father-Son picnic. It certainly would have been a different learning experience and a lot more fun growing up in a traditional family setting for all of my early years. In reference to the Bible, parents are held responsible for the raising and education of their children, and all these men now failing as fathers and heads of families should read *1 Timothy 5:8,* which says that any not providing for his own, especially for those in his own house, have denied their faith and are worse than unbelievers. Death is one thing. Having both parents living but separate is another. It would be great if more fathers and mothers these days lived in the same home and were committed to the joint upbringing of their children, but only faith will return families to being as they were in the past.

Fear - People live in fear every day; in their homes, at work, on the streets, in schools... *Fear* is the feeling or condition of being afraid, whether real or imagined, and is aroused by impending danger, evil, pain, etc. A Gallup Poll conducted in 2005 revealed that the most common fears for teenagers in our country then were terrorist attacks, spiders, death, failure, war, heights, crime/violence, being alone, the future, and nuclear war. Then during these tough economic times many people have great fears about losing things, like their jobs, money, investments, homes, cars, marriages, health, and especially faith. Every person has fears about at least one thing or another but should never allow any to consume them. As the Bible instructs, I have learned to place most of mine in the hands of the Lord, where I feel safe.

King David said that even though he walked through the valley of death he feared no evil, for the Lord was with him (*Psalm 23:4*). In his combat with Goliath, he stated that the battle was the Lord's (*1 Samuel 17:47*) and that's where he drew his strength and courage. It's the same with us as the Lord is with us through all of our challenges. In *Psalm 34:4,* David goes on to say that he sought the Lord and was answered. He was then delivered from all of his fears, just as the Lord will do with us when we are troubled and call on Him. Those who fear Him will lack nothing (*Psalm 34:9*). However, we also have to be wise when it comes to fear for, just as *Jeremiah 6:25* warns, the enemy and fear are on every side in the fields and where we walk, meaning that we should be careful not to place ourselves in situations where safety may become an issue.

Fellowship - An association with others is called *fellowship,* and I didn't do much in the beginning at my present church. I was comfortable and had no problems with the women but felt that most of the men didn't care much for me. My quiet nature gave some the wrong impression and they seemed to be unwilling to take any time to really get to know me. Things changed when I began to approach them on a more personal level than just our religious association, upon the urging of my ex-wife. As a result, friendships have resulted with many of the men from conversations that revealed we had a lot in common even beyond our church and faith. I believe it's a great thing for that to have happened because the fellowship of believers is most important and beneficial as we support each other and worship together in our fellowship with God and Jesus.

With my different church affiliations and the sharing of my inspirational writing, there has been a dramatic increase in the number of people I fellowship with. I now communicate with Christian folks from all over the country, many that I have never met personally. We all, as I am trying to do, should proclaim what we have seen and heard in fellowship with each other, as our true fellowship is with God and Jesus (*1 John 1:3*). Then *1 John 1:7* tells us that if we have fellowship with God and walk in His light, we have fellowship with each other, and the blood of Jesus will cleanse us from all sin. Therefore, fellowship is very important for our salvation. However, Paul warns us against having any fellowships with devils that don't sacrifice to God as we do (*1 Corinthians 10:20*). Believers have nothing in common with unbelievers.

Fight - At times I feel that my life has just been one continuous fight, over the past few years, as I have faced one struggle after another. However, while some may have given up by now, I have persevered and learned how to fight harder, especially through my faith. As a result, my victories have begun to greatly outnumber my defeats. It's very sad though that I have had to fight some that should be in my corner fighting with me rather than in another fighting against me, but it's pretty typical for people with ungodly spirits to turn their backs on others or try to make things even more difficult for them. However, I have learned to distance myself from those kinds of people because, in agreement with *Acts 5:39*, it's a waste of time that may only result in me fighting against God as they really are.

Through it all, I have continued to fight a good fight and in keeping my faith, as *2 Timothy 4:7* reads. There are still a few more battles to be won however, but I know that the Lord is fighting with me and I can hold my peace because of Him *(Exodus 14:14)*. And I don't have to worry about those that may be against me because, as with *Psalm 35:1,* I can plead my cause to the Lord and call on Him to fight against those who fight against me. In remembering the Lord's greatness, I know that there is nothing for me to fear, and am now more confident in fighting for myself, along with being encouraged to fight for my brothers, sons, daughters, wives, and houses, as with *Nehemiah 4:14*.

Flee - In life we face many battles, with some being never ending. As humans, for example, we will always commit sin no matter how hard it is fought against, and the devil will continue to attack us no matter how many times we defeat him. In those and other battles, we may have to decide when it's better to fight or to flee in gaining any kind of advantage. Let's say that I had a drinking problem and some friends invited me out to a place that served alcohol. I could go and have to fight the urges of taking a drink, but a wiser decision would be to just steer myself away from there. It would probably be a good thing too to have friends that would be more considerate of the problem.

A parable tells us in *John 10* that Jesus is *the door* and our *good shepherd.* We that know the Lord's voice can follow Him through His door. However, we should flee from any person trying to enter the door improperly (like a person trying to break into another's home) or has the voice of a stranger, as they are considered to be thieves and robbers. As sheep, we should follow our shepherd. He will lead us in ways that are good, and help us win our battles. We should always listen to the Lord's voice and have Him before us as we fight, while having a deaf ear and fleeing from our enemies and others, including some false friends, whose encouragement may only lead us astray or to imminent defeat.

Following - I'm following Jesus and my writing is in testimony to that. After many years of trying, I had finally realized that I couldn't accomplish many things on my own. Decided that it was time to accompany Him on my journey through life. I have faith in Him and who He is, and have accepted the offer of eternal life that He has extended to us. On my daily journey, I am relying on Him to lead the way. In submitting myself to Jesus, my relationship with Him is placed above all else, and I know He will lead me to a better, hope filled, and blessed life.

I've lived a fairly successful and happy life, but have fought a few battles by myself where I could have used the Lord's presence and direction to light a path to victory. I just didn't fully understand then how easy it was to call on Him. But in reality, He had called me many times but I wasn't listening. He knows best when we need Him. All we have to do is accept His invitation when He calls on us and says, "follow me", as in *Matthew 19:21*. I now know that in following Jesus I never have to go it alone or in darkness. He is the light of the world and, in walking with Him, I have the light of life (*John 8:12*).

Forgiveness - I have always had a very forgiving nature, and try to resolve conflicts with others quickly, especially when feelings have been hurt. However, a few years ago, I experienced a situation where a person just quit talking to me and wouldn't offer a reason as to why. After months of trying to clear things up with no luck, I just decided to forgive the person and move on. Then one day we came face to face on a street corner. It was a most awkward moment, and I wasn't sure as to whether I should speak or just walk on by. Being myself, I chose to speak and was quite pleased to receive a response. We were then on speaking terms again, even though I still didn't know why there had been a problem between us. I just rejoiced in that there was now forgiveness on both of our parts, and was certain that the Lord had arranged our chance meeting.

It is just human nature for people to have their differences and disagreements, with some even becoming enemies with another. Therefore, we may fight or hold grudges against those that may have wronged us in one way or another, while we should find peaceful ways in settling our issues and practice forgiveness, as the Bible instructs. When Peter asked the Lord if seven times would be often enough for him to forgive his brother who had sinned against him, Jesus told him that it should be more like seventy times seven (*Matthew 18:21-22*). Then *Matthew 6:14-15* says that our heavenly Father will forgive us if we forgive those that sin against us, and He won't forgive us if we don't. Also, we should have a spirit of forgiveness in doing it from our hearts (Matthew 18:35), and *Romans 12:8* says that we should express our mercy to others in cheerfulness.

Forgotten - During the bad times, people may look to others for comfort and strength, but often only feel alone and forgotten. It's like those being counted on suddenly went away on an extended vacation. And they have! Just away from you. They may say that they were giving you some space while you worked things out, but really may have been more worried that you would look to them for help. However, for whatever reason, during some battles one may find a few of their soldiers running off rather joining in on the fight. These are the times when a person's faith is really tested also, as people may question God's presence too when things aren't going well for them.

The thing to remember is that God is always with you, through the good and the bad. He'll never forget you or pretend to have forgotten you as some people may do. As they faced captivity by King Nebuchadnezzar and the Babylonian armies, the people of Israel wondered if God had forgotten them in the midst of their continued struggles. Their concerns were unfounded though, and *Isaiah 49:15-17* tells how God answered them, through the prophet Isaiah, saying that He hadn't forgotten them and was going to deliver them away from their destroyers. He even had their image engraved on the palms of His hands. For us today that are strong in faith, ours is there as well.

Freedom - *Freedom* is the quality or state of being free, with the absence of being denied to do as I choose. With it, I am supposedly liberated from slavery, restraint, or the power of another, along with the ability to make my own choices. Therefore, in spite of those that tried to convince me to do otherwise, I exercised my free will in deciding to follow Jesus. Nonetheless, I often question what true freedom is. I've seen people going to work on Halloween wearing costumes, including some dressed as devils. Then for Christmas, where I worked, I wanted to post one of my poems on the office bulletin board, and placed a message in one of my weekly company newsletters telling people to contact me, if they wanted copies of it and others. The response was great but my bosses threatened to write me up for insubordination, then my responsibility for writing the newsletters was later taken away from me. Imagine that! There was freedom for some people to celebrate the devil at work but not the birth of our Lord.

The experience at work disturbed me a bit, but there will always be those that will deny or continue trying to take away the freedom of others, even in a democratic society as ours. However, while freedom is never a guarantee in man's world, it is in Jesus. In *John 8,* Jesus told the Jews, who believed in Him, that even though the children of Abraham had never been slaves to anyone they were still slaves to sin. If they held to His teachings they would learn and know the truth, which would give them freedom. It goes on to say that the slave of sin has no permanent place in the family but Jesus belongs to it forever, and He is the one that shall grant true freedom. *Romans 8* then explains that there is now no condemnation for those that are in Jesus Christ. They are granted freedom from the law of sin and death, while given life and peace. The sufferings that man may place upon them in the present are not worthy of comparison to the future glory that will be revealed through the Lord.

Friends - Good friends are truly a blessing. Good friends are friends for life. Good friends believe in you and want you to succeed. Good friends share their wisdom and encourage you to do right rather than wrong. Good friends stick with you through the thick and thin. Good friends are loyal and are the first to volunteer when you need help. Good friends will stand watch and fight with you during your toughest battles. Good friends share your core beliefs, hold the same value systems, and are usually headed in the same direction as you in life. Good friends will tell you what you need to hear rather than what you want to hear. And good friends, with Christian beliefs, will hold you accountable and guide you back to God when you run astray. *Exodus 33:11* says God spoke, face to face, to Moses as a man does with his friend. He'll do the same for you, as will Jesus.

Chapter 19 of *Job* tells how his friends only treated him with cruelty, when they believed he had gone astray. Some friends forgot him *(verse 14)*, while others detested him and turned against him *(verse 19)*. All he could do was ask for their pity *(verse 21)* and question why they were persecuting him *(verse 22)*. Good friends shouldn't behave like that as *Proverbs 17:17* says they should love each other at all times. And there is no greater love than a man who will sacrifice his life for his friends as Jesus did *(John 15:13)*. He commands us, in being His friends, to love one another as He loves us *(John 15:12,14)*, and to recruit other friends. *Mark 5* tells of Jesus healing a demon-possessed man, who then wanted to follow Him. Jesus told the man to just go home to his friends and tell them of the Lord's compassion and the many great things He was doing.

Fruit - A definition of *fruit* is that it is a result, consequence or product of something, and God wants us to live *fruitful* lives that make us worthy of the fruits He blesses us with. The labor of the righteous gives them life, while the fruit of the wicked only brings them punishment *(Proverbs 10:16)*. God wants to see us grow spiritually and be committed to devotional lifestyles that will create and strengthen the bonds between Himself and those that choose to be His followers. As with the prayer from *Colossians 1:10,* we should try to live lives that are worthy of the Lord and that may please Him in every way, being fruitful in all of our good work, and always looking to increase our knowledge in God. The fruit of the righteous is the tree of life and they will receive many more blessings than the wicked and the sinner *(Proverbs 11:30-31)*.

Romans 6:22 says that in becoming servants of God, we reap the fruit of holiness and in the end there is everlasting life. However, *Hebrews 12:10-11* additionally says that God disciplines us for our own good, so that we may share in that holiness. His discipline may be a little painful at the time, but afterward it will yield a fruit of righteousness and peace for all those trained by it. Also, according to *James 3:17,* we should harvest our wisdom from above, as it is first pure while later being full of mercy and good fruit, peace loving, considerate, submissive, impartial, sincere, and etc. Then *Galatians 5:22-23* instructs us to live by the Spirit, because in it's fruit are things like love, peace, patience, kindness, goodness, faithfulness, and self-control, for which there are no laws, and we will be recognized by our fruit on the day of judgment.

Funerals - One semester in college, I took an elective course called *Death And Dying*. My core schedule was going to be a little tough and I had heard that this class wouldn't be too difficult. For one assignment though, we were told to go to a funeral home, on our own, and get information and pricing for the planning of a funeral. A greater portion of our grade was to be based upon a paper we were to write. However, especially after my father's death, I had a thing about funerals and had no plans on visiting a funeral home. My way out was to just change the numbers a bit, that a friend had gathered, and put my writing skills to work. The result was a very descriptive story of me visiting a funeral home and feeling like a stranger, riding into a dangerous gun-slinging town in the old west, with an undertaker already sizing me up for a casket. My paper, also, included the planning of a very nice and affordable funeral. I was given the highest grade, and my instructor said it was the most informational and entertaining he'd ever read.

Though a Christian now, funerals are still a little uncomfortable for me, as I seem to find myself attending far more of them than the parties of my college days. Funeral processions are said to have begun over 3,500 years ago in ancient Egypt, out of the necessity for transporting bodies to their resting places, and *funerals* are defined as being ceremonies for celebrating, sanctifying, or remembering the life of a person who has died. However, it is only human for us to grieve over the loss of loved ones and, according to the Bible, Jesus even experienced sorrow and shed tears. Once was when He returned to Bethany, near Jerusalem, four days after the funeral of Lazarus, a good friend. While at the burial site in the midst of many mourners, including friends Martha and Mary, the sisters of Lazarus, upon hearing their cries of pain and loss, *John 11:35* simply says, "Jesus wept". He had felt their sorrow and wept in spite of knowing that He soon would be raising Lazarus up from the dead; just as we grieve even in believing that our lost loved ones have only moved on with Him to a better place in Heaven.

Future - My writing details a lot about my past and how I've arrived at where I am today. I've had my struggles but have accomplished much to be proud of. There are times that I may think back about how things would be for me today if I had done some things differently, like maybe attending a college where I could have continued my competitive running as a sprinter in track. However, I've learned to never worry or dwell too much on the past, but to use my experiences as learning tools in dealing with my present concerns. The result is that I'm running and winning different kinds of races, and continue having some high hopes and dreams for the future, while also understanding that the future is really now. God controls what lies ahead for me and my relationship with Him must be today, not tomorrow.

I'm positive that things will work out for the best. My trust is in God and I faithfully believe that He still has many good things planned for me. As with *Jeremiah 29:11,* I know that His thoughts are of peace, not of evil, and will give me hope and a future. Then with my present life under control, I won't have to worry much about my next either, if I maintain a positive relationship with God. In *John 6:47,* Jesus tells us that our belief gives us everlasting life, and I can't think of a better future than that, especially with the promise of a new life void of any sufferings. My tears will be wiped away and I'll never again have to worry about any of the things that are troubling me now or did in the past *(Revelation 21:4).* I can see a great future ahead here on Earth and in Heaven, but only if I continue drawing nearer to God, as I know He will to me *(John 4:8).*

Gifts - God blesses everyone with their own unique individual gifts, however you don't necessarily have to be the most gifted to accomplish some great things. Having determination and the willingness to put in a lot of effort are also important. I may not be the best writer or singer but I'm now working harder than ever at it. There are just people, many more gifted than myself, that are wasting their gifts as I once was. We need to put our gifts to work and encourage others to put theirs to work too. Just look at Ben Carson, considered to be the world's best neurosurgeon, who went to both Hunter Junior High and Southwestern High School in Detroit, as I did. In his book, *Gifted Hands,* I like where he says to *think big* and that *being a member of a minority race doesn't mean being a minority achiever.* He was a smart student but says that he went from the top of his class to underachieving and straying from the *important and basic values of his life.* However, his mother, Sonya, was determined not to let him waste his gifts. She sacrificed her life and helped push him to where he is today. An important thing to see though is that you don't have to be as intelligent as Ben Carson to achieve similar greatness. Use any gifts God has blessed you with, big or small, as best as you can.

1 Corinthians 7:7 says that each man has his own gift from God; one has this gift and another has that. Therefore, I am blessed with gifts that another is not, just as you are. *1 Timothy 4:11-16* tells about the Lord encouraging young Timothy to devote himself to publicly reading the Scriptures, teaching and preaching. He was to set an example for the believers in speech, life, love, faith and purity. In doing so, he wouldn't neglect the gift that was given to him through a prophetic message when the body of elders laid their hands on him. And in giving himself wholly to his gifts, watching his life, and continuing his teaching, all would see his progress, which would ultimately save himself and his hearers. I don't have the gift of prophecy, however I am trying to follow the ways of love and most desire being given spiritual gifts as says *1 Corinthians 14:1*. Many see me as having the gifts of writing and singing, but I view my good nature as being a great gift too. I have a very giving heart and am always doing whatever I can to help others, plus leading by example. My greatest gift came though when I did as Peter instructed in *Acts 2:38*. In repenting and being baptized in the name of Jesus Christ, I received the gift of the Holy Spirit.

Giving - There is a lot of greed and selfishness in the world, and this can be said of non-believers and believers as well. Some people just lack giving spirits and will seldom, if ever, share their God-given blessings with others. God desires us to be more givers than receivers and greatly blesses those that are. You surely can't take things like wealth to the grave with you but it seems like there are those who think that they can. Some of the stingiest people around may die with more money in their bank accounts than anyone could have ever imagined; money that only sat for years when it could have been put to many good uses. Then other people may flaunt their wealth and only look down upon others they could be a blessing to. I may never become as wealthy as some but will always have a giving spirit in sharing whatever I have.

I have always been a generous giver in giving as much as I have been able, and even beyond, as the people of the Macedonian churches are said to have done on their own in *2 Corinthians 8:3*. However, God wants there to be equality. According to verses *14* and *15,* my abundance should be used to help others just as theirs should be used in helping me. People should not have beyond or below their needs. There are certainly very few people in today's world willing to give to the extent where everyone would have the same of everything. As some people, my giving is more based on *2 Corinthians 9:7.* God loves a *cheerful giver* and I give according to my heart, and not out of necessity or what others tell me. Jesus Christ set a great example for us to learn from though. He was rich but became poor so that through His poverty we could become rich (*2 Corinthians 8:9).* We don't have to give as much to each other but surely can give in the same spirit.

Glory - We are born in glory and then may enjoy many other moments of glory over the days of our lives. Some of mine include the winning of awards and setting records running, earning awards for being an honor student in high school and college, celebrating my graduations from high school and college, my church wedding, being baptized and becoming a Christian, being a coach in the delivery room and witnessing the births of my children, singing my first Christmas song at a church concert, receiving writing awards for my poetry, and the writing and self-publishing my first inspirational book. While *glory* is any praise, honor, or splendor that we may enjoy, it is also defined as the bliss (joy) of Heaven. In living right, that is where we will experience our final and greatest glory.

Proverbs 3:35 says that wise people inherit glory, while shame is the promotion of fools. That tells me that those that live righteously and are believers in God shall surely enjoy much more glory than those that don't. And as *Psalm 3:3* says, God is my shield, glory, and the lifter of my head. Therefore, just being able to open my eyes every morning is a moment of glory that none on Earth can ever deny me. Then as with *2 Corinthians 4:16,* I can tell, by my growth as a Christian, my outward self is decaying while my inward self is being renewed day by day. Any troubles that I may experience are only temporary for me in achieving the eternal glory that will far outweigh them all (*verse 17).* I believe as *2 Corinthians 3:18,* which says that, in having open faces reflecting the glory of the Lord, we will be transformed into His image with ever-increasing glory.

Gluttony - There is a very large number of people that eat more than they need to on a daily basis, and then on some days, like Thanksgiving and Christmas, a lot of us become guilty of just plain *pigging out.* However, when overeating becomes an obsession it's called *gluttony,* which is a sin. This type of person will waste food through their abnormal and excessive desire for the taste, and have been condemned for not giving food to the needy, even when having more than they can possibly eat before them or stored away.

In the Bible, gluttonous people are viewed in the same bad light as alcoholics are, and we know what a danger alcoholics can be to themselves and to others. Both overeating and overdrinking can lead to some serious health issues; like obesity and heart problems for the glutton, and liver disease for the alcoholic. Then to others, the gluttonous person may not be willing to even share food with a person starving from hunger, while the alcoholic may kill or injure another while driving drunk. *Proverbs 23:19-21* says that drunkards and gluttons will only become poor. We should keep our hearts on the right track and avoid those that drink too much liquor or eat too much meat.

Goals - We all should have *goals,* which are the result or achievement toward which our efforts are directed. They should be specific, measurable, attainable, realistic and timely. There are short-term goals that drive us through a sense of urgency, longer-term goals that provide the satisfaction that we are on the right road and going somewhere, and life goals where we ask ourselves what we want to achieve with our lives. It's usually the short-term goals that we have to be more careful with, as people can be impatient and may make quick decisions that they will only regret over the longer term; like purchasing something on credit without reading the small print or fully understanding the contractual agreement being signed. Take your time and pursue your goals with intelligence and purpose. And maybe you should first make your goals more directed to the Lord than yourself. Achieving any goal is most possible through Him.

It's sad but true that there are many people that have no set goals or plans. Then there are those that only pray and wait for the Lord to answer and direct them. Then others that have some goals that are most disturbing to me, like the young men I hear saying they want to become drug dealers rather than aspiring to live lives of a more positive and honest nature. I have met or surpassed many of my previous goals. However, my goals for the present and the future are more Spirit-led than they ever were in the past. I am very determined to be the best Christian that I can possibly be, while encouraging others to do the same. Beyond what Paul says in *Acts 15:36,* I want to speak, sing, and write the words of the Lord to all my brothers and sisters, and then hear how they are doing in respect to their goals. In Him, all of our goals have purpose and power. Therefore, I will always expect great things from you and from myself.

God - One problem that I had with God was in not having a visual image of Him as we do with His son, Jesus. Another concerned His origin. Where did He come from? The Bible tells how He created all things, including us. But who or what created Him? However, I learned that the most important thing for us is to just believe. And I do! I am developing a strong relationship with Him, and have witnessed His presence up close and personal, beyond all the things I had already seen and heard that only bolstered my belief that there is a real God. He gave me a beginning and is offering me an existence with no end, if I only trust, fear, worship, and abide in Him. I've heard His voice and have seen His light of love and healing. God is with me and in me. It may not be for us to ever know the answers but somehow and someway He lives and makes the impossible possible with His majesty and power.

I don't have my own perception of what God may look like, but as a believer am just satisfied in knowing who He is. The Bible opens with the fact of God when *Genesis 1:1* states that in the beginning it was He alone that created heaven and earth. Then on the sixth day of His seven days of creation, *Genesis 1:27* says that God created man in His own image. So we know that God has a human form, and Isaiah witnessed it according to *Isaiah 6:1.* He was being called upon to become a prophet and saw a vision of God seated on His throne in Heaven. While we can't physically see God as Isaiah did, we can certainly experience His presence. Like Isaiah, we should confess our sins and seek God's forgiveness, along with discovering and understanding what He desires to be the purpose of our lives. In living for Him, we can truly experience His greatness and pass on our experiences to others, as I have been trying to do.

Goodness - The Bible describes *goodness* as being excellence, and it is first mentioned in *Genesis 1,* where God proclaimed it as He spoke each phase of creation into existence. He saw everything as being good because it met His expectations, which is how the idea of goodness should be manifested in our lives. God's goodness is defined by His love, and He displays it through His blessings and the forgiving of our sins. There are times that I step back and just admire all the great things that were created out of the goodness of God. However, as many, in the past I questioned His goodness when things were going bad. But I realize now that there is goodness in all that He does, because God is excellence. There are just times that we may have to reconsider our thoughts of *good* or *bad*, and alter our expectations a little. I may not always wake up in the morning feeling well, for example, but it's the goodness of God that allows me to even wake up at all.

Moses met the Lord God on the Mount Sinai where the tablets of stone were to be replaced that contained the words of the Ten Commandments. He had broken the first. There, according to *Exodus 34:6-7,* he was told of God's goodness and truth. God was said to be merciful, gracious, and slow to anger. He would forgive thousands for their iniquity, transgression, and sin, but would not leave the guilty unpunished. Moses had also asked God to be with them as he led the people. God answered with *Exodus 33:19,* saying that He would make all of His goodness pass before them with grace and mercy, as He had been pleased with Moses. That promise was verified as Moses and the Israelites never lacked any of the necessities, like water, food, and clothing, as they wandered through the desert for many years. Also, in *Psalms 33,* David said that God should be praised for His goodness. It was just by the Word of God that the Earth had become filled with His goodness. Everything He created was in excellence and every person should have stood in awe of Him, as I have often done.

Gospel - A *gospel* is an account, usually written, that describes the life of Jesus Christ and refers to the *Good News* message of the *New Testament.* Many gospels were written in antiquity, but it appears that Irenaeus of Lyons, in the year 185, is given the credit for recognizing that only four were worthy to be accepted as part of the *New Testament:* The gospels of *Matthew, Mark, Luke,* and *John.* He insisted on the four and denounced some early Christian groups that used only one gospel; like the Ebionites that may have used an Aramaic version of *Matthew.* According to Irenaeus, the four gospels represented the four *Pillars of the Church,* and he was ultimately successful in declaring that they contained the truth collectively and exclusively. Each gospel was to be read in light of the others, and he made of *John* a lens through which to read the other gospels.

I've read that there were at least twenty gospels that weren't included in the Bible. Some disappeared and may still survive at unknown locations, while some appear to have been found during modern times. They are known about because of them being mentioned in other writings. Also, several lost gospels may well be parts of *Matthew, Mark, Luke* and *John* as researchers have identified certain characteristics indicating that some of the words may have come from other writings. So it's possible that earlier writings may have influenced the authors of the *New Testament* gospels. Some of the excluded gospels include those of Simon Peter, Mary Magdalene and Judas Iscariot. However, while fragments or secondary translations have been found, the complete originals remain lost. Also, their real authors are unknown. Some other gospels that have been mentioned and may no longer survive include the *Gospel of Matthias*, the *Gospel of Perfection*, the *Gospel of the Seventy*, the *Dialogue of the Savior*, the *Gospel of the Twelve*, the *Gospel of the Hebrews*, the *Gospel of Eve*, and the *Secret Gospel of Mark*. Then other gospels may have been lost along with even their names.

Greatness - As a professional baseball player, Ricky Henderson defined *greatness* for me. He was the best player that I ever saw, combining excellent hitting skills with his unmatched base stealing ability. Never have I seen a player that could just take over and win games in as many ways as he did so often. However, it wasn't just his superior athletic ability that drove him to a level far above the average player. He had a true passion for the sport of baseball. His passion was baseball and baseball became him. Without having a passion for something great things may never happen for you. With it we are all capable of greater things than we can ever imagine. One must realize too that all greatness comes from the grace of God, for He places the passion, ability and potential for all things within us. Therefore, whenever we talk about the greatness of any person, we should also mention the greatness of God.

Just as I am telling about the greatness of Ricky Henderson, we directly or indirectly hear about God's greatness from others. Through our interactions with God we are able to witness His goodness and power directly, and should always look for opportunities to make Him known to others. Telling friends, family members and others about God should be a part of our everyday conversations. And just as I am telling about the greatness of my favorite baseball player, I should be and am even more excited when telling anyone about God, just as David does throughout *Psalms*. Then *Jeremiah 9:23-24* tells us that God delights in those that understands and knows Him. Whether wise, strong or rich, we should never boast of ourselves. Our boasting should be reserved for God as He exercises His kindness, justice and righteousness on Earth. I've never met him personally, but I am sure that Ricky Henderson boasts a lot about how God made him the player that he was.

Greed - It's *greed* when a person wants more things than they need or deserve, especially concerning wealth, status and power. There is an excessive desire for them to possess all that they can with the intention of keeping it all for themselves, and things like violence, trickery, and manipulation of authority may result from their greed. God wants us to achieve and acquire more than we can ever imagine possible. So, in that respect, we never have to lower our ambitions or expectations. However, greed is inappropriate expectation and a sin. St. Thomas Aquinas (1225-1274), philosopher, theologian and priest of the Catholic Church, wrote that, like all mortal sins, it was a sin against God because the greedy person condemns things that are eternal for the sake of temporary things.

Proverbs 1:15-19 warns us to not walk in the path of the greedy. It tells of the ways and fate of some bird hunters that were driven by greed. Their feet ran to evil and they were hasty for blood. However, those going after the ill-gotten gain would only end up lying in wait for their own blood and lives. Then *Isaiah 56:11* refers to those that can never have enough as being *greedy dogs.* They lack understanding in only looking to themselves and seeking their own gain, while God wants us to practice generosity with our gains. *2 Corinthians 9:6-15* says that those who give generously will be rewarded generously by God. We should be *cheerful givers,* giving from our hearts under no reluctance or compulsion. In doing so, God will make sure that we have all that we need in all things at all times.

Grief - If memory serves me right, it's Charlie Brown, the cartoon character, who often utters the words, "good grief", whenever a friend plays a trick on him or something else of an unfortunate nature happens. Of course it is said in a sarcastic tone because how could there possibly be any good concerning grief? Many think of *grief* as the mental anguish that arises from bereavement when a loved one dies. However, it may also result from annoyance, frustration, trouble, difficulty, or losses of health, jobs, relationships, dreams, safety, etc. And according to psychiatrist Elisabeth Kubler-Ross, in 1969, there are "five stages of grief" - *denial, anger, bargaining, depression, and acceptance.* Immediately following my stroke, I was in the denial mode, as I just couldn't believe what was happening. However, when I felt God's presence, while I was in the hospital, I was in acceptance and at peace with what had happened. At that point, my bad thoughts of grief turned to good, especially upon finding out that things could have been much worse for me.

The Bible defines *grief* as being sorrow or affliction, and *Jeremiah 31:15-17* tells how the Lord may be a comforter to one that is in grief. A woman named Rahel (Rachel) was weeping because of the loss of her children but had refused to be comforted because they weren't. However, she finally stopped grieving and was comforted when the Lord told her to stop her voice from weeping and her eyes from tears. He promised that there was hope for the future, as her good work would be rewarded. The Lord was going to make sure that her children were returned to their own land from the land of the enemy. Therefore, if we are right with the Lord, He may turn one's grief into joy, even without our asking. Then we may call on Him through prayer, as David did in *Psalm 6*. David was consumed with grief and prayed to the Lord that he be delivered from his ailments and enemies rather than to face His wrath. He says that the Lord heard his weeping and cry for mercy, and that the Lord had accepted his prayer. As a result, all of David's enemies were to turn back in disgrace while being ashamed and dismayed. Through prayer, we can fight our ailments, enemies or whatever else grieves us in the same way.

Growth - *Growth* is defined as an increase in the size, number, value, strength, extension, or expansion of something, and I would include the words *positive change,* which would best describe my growth. I see myself as having grown much over the past few years as a person and a Christian. I know what is missing in my life, what can be improved, and am actively working on it through education, new knowledge and increased awareness. I have taken a good look at my belief system and have made changes in becoming a more focused and dedicated Christian. I have changed my outer identity to one that more closely matches my inner self, and have become more knowledgeable about who I am and what I want in life. Further, I have experienced God's love, greatness, and forgiveness, am filled with the Holy Spirit, am walking more in the Spirit, am telling others about my experiences and knowledge concerning God and Jesus, am loving by faith, am praying with confidence, and am even more of a giver now.

Growth and positive change can start with the *new beginning* a person is given in being *saved*. God wants every person to hear the Gospel so that they may believe in Jesus and be saved, and *1 Timothy 2:2-6* tells us that God wants us to live peaceful and quiet lives in godliness and holiness, for it pleases Him as He wants all people to be saved and to acknowledge the truth that there is one God and one man who is the mediator between Him and His children - Jesus, who gave Himself for us. That knowledge can prompt and promote a healthy personal and spiritual growth that may be exhibited and experienced in every area of one's life. *2 Thessalonians 1:3* tells us that we can grow in faith as our labor is promoted by love and our endurance is inspired by our hope through Jesus. *2 Peter 3:18* tells us to grow in the grace and the knowledge of Jesus and worship Him, for He is our glory both now and forever. Then *Mark 4:30-32* tells us that we can grow to greatness no matter how small or difficult our beginning was. Therefore our growth has no limits or boundaries if we are saved and live lives of knowledge, belief and faith.

Guidance - During my early battle with diabetes, I faced a number of other problems that really compounded the degree of my troubles. However, rather than allowing God to guide me through His words or listening to the advice of others I trusted, I stubbornly moved ahead on my own. As a result, I made some bad choices and had to suffer the negative consequences of doing so; like almost falling into a diabetic coma because I had refused to see a doctor when I first began passing out from my illness. I should have taken my time in prayerfully considering my choices and would surely have made better ones. Things began to turn around in a more positive direction when I stopped ignoring God's warnings and began turning to Him for guidance. He now guides me through all things, as I'm listening and making wiser decisions concerning my health and other issues; things like eating healthier, exercising more, doctor visits, stress management, and having stronger faith in God, myself and others. I know especially that God is making something good come out of some things, even in some cases where I can't yet see it. Plus, I can sense that He was there all along from the beginning of my troubles. He was just waiting for me to turn to Him for His guidance and care, but making sure that I didn't allow my troubles to totally down me.

Guidance is something that provides direction or advice in relation to our decisions or courses of action, and normally we can rely a lot on our own inner wisdom to guide us as needed. Our inner wisdom is an inborn and natural gift given to us by God, and it may operate in our lives on a daily basis, even with us having no knowledge of it. Then it's during those troubled times that we may not use it to our advantage. However, when we begin to make the bad decisions or lose direction, some regular prayer or meditation can help us to re-connect us with our inner wisdom, as will accessing the spiritual wisdom of God and others that may be able to provide some good advice or beneficial help. *Isaiah 58:11* says that God will guide us always and satisfy our needs. Therefore, He is there to guide us through all of our troubled times. We just have to call on Him. *2 Kings 4* tells the story of a woman in crisis. Her husband had died and she was afraid of losing her sons to the slavery of a creditor. She called upon a prophet, Elisha, who asked her what she had in her house. The widow said that she only had a little oil and was instructed as a first step to gather empty jars from neighbors. Then as she filled each jar, God multiplied the oil. After the oil stopped flowing, Elisha told her to sell it to pay off her debts, and then her and her sons could live off of what was left. God had guided the widow through the crisis and her faith was multiplied, just as the oil had been. We too can be guided through our difficult times if our first step is obeying God.

Guilt - *Guilt* is the state of having committed an offense, crime, violation, or wrong, especially involving moral or penal law. At first thought, I would say that I presently have no reason to feel any guilt concerning anything. However, that is in reference to the rules and laws of man. According to God's, I may be guilty of several things as we all commit sin and are never totally guiltless at any give time. I may not do anything today that man may frown upon, but may surely do something that will make God do so.

James 2:8-11 tells how strict God is concerning guilt if we truly keep the royal law according to the Scripture. We are doing right if we love our neighbors as we do ourselves, but we are guilty of sin and considered to be lawbreakers if we show any favoritism. Then breaking one law makes a person guilty of breaking the whole law. So if you are to stumble just once over the course of a day, you have totally sinned and are in guilt. You may not commit adultery, for example, but if you committed murder you are just a lawbreaker - period!

Habits - *Habits* are an acquired pattern of behavior that often occurs automatically and, in that, we may find ourselves doing the same things day in and day out. Most of life is habitual and our habits, good or bad, define us and make us who we are. The key is in controlling them and, if we know how to change our habits, just a small effort can result in some big changes. I, for example, had a bad habit of keeping my problems to myself. Just didn't want anyone to know that anything was troubling me. But how could anyone offer their help when they didn't know that I needed it? Also, rather than turning to God for His help, I was turning away from Him. I finally realized that I needed to develop a good habit of sharing not only my successes with others but my failures too. Now I have a good habit of confiding more in the people I respect and trust, along with praying to God every night with my concerns and giving thanks. One thing I read about habits was that many are done on an unconscious level; it is estimated that out of every 11,000 signals we receive from our senses, our brain only consciously processes 40. That's why sometimes we just may not know why or realize that we have certain habits.

We develop habits when we do certain things day after day, and eventually we begin doing them automatically, with no conscious thoughts about it. That's the way it should be in relation to God. We should make it a habit to serve Him in any way possible, each and every day. He should continually be in our thoughts, decisions, actions, etc. The Bible tells of the holy habits of the prophet Daniel. He had been thrown into a lions' den after some men had reported wrongdoings on him to the king *(Daniel 6)*. However, he had done no wrong and was not harmed because of his trust in God. When the king saw that, he released Daniel and then had the false accusers thrown into the lions' den, along with their wives and their children. All were killed before they even reached the floor. Daniel prospered after that and the king issued a decree declaring that everyone in the kingdom had to fear and revere the God of Daniel. It is said that Daniel had a habit of holiness that extended from his *steadfastness, strength of character and faith.* The more he did the right things, the harder it became for him to do wrong. And he had a daily habit of praying to God three times a day, same time and same place. So his habits defined him and his life as he served God continually. Many of us should follow Daniel's example and strengthen our relationships with God.

Hands - Years ago, when I worked construction, I was told that I had small hands for a man. However, I was still more productive than most of the other men on the jobs. And in many ways then and now my hands are much larger than most men's. I've used my hands for employment and doing a number of things around the home and other places but, most importantly, in the church and my community I have always had my hands being utilized in other good ways. With my nature of giving, I am always anxious to provide some assistance in projects for the benefit of others, just as I am doing now. If someone needs a helping hand, I am often there to lend one or two. Then be there if someone just needs a hand to give them a pat on the back of support from time to time. So my hands may be a little small in size but quite large in spirit of the Lord.

The Bible speaks much of our hands being used, both figuratively and physically, in improving the quality and success of our lives. *Psalm 24: 4-5,* for example, says that in having clean hands and a pure heart, while not worshipping idols or swearing by things that are not true, we will receive blessings from the Lord and vindication from God. Then in *Psalm 90:17,* Moses prays for the favor of the Lord to be upon us and establish the work of our hands for us, meaning that through the Lord we would be able to use our hands to do many things for ourselves. And *1 Thessalonians 4: 11-12* says that we should make it our ambitions to live quiet lives, mind our own business, and work with our own hands. In that way, in our daily lives, we will gain the respect of others that are less fortunate and never be dependent on anybody.

Happiness - *Happiness* is a state of being content of mind and we should all try to find ways to maintain our good feelings no matter what is occurring in our lives. There are going to be some periods of unhappiness, as things won't always go as we would like. We just have to find ways to limit it as much as possible in keeping our peace of mind as we weather our storms. And we especially have to distance ourselves from those that may become a source of our unhappiness. There are just some, even close to us, that can intentionally or unintentionally bring us down, as they are unhappy and want their unhappiness to be shared by others.

In spite of any circumstances, we don't have to allow ourselves to be overcome by unhappiness. We have a God that protects us and in His strength and blessings we can always find reasons to be happy, even when we are faced with the most difficult of problems or those that may be against us. We can react like Paul in *Acts 26:2*. He stood before King Agrippa to defend himself against some false accusations of Jews that wanted him dead, although he done nothing wrong deserving of his life being taken. However, Paul hadn't allowed the circumstances to rob him of his peace of mind or faith. His first words to King Agrippa were "I think myself happy".

Hate - By watching television news reports, reading the newspaper, walking the streets, visiting some homes, or just listening to people when you're riding the bus, it's easy to see that there is absolutely too much hatred among people in our world today - family hating family, friends hating friends, religions hating religions, politicians hating politicians, countries hating countries… It seems that murder, destruction, violence and negative propaganda have become a normal and acceptable way of life, just like in some of those unholy and wicked civilizations they speak of in the Bible. *Hate* is a deep and emotionally extreme dislike, directed towards things like inanimate objects, circumstances, one's self or another person, groups of people, life and people in general, or just the entire world. In relation to people, hatred may be associated with feelings of anger that may linger and there exists the possibility of hostility being taken out against others or one's self, including behavior like the violence, murder and war we see.

In the Bible, much is said about hating evil, the rewards for living lives of goodness, and God's desire for us to not hate one another. *Psalm 96:10* says that those who love the Lord should hate evil because He guards the lives of the faithful and delivers them from the hands of the wicked. *Amos 5:14-15* says that the Lord will be with us who hate evil and love good, while seeking good and not evil. In that, one who loves the Lord and hates evil can have security and confidence when facing any of life's storms. Then *John 3:20-21* tells us that evil-doers hate the light of the Lord and will refuse to come into the light for fear of their evil deeds being exposed. Those living by the truth of the Lord will come into the light to make it clearly seen that their good deeds have been done through God. Finally, regarding people living in peace with a love for each other, in *Leviticus 19:17,* the Lord told Moses that one should not hate their brother in their heart. Sad to say but nowadays many don't even know their neighbors or see them enough to love or hate.

Healing - *Healing,* in Christian terms, focuses on restoring the wellness of one's mind, body or spirit. There just may be times that we find ourselves suffering through the pains of life from things like illness, physical injury, unfortunate circumstances, financial problems, emotional distress, loss, or being hurt by others. We then need a remedy and a healing and can just place all of our pains before God. Faith healing has not been scientifically proven. However, through prayer, "laying of hands", and positive mental thinking, there are many stories of people being miraculously healed from incurable diseases, having eyesight restored, regaining use of their legs, and being relieved from an assortment of non-physical problems. So, whenever we have any form of ailments, we should rely on our faith and trust in God. I did and truly believe that I have been healed and was spared from suffering the more serious consequences of a stroke because of Him.

Psalm 103:3 says that the Lord is the Divine Healer and He will forgive all of our sins and heal all of our diseases. Then *James 5:14-15* tells us that we can call upon the elders of the church when we are sick. They will pray over us and anoint us will oil in the name of the Lord. The prayer of faith can save us from our sickness and have our sins forgiven. One problem I see with some sick people though is their lack of faith or trust in doctors or medicine. Some will refuse to rely on either, only to find themselves ailing more as they wait on a healing from the Lord. But think about it. *Luke 9:1-2* tells how Jesus called his twelve disciples together and gave them the power and authority to cast away devils and cure diseases. Then they were sent out to preach about God's Kingdom and heal the sick. Doesn't it stand to reason that many doctors are given that same kind of power and authority today? And in *2 Kings 20:7* it says that Hezekiah was healed from a boil after Isaiah gave instruction for a lump of figs to be placed upon it as a healing medicine.

Health - In spite of my personal problems, diabetes, stroke and other things, I believe that I am presently in pretty good shape health wise, with a soundness of mind, body and soul. I'm exercising, watching my diet, taking my medicine, controlling my stress, and relying ever more on my strength of faith to help keep me healthy; physically, mentally, and spiritually. In health,

I am very optimistically looking to the future; in being able to continue doing some things that I had fears of no longer being able to, and doing even more.

I'm trying to live as righteous as possible and, in doing so, *Proverbs 4:22-23* says that it can give health to my whole body, while guarding my heart will be a safeguard of my life. And when my health is failing, *Jeremiah 30:17* assures me that the Lord can restore it. *Proverbs 12:18-19* also tells me that, in seeking the Lord's favor, if I am wise there will be health in my tongue, and in having truthful lips will endure forever. Then like in *3 John 2,* I always pray for the prosperity and health of others, as I hope some will continue doing for me.

Heart - I think that I have always had a good heart. Even during the most troubling of times, I still see myself as giving far more to others than I will ever expect to receive in return from them. However, that has never been a problem for me because of my generous heart, and the knowledge that God desires for me to always be more of a giver than a receiver. I know that the recipients of my good deeds may never return the favor or give proper thanks, but I always give without expectation, for I know that my rewards will be from God who blesses giving and goodness. My belief is that one's heart defines their character, nature and spirit, and I also believe that mine are viewed favorably in the eyes of the Lord and most that know me.

In having a good heart as the Lord desires, I know that I will continually be blessed, for *Deuteronomy 11:13-15* says that there are blessings for obeying the Lord's commands in serving Him with all our hearts and souls. And we have to be careful because He will test us to see that we do (*Deuteronomy 13:3).* Then *1 Samuel 16:7* tells me that while some people may only view me by outside appearances, the Lord looks at my heart. I'll always have a giving heart as we all should, because *Ephesians 6:6-7* says that if I do the will of God from my heart I will be rewarded for all of my good deeds. I must have a little wisdom though, as *Ecclesiastes 8:5* says that men with wise hearts know when and how to do good concerning all matters.

Heaven **-** When I think of Heaven, I think of God, Jesus and all the people I hope to see there; family, friends, fellow church members, and possibly some of the many great people that I have admired or read about during the course of my life and over the pages of history. However, I know that there will be a few surprises as some I may expect to see won't be there. I am just working as hard as possible in the Lord's will to make sure that I make it there myself. Hell is not an option for me. My desire is to spend my eternity in Heaven with all of my worries, troubles and concerns left behind. It will be a new life and existence of total peace, contentment, health and joy that can't be experienced on Earth. For now I'm trying to enjoy the best Christian life here as possible, especially in the company of those that, in great sadness, I may never see again some day.

Heaven is the prepared home for the redeemed where people who have died will continue to exist in an afterlife, and according to a recent ABC News poll nearly nine out of ten people in the United States believe that. However, there is the question as to whether or not people are doing what is required for admittance, for different religions differ on how (and if) one gains entrance into Heaven. For many religions it's on the conditon of having had lived a "good life" in terms of spirituality or having accepted God into one's heart. One exception is the "sola fide" belief of many Protestant Christians, where if a person accepts Jesus as their saviour, He will assume the guilt for their sins. Therefore, believers are to be forgiven, and accepted into Heaven, regardless of any good or bad works done during their lives. That differs from *Hebrews 12:14,* which says that a man must live in peace and holiness to see the Lord.

Help - In these continually poor economic times, many are hurting and need help. People are losing their jobs, homes, cars, finances, health, sanity, etc, and that has led to increases in murder and other crimes, divorce and broken families, stress and hopelessness, alcoholism and drug abuse…Then a really bad thing about it is that there doesn't appear to be much relief coming in the near future through our leaders and politicians. They just don't have many real answers that I can see, and seem to be doing more finger pointing at each other than finding solutions. However, all is not lost if one keeps the faith. Our help will come through God and those that He is sending our way to help us. For in faith, you can expect blessings without having any advanced knowledge of how and when God will be sending them. Just never give up as your help may well be on its way to you. I am most positive that mine already is, and that things will be turning around for me in many good ways soon.

Luke 18 presents a parable that tells much about persistence and faith when any help is needed. In it Jesus wanted to show His disciples that they should always pray and never give up. The parable tells of a judge in one city that didn't fear God or have any regard for man. A woman came to him, asking that he punish a person that had been troubling her. He had first refused but she kept coming back to him with her plea. Finally, so that she would stop bothering him, he agreed to see that she would see justice, and not continue to wear him out from her visits. After Jesus finished the story, He told the disciples to listen to what the un-just judge had said. Then He asked them if God would bring about justice for His chosen ones, who cry out continually to Him, or keep putting them off? The Lord's answer was that their justice would come quickly, though He further questioned if He would find faith on Earth upon His return? I have much faith and have been very persistent in my prayers for help, just as that woman had been with her pleas.

Holidays - We all have our favorite holidays, from the religious celebrations of Easter and Christmas to those established by man, like Thanksgiving, the 4th of July, Labor Day, Memorial Day, Mother's and Father's Day... However, we don't have to limit ourselves to just those that are presently marked on our calendars. A *holiday* is any day that is designated as having a special significance for which *individuals,* governments, or religious groups have set aside for observation. To me, that means that I can establish and celebrate my own holidays too. For example, on October 20th, 2011, I will be celebrating a year of good health since my stroke. Surely a day of significance for me that I can consider as being a holiday, and I'll be celebrating in prayer and giving much thanks to God and Jesus, this year and hopefully for many more to come.

I can remember the days when Easter and Christmas were holidays and sabbath days of rest. I wouldn't see anyone going to work and most everything was closed. But what about a holiday that was celebrated every day of a year like that? In the Bible, the holidays of Easter and Christmas are certainly written about, but then it is spoken of what were called *sacred seasons,* just as we refer to the period from Christmas to New Year's Day as being the *holiday season.* One sacred season was called the *Sabbatical Year,* which occurred every seven years and was a year-long sabbath with no work being done of any kind. And all debts were cancelled. Imagine that! Every day was a holiday with no work or having to worry about paying any bills. It was designed to just be a year of quiet religious worship and meditation.

Holiness - *Hebrews 12:14* says that we shall not see the Lord without holiness and, since turning myself over to Jesus as commanded by God, I have tried to live as holy of a life as possible. *Holiness* is a state of being clean or pure, and like God. In becoming true Christians, we are *born again* as the old person in us dies. And in desiring to live holy, I would recommend the reading of *Holiness* by J.C. Ryle (1816-1900), which is considered by some to be the best book ever written on Christian life. In it, he wrote that a holy man would try to shun every known sin and to keep every known commandment, while striving to be like Jesus. A holy man will also follow after meekness, patience, gentleness, kind temper, government of his tongue, temperance, self-denial, charity, brotherly kindness, a spirit of mercy, benevolence towards others, purity of heart, the fear of God, humility, faithfulness, and spiritual-mindedness. It's surely quite a list, but the rewards of God's promises make the pursuit of holiness well worth it.

In the Bible, *Colossians 3* presents God's rules for living holy. We must set our hearts and minds on all things above, while putting to death the earthly ways of sexual immorality, impurity, lust, evil desires, and greed, for they are the worship of idols. We should have a new walk and rid ourselves of such things as anger, rage, malice, slander, and filthy language from our lips. We should not lie to each other, as we have put on new selves being renewed in the knowledge of God. We should clothe ourselves with compassion, kindness, humility, gentleness, and patience. We should bear with each other and forgive our grievances against each other, forgiving as the Lord has forgiven us. We should let the peace of Jesus rule our hearts, be thankful, and let the Word of Jesus dwell in us as we teach and admonish each other with wisdom, while singing in gratitude. And in all of our deeds, we should do it all in the name of Jesus, while giving thanks to God through Him.

Home - As I was thinking about a direction to go in writing about the word *home,* I turned on my computer to read a very disturbing headline on the Internet concerning my *hometown* of Detroit, Michigan. An article by *Forbes* lists the city as having been the most dangerous in the entire country for 2010. There were 345 murders reported in the area, with there altogether being 1,111 violent crimes (murder and non-negligent manslaughter, forcible rape, robbery, aggravated assault) per 100,000 residents. The reasons cited were the continued drop in population and employment rates over the past many years. The city has been strapped of funds that had been devoted for basic services like education and public safety. Then the people who are moving aren't the ones who were committing any crimes. So while many hard working and honest citizens are moving out of Detroit, the criminals remain to continue their siege. We surely must find ways to make our Detroit home a better, more prosperous, and safer place.

No matter what, Detroit is where my heart is and will always be. And I'm praying hard that God will soon bless my hometown and become a visible resident, as there is no place better than one in which He resides. In the Bible, it is said that David prayed for his home, and in a non-structural sense as I am. He prayed that the members of his home would always find acceptance and approval from God. Then wherever life took him, he never wanted to be away from God's watchful eye. His desire was to live in an atmosphere and awareness of being in

God's favor, and that was surely to have included things like health, prosperity, and safety. Therefore, I have the same prayers and desires for all the good people having homes in Detroit, especially our religious community that appears to be thriving in spite of all the city's hardships. Through faith and in having a leadership in Detroit that is truly commited to positive change, Detroit can return to a home of prominence, respectabilty and much less crime. Sad when also reading that some of our politicians and leaders have helped to create many problems beyond those of the criminals.

Honesty - I have always considered myself to be a most honest person, but have known people that made me think really long and hard whenever they would tell me anything. Some just have dishonest natures and may often use their lies and deception to confuse, hurt, persuade, trick or cheat you in any way that they can. However, I never have it in my heart to do things like that to others and learned long ago that you may reap what you sow, as some lies will only come back to haunt you. So it's best to take the honest approach from the beginning, even in situations where you may be trying to save face or find it difficult in admitting to doing something wrong. Being continually dishonest will only damage your character, reputation, image, and relationships, along with it being considered as a sin by God. He wants us to be honest with each other, and especially in our prayers and communications with Him. But whether you hold back some things or be dishonest with God, He already knows the whole truth, and the content of one's heart. Therefore, I try to be as open and honest as possible with Him.

Hebrews 13:18 says that we should have trust in ourselves and in good conscience desire to willingly live honestly in all ways. Then when others may be dishonest with us, we should never repay their evil with evil. Rather we should be careful to do what is right and honest in the eyes of everyone *(Romans 12:17)*. *Romans 13:12-13* goes on to say that we should cast off the works of darkness and put on our armor of light. In that, we will be able to walk honestly and not behave in any sinful ways. An example of honesty is presented in *2 Kings 22:3-7*. Money had been collected from the people by the doorkeepers and brought into the temple of the Lord. It was to be used for some work to be done on the temple and was entrusted to the men who had been appointed to supervise it. They were to pay the carpenters, builders, and masons, along with purchasing the materials required for the repairs being done. However, they weren't required to give an accounting of the money being paid out or spent because they were dealing faithfully, and honestly, just as God always desires us to.

Hope - I have faced a number of struggles and unfortunate circumstances recently but remain hopeful in the belief that some really good things will arise from it all. Things are surely going to turn out the best for me and in my faith are most confident of that. *Hope* is expectation in reference to the fulfillment of God's promises. In Him, I can anticipate there being some favorable outcomes through His love, devotion and guidance. Plus I am even more confident because of what He has done for me in the past. If I remain faithful, patient, and follow His direction, He will surely do more for me in the future. Therefore, all of my hope and continued strength is and will always be in God, who will never abandon us or give us a reason to give up, though we may certainly give Him reasons to.

When things aren't going well, it's hope that can sustain us. And we don't have to just wish that things would turn out better. We should know that they will as God can turn anything bad to good, as well as our mourning to happiness. *1 Corinthians13:13* says that *hope* is one of God's three graces, with the other two being *faith* and *love,* and we should abide in them. Then in presenting the grounds for hope, *Psalm 33:18* says that the eyes of the Lord are on those that fear Him and whose hope is through His love. Also, *1 Timothy 1:1* describes Paul as being an apostle of Jesus by the commandment of God, and of Jesus, who was his hope and is ours. A finality of hope is mentioned when *Hebrews 6:10-11* states that in order for our hope to become a certainty, we have to be diligent in all of our work, especially in God's name, to the very end.

Huggy - As I am writing about myself on this day of October 7, 2011, my life is a continuance of uncertainty because of some issues still needing to be resolved. However, there is much anticipation and hope, as all of my problems have been placed in the hands of God and Jesus, along with my prayers and dreams. Then right in the middle of my thoughts, I received a telephone call from the Detroit Free Press. A reporter is writing a newspaper story about some volunteer work that I have been doing to help seniors and others, concerning a variety of health care related matters. There is also the possibility of an additional article being written that will be about my first book, *Forever A Man With The Lord.* That being said, maybe I am an example of how God desires us to be; by continuing to do good things and inspiring others in spite of my own personal needs and challenges. So, maybe my deeds will help to define me?

Some people won't be surprised upon hearing about some of the things that I've been doing, as they have always known me to have a caring and giving nature. Others may not know because I really don't talk about myself much. However, there have been times that the recipients of my good deeds have done my talking for me. I will say that most have no knowledge about the extra effort that has been required of me on occasion. Presently, without a running vehicle, I may have to catch two buses to attend or speak at some outreach events, plus some walking. One day after leaving one, my bus wait was over two and a half hours. For another I walked about 5 miles in order to be there on time. That's devotion and dedication! But I don't do it for any personal rewards from those that I talk to or help. God will bless me as I am showing great faith by what I do *(James 2:18)*.

Humility - I can remember a couple of my mother's old friends having to call and tell her about me being a star runner on my high school track team. She was so happy but maybe a bit surprised. The friends had been at a track meet to see some other runners and saw me win some sprint races. However, I was never one to talk much or brag about things like that when I got home. So, I don't know if my mother knew that I was even doing any running. Sports were just something that my friends and myself were always involved in, and I took it for granted.

In *humility* one is humble, modest and free from pride. Their good deeds and accomplishments often just speak for themselves. And God blesses humility. *Proverbs 22:4* says that the rewards for humility and fear of the Lord are riches, honor and life. Then *Matthew 23:12* says that those who exalt themselves will be humbled, while those that are humble will be exalted. That means that the Lord looks down upon those that are boastful and driven by pride, and looks up upon those that don't allow their victories and successes go to their heads.

Idols - Some people only think of idols as being the statues of worship that may be seen in certain parts of the world today and spoken of in the Bible. However, *idols* are defined as being any person or thing being regarded with blind admiration, adoration, or devotion. Certainly money is viewed as being an idol for some driven by greed. But how about things like automobiles, televisions, houses, hobbies, one's self, political parties, causes, jobs, sports, art, music, addictions, astrology, lusts, pleasures, stubbornness, covetousness, selfishness, success, investments, popularity, pride...? Pretty much anything may be considered as being an idol if it takes on too high of a degree of importance in one's life, especially when even more important than obeying God. Idols are an abomination to Him. He is a jealous God and curses those that make, possess, or worship idols. Placing anything above Him in any form is considered to be a sin, and we are clearly told in the Bible many times not to do it. Therefore, it may be a great thing for some that the Detroit Lions in 2011 may finally have a winning season after many years of losing. But let's not get too carried away and place their quarterback and other players on a pedestal over God's. Plus even the players have to be mindful of idolizing themselves too, as a promising season can easily turn to one of defeat. Hype, press clippings or overconfidence can't guarantee any victories, on or off the field. God can though.

The Bible describes *idols* as being false gods, and our God tells us to worship none other than Him (*Exodus 20:3*). He also says that we should never make any idols of any kind to bow before and worship; for He is a jealous God who punishes sin but shows love to all that love Him and keep His commandments (*Exodus 20:4-6*). However, there were still those that worshipped idols during biblical times, and *Acts 17:16* tells of a city that did just that, as many cities across the country and world may now do on days like Super Bowl Sunday. God becomes the furthest thing from the minds of many as they enjoy the championship of professional football and worship the idols of the game. But God will forgive us if denying Him isn't an every day occurrence. If not we could face the fate that was prophesized according to *Isaiah 2*. Isaiah told of the coming of the Lord's Kingdom, and in *verse 8* describes Judah and Jerusalem as being a land full of idols, with people worshipping the work of their own hands and which their own fingers had made. *Verse 9* goes on to say that they would not be forgiven, as man would be brought low and humbled. The Lord alone would be exalted on that day, with the abolishment of idols, and man fleeing from fear of the Lord, while casting away their idols that had been made for worship *(verses 17-20)*. Rather than facing a similar punishment though, we can turn to God in repentance and away from any forms of idolatry or other practices that may be deemed as abominations by Him *(Ezekiel 14:6)*.

Ignorance - Ignorance is a state of being uninformed or having a lack of knowledge concerning something, and spiritual ignorance is a most serious matter. I've read where it has been described as being *a shoreless ocean of darkness, the product of false ego,* and *the sense of limited individuality.* I've also read that it is believed that there are more people in the world that have absolutely no knowledge of God and Jesus than those having at least some. However, those lacking a personal relationship with the Lord aren't the only ones that are spiritually ignorant. Some Christians may just choose to be so when behaving contrary to God's Word or principals. The Bible refers to them as being *willingly ignorant,* and they will commit sins and try to deny any knowledge to themselves or others of their actions as being sins. But according to God, ignorance is never an excuse for sin, just as under our legal system ignorance of the law is not an acceptable excuse for breaking any.

In *Ephesians 4:17-19,* Paul speaks of people who were without Jesus and how they were alienated from the life of God because of their own inner ignorance. He says that in walking with Jesus one can't walk as other Gentiles walk. There is vanity in their minds, their understanding is darkened, and they are alienated through ignorance and the blinding or hardening of their hearts. They also lack true feelings and will indulge in every kind of wrongful action, like being unclean and greedy. *Verses 23-24* go on to say that people should be renewed in the spirit of their minds, while putting on new faces in being like God in righteousness and true holiness. However, willingly ignorant people will ignore those words of Paul and of God by refusing to accept and receive them. *2 Peter 3:3-5* says that in the last days the scoffers will come forth continuing to follow after their own lusts, questioning the promise of the Lord's coming, and being willingly ignorant or deliberately forgetting how the Word of God transformed the heavens and Earth.

Imperfection - During the writing of my first book, *Still A Black Man With The Lord (*later renamed *Forever A Man With The Lord),* I joined a couple of Christian writing groups on the Internet for information, advice and fellowship. In these groups we could communicate with each other concerning our writing projects or on a more personal and religious level. After some time, I offered to share some of my writing to receive feedback about it. Most wrote that they were very impressed and inspired by my samples. One woman wasn't though. She criticized the title and complained of simple things like the misplacement of a couple of commas. She also wrote that she was a teacher of writing and demanded perfection from her students. To her, my work wasn't up to her standards and she refused to read beyond more than a few pages. I'm still not sure about where the errors, if any, were actually made but had never expected my book to be perfect. I believe however that it was more about the title that she couldn't get beyond, as she said it made my book sound racist. It certainly wasn't but eventually I changed the title, while finding very little else needing to be. All criticism aside, I wrote the book to inspire and uplift all possible readers, in spite of any imperfections concerning my writing or myself. And God often chooses imperfect people like me to do His work. What if the people of Israel had refused to listen to Moses just because of his stuttering problem?

Through the direction and guidance of God, there are no limits to what imperfect people may accomplish. We never have to feel overwhelmed in thinking that something is greater than our abilities. He chooses us for certain tasks and all we have to do is ask Him to use us. Then if we are faithful, the end results will be favorable, as He will place them in His hands. A great thing to read about imperfection is *1 Corinthians 1:26-31.* It tells how God may call on imperfect people, while many wise, mighty and noble men are not. God chooses foolish and weak things to shame the wise and the mighty. He also chooses the lowly, despised and things that are not to nullify the things that are. In that way none should glory (boast) in His presence. Man's glory is in the perfection of the Lord, where there is wisdom, righteousness, sanctification and redemption. In *2 Corinthians 12:9-10,* Jesus tells Paul that His grace was sufficient for him because His strength is made perfect in weakness. Paul then says that he would rather have glory in his own infirmities (weaknesses), so that the power of Jesus would rest upon him. He would take pleasure in any infirmities, reproaches, necessities, persecutions, and distresses for the Lord's sake, as he would be strong in his weakness. That also means that Paul recognized and accepted his imperfections but through Jesus would be able to use them to his advantage in any situation he was confronted with, just as we all can.

Independence - My high school and college years were really tough without a father living in our home for financial support, instruction or advice, and I set a goal for myself of reaching a point in my life of being an independent person. In that way, I would not be influenced or controlled by others concerning my thoughts or actions, or theirs. I would be free and not subject to anyone's authority or jurisdiction. Plus, I would not have to rely on anyone for any aid, support or sustenance, or have my existence contingent upon something else in any way. The result was that I often kept my thoughts, ambitions, desires, problems, needs, etc. to myself. Even those closest to me at times had no idea of what was going on in certain areas of my life. However, everything changed years later when I realized that I couldn't do it all alone, as there had been success but failure too. Upon finally turning myself over to the Lord, I also discovered that I hadn't been as independent over the years as I had thought. He had been there all along doing some things for me while waiting for me to call upon Him for others.

Many people, at one time or another, think that they can be totally self-reliant and go at it alone, no matter the task or challenge. In some cases independence may make sense, but it could present trouble if one attempts to apply it to every area of their life, especially in regards to God. *Judges 17* tells about the independent actions of a man named Micah. *Verse 6* says that a man could do anything he thought was right because there was no king in Israel. Micah had stolen money from his mother, gave it back, and then some of it was used for idols and a shrine. Then he even invited a man to live in their house as a priest. Essentially, he had decided that he could honor and worship God in totally his own way. But it's easy to see that he was only headed for a really big problem, as God surely doesn't condone what Micah did. Micah may have done what he thought was right in his own eyes but not in those of God's. Just as Ezekiel, in the Bible, was appointed by the Lord to be a watchman over Israel, we may need friends or others to watch over and advise us. If Micah hadn't acted independently, he probably wouldn't have made the big mistake that he did.

Injustice - For me *injustice* occurs whenever a person isn't treated fairly or equally as others may be, and I have certainly experienced a few injustices over the course of my life. It may involve the violation of one's individual liberties, denial of voting rights or due process, infringements on the rights of freedom of speech, inadequate protection from cruel and unusual punishment, religious, ethnic, gender or racial discrimination, discrepancies in access to food, housing and wealth, unfair hiring practices, lack of available jobs and education, insufficient health care, murder, crime... I can remember well the injustice of being denied a job many years ago because I wore an Afro hairstyle. I've read in the paper where people haven't been granted homeowner loans because of their race, even though they were in a better financial position than others being approved. People in richer neighborhoods pay less for car insurance than those in poorer. Prayer has been taken out of the schools, not because of the children, but because of the complaints of their parents. We just live in a society of injustice where some dictate and others are dictated to, whether it is unfair or not. Most of us just have to deal with it in one way or another. My way is turning to God. In faith I am able to overcome any injustice as He has the final word. I didn't get that one job but was blessed with a better one.

Leviticus 19:15 says that we should judge each other fairly. Justice should be applied without prejudice and the great should never be honored or the poor disrespected. Those are among the laws that the Lord spoke unto Moses as to how He wants people to treat each other in sameness. Then according to *Proverbs 29:27*, the righteous and the wicked despise each other. Therefore, there could only be injustice, as an unjust man will never treat a just man favorably. Also, as Christians we should not be surprised or find it strange to encounter suffering and injustice (*1 Peter 4:12*). That's just one of the trials in proving ourselves. The remaining verses of *1 Peter* says that we should rejoice in being able to participate in the sufferings of Jesus, and we can all do so on an equal basis, plus share in on the joy when His glory is revealed. We should not suffer as murderers, thieves, evildoers or meddlers, but in suffering as Christians we should not be afraid and should praise God in being Christians. It goes on to say that judgment will begin with the family of God, and also questions the fate of the ungodly and the sinner. Those who suffer according to God's will and commit to Him will do well, while the others won't. There would be no injustice as God will be equally faithful to all who are faithful. So, we don't have to concern ourselves about the distribution or fairness of God's blessings. We can rejoice in spite of any circumstances, knowing that God can turn injustice into justice.

Integrity - *Integrity* is derived from the Latin adjective *integer,* meaning to be *whole* or *complete*, and people with integrity act according to the values, beliefs and principles they claim to hold. Someone who has integrity may be described as being principled, honest, scrupulous, truthful, fair, faithful, open, whole or trustworthy. There is also a consistency in their actions, methods, measures, expectations, outcomes, etc., as others won't view a person who displays unpredictable behavior, from one day to the next, as having integrity. I believe that I am a man of integrity, though I could maybe be a little more open. Am just a little cautious with people I don't know, respect or trust much. However, I refuse to allow any circumstances or pressures to change my values, beliefs or principles, and being in the Lord has made me whole and completed me. I may always have a few problems but through faith never have to compromise my integrity in solving them.

In the Bible, chapters 1 to 3 of *Daniel* tell about men of integrity as Daniel and three friends stayed with their principles, despite pressure to the contrary. Daniel, along with Hananiah, Mishael, and Azariah had been taken out of Israel and transported to Babylonia where they received special training and treatment. They adapted to their new home but remained true to the God they knew as children back home. In one instance Daniel had refused to indulge in the royal food and wine, though it would anger the king. However, he proved that all the young men would be healthier and better nourished in eating vegetables and drinking water as he always had. Later the friends renamed as Shadrach, Meshach and Abednego faced death for refusing to worship an idol the king had made. They were unwilling to serve or worship any god except their own God, and after refusing a second time were thrown into a furnace. They were not harmed in any way though, and the king saw a fourth man in the fire that some believe was Jesus.

Investment - *Investment* is when you place time, effort, money or etc. in something with the expectations of receiving a gain or return. And in putting God first, I am investing in my life and future to secure the spiritual rewards that are promised. I'm trying my best to take advantage of the gifts and opportunities that God has blessed me with, as He is investing in me too and looking for a return in my being faithful, obedient and doing His work. Through spiritual investment the rewards are great now and will be even better in the future as the ultimate return on my investment will be Heaven.

Matthew 6:19-21 says that we should not invest in treasures of the Earth that moth or rust can destroy, or thieves can steal. Our investments should be in Heaven where there won't be any lost treasures, and wherever our treasure is, our hearts will be too. Then it is impossible to serve both God and money (*Matthew 6:24*), so we have to beware of placing our financial investments over those in Him. We need to first seek the Kingdom of God and His righteousness, and in that investment will have not have to worry about our needs for today or for those of tomorrow (*Matthew 6:33-34*).

Jabez - The story of Jabez is an interesting one that many have written about. He is an intriguing person because so little was mentioned about him in the Bible, though he appears to have been highly regarded. My take is that he was an illegetimate child. In that, his mother was disgraced and it made things very tough for his family. Yet, in spite of it all, he grew up to enjoy a life of greatness and prosperity. Included in his story is a much discussed prayer where he asked God to have his territory enlarged. I've read where some believe that he may have been seeking to recover an inheritance lost at his birth. However, I believe as others that it was more about being a witness for God. Many had seen him rise from nothing to prominence, but he probably wanted to be able to reach out to those that didn't know him but needed to hear his story. He would be the example in showing them that, through God, all things were possible as he had done, against all odds, what no one would ever have expected of him considering his birth and subsequent upbringing - to succeed. I wrote about Jabez in my first book, but have since expanded my thoughts a little. Jabez was born in sin only to become a survivor, conqueror, and a man of God.; surely looked up to by many.

Over the pages of *1 Chronicles* are historical records with the names of the many kings and families from Adam to Abraham. Jabez is named in *verse 4:9* with no mention of a father, his mother's name, or even the names or number of his brothers. The ommission tells me that their names had been disgraced. Jabez (defined as *sorrowful* in the Bible) was probably born out of sorrow because his mother had been shamed by infedelity. He, also, must have been the youngest son with a different father than his brothers. However, Jabez grew up to be more honorable than them as he didn't allow the hardships, most likely endured because of the wrongful actions of their mother, to doom him to failure as they obviously did. Then by being mentioned in the same breath as kings, I am sure that Jabez most likely acquired all the wealth, power, and territory (land) that he needed. God blessed him with all that he asked for because his prayers were far more for the benefit of others than for himself. He wanted to tell those beyond his terrority of the goodness of God, along with sharing his blessings with them. Only God could make that possible though for, in those days, even those bearing the knowledge and gifts of God were not always welcome in many places. That's probably why *1 Chronicles 4:10* says that he prayed for God to be with him, and keep him from evil and grief. In having his prayer answered I believe that, beyond all obstacles and barriers, Jabez rose to the status of a king and accomplished much pleasing to God.

Jesus - I learned of Jesus Christ at an early age because of a Baptist family upbringing. We were taught about God and Jesus at home and Sunday morning church service was mandatory, as it appeared to be for most of the children in my neighborhood during those days. Christian prayer was approved of in school and I never heard one person complain or protest about it during my high school or college graduations. On Good Friday banks, stores, gas stations, restaurants and most other places of business would close from noon to 3 pm in commemorating the crucifixion of Jesus, and they would be closed all day on Easter and Christmas. I don't believe that there was even any bus service during those times either. It was like the whole world would just temporarily shut down. Then during some Christmas holiday seasons, we would enjoy walking door-to-door singing carols, and every company I worked for had some kind of special Christmas celebration planned. However, things are quite different these days. In a democratic society, where majority rules, it's been a minority of non-believers now dictating how, when and where we can worship and honor Jesus, with many children being raised having little or no knowledge of who He was and is. Good Friday is now a full day of business and for many Easter and Christmas are workdays.

I truly believe that Jesus Christ is the Son of God and my Savior. Through His life and teachings are all my hope and way to peace, success and happiness, among many other great things. Historians report that Jesus lived anywhere from 7-2 BC to 30-36 AD, while my Bible says He was born between 4 to late 5 BC. He was born of a virgin (Mary), was baptized by John the Baptist, performed miracles, founded the Christian Church, was crucified in Jerusalem on the orders of Pontius Pilate (the Roman Prefect) after being accused of sedition (stirring up discontent) against the Roman Empire, rose from the dead, and ascended into Heaven from where He will return. His name, *Jesus,* signifies that He will save His people from sin *(Matthew 1:21)* and was announced by an angel as it being the divinely chosen name for Mary's son. Then the name *Christ* (anointed one) was the official title given by Jesus as the Messiah *(John 1:41)* and as the Son of the living God in a answer from Simon Peter proclaiming who Jesus was *(Matthew 16:16).* In *Matthew 5:17-20,* Jesus tells us that He had come to fulfill the Law of the Prophets, even until Heaven and Earth disappeared. The righteous obeying His commandments will be granted entrance into Heaven, while those who aren't and break His commandments will be denied.

Job - There may be times that we all are tested, endure hardships, and face many different challenges, as God never promised us life without difficulty. No person is exempt from trouble, no matter how righteous. And when going through some things, it doesn't mean that one has done any wrong in the eyes of God and is being punished. I believe myself as being a good person but realize that bad things may happen to good people. Certainly much has happened to me that I never expected and am continuing to fight back from some unfortunate circumstances. However, while my expectations are high that I will soon regain control of my life and possibly be rewarded with more than I lost, it has bothered me hearing the suggestions by some that my problems may have stemmed from me not being the Christian I had claimed to be. They question that if I was doing right how could so much be going wrong, but I understand too that some rejoice in the misfortune of others. So I just try to lend a deaf ear to the negative voices as my battles continue to be fought through faith, and I am inspired greatly by the Book of *Job* in the Bible. Through it's reading, I have learned that bad things may happen to good people without us knowing or needing to know why. If God wills it, we should be willing to suffer than to be in health and prosperity, as God rewards an abiding faith. I may be suffering a bit now but trust that God will deliver me from it in many good ways.

Job was considered to be a pure and upright man but was punished in a contest between God and Satan, who had contended that Job's loyalty to God was based solely on the blessings he was receiving. So, in testing Job, God allowed all that was important and treasured by him to be taken away. Job was known to be *blameless* by God and Satan, but had to deal with the painful irony of his situation in an interaction between his friends and himself. Job wanted to find a way to justify God's actions, but he had trouble understanding things like how evil people could harm a widow *(Job 24:21)*, only to be rewarded with long and successful lives. Then Job's friends said that God distributed outcomes to people based on what their actions deserved. In that belief, they insisted that Job had to have done something wrong to merit his punishment. Therefore, Job had to work through his confusion and the lecturing of his friends. However, God suggested that people shouldn't discuss divine justice, as His power is too great for us to possibly justify His ways. Job had to admit that he lacked the power for doing anything that God could do. Then in refusing to yield his integrity to Satan, he knew he would be vindicated, though once driven to even curse his birth. As a result, he was blessed with twice that of what he had before *(Job 42:10)*, and a major theme, of the Book of *Job,* is that we should always trust God whether or not the conditions are known.

Journey - A *journey* involves the taking of a trip from one place to another, and in my first book I wrote that mine was one of faith as I am on a spiritual journey. People, having a hard time, may look for something to hold on to. In the past many went to churches for answers but as time goes on some will search for their spiritual enlightenment beyond religious institutions. However, in spite of a downturn in Sunday church service for many years, there has recently been more attendance. It has been reported that an increasing number of minorities are in our country and seeking answers for their problems; with a large number of new churchgoers said to be Catholics. But still many remain on their own personal journeys for a spiritual awakening, whether in church or not. Every person journeys on in their own way and many lessons are learned along their chosen routes. Our journeys take us from where we were to where we are today and, as a Christian, I'm hoping that my final destination will be Heaven, in utilizing my faith, beliefs, experiences and increased wisdom to guide my every step.

Any journey can become a tiring and weary one, and one may need to find a source of strength to continue. *1 Kings 19* tells about a journey taken by Elijah as he fled from Jezebel, who threatened him and already had killed other prophets. He was afraid and running for his life. His journey first led him into the desert for a day, where he wound up sitting down and praying that he would die. After he laid down under a tree and fell asleep, an angel of the Lord touched him and told him to eat. He ate and drank some bread and water that was placed by his head, only to lie back down. Then the angel came back a second time telling him that he had to get up and eat because the journey was too much for him. He ate and drank again, and was so strengthened that he was able to travel for forty days and forty nights until he reached Horeb, which was the mountain of God. As Elijah we may feel overwhelmed by our journeys, but we should never consider giving up as an option. I continuously pray that through God's will my journey will be a successful and prosperous one in leading me to Him, as *Romans 1:10* says.

Joy - A niece of mine was telling me how she had enjoyed the wedding of a friend, only to find out later on in the day that she would also have to make plans for attending the funeral of another friend that had died suddenly. That got me to thinking about how one's joy can easily turn to worry or sadness in the blink of an eye. You make that final car note payment, only to find out that the vehicle is in need of major repair. You receive a pay raise or a promotion at your job, only to hear rumors that the business you've worked at for many years faces an imminent shutdown. You finally get your finances in order, only to have an illness, bad investment, or another unfortunate occurrence place you back into more debt. The fact of it all is that bad things can and will happen. We just have to find ways for not allowing them to totally rob us of our joy, in spite of the circumstances. Having a strong faith is one, as it can give a person the power to maintain their joy during even the most troubling of times.

I admit to experiencing some times where I have felt less joyful than others, allowing people, health concerns, financial issues and other concerns to dim my spirits. However, in now placing my faith and trust in the Lord, I am maintaining my joy through the feelings of peace and well-being. I know that I will always be a part of His plan, through the good and the bad. In that, I also know that any compromises of my joy will be temporary, and it allows me to be more able to concentrate on the things that bring me joy through Him and for Him; like the volunteer work I have done helping senior citizens with their healthcare related issues, along with the inspirational writing and singing I do. *Jeremiah 31:13* tells me that the Lord can turn my mourning into joy, comfort me, and have me rejoicing over any sorrow. Therefore, through Him, my life can always be one of continued joy, even when going through things like stroke, diabetes, job loss, divorce, financial issues, death of loved ones, and etc.

Justice - *Justice* is the fair rendering of what is right, just or due. For me there is justice when I treat people nice and am treated nice by them. There is justice when purchasing something needed that meets or exceeds my expectations. There is justice when a person is chosen for a job based on their qualifications and not by race, gender, favoritism, age, connections or etc. There is justice when people who are equally yoked in crime are judged and sentenced as equals. There is justice when all people enjoy the same rights, freedoms, and opportunities. There is justice when a person can safely drive or walk through any neighborhood without any fears from being just who they are. There is justice when warring nations can sit down and discuss ways to peacefully settle their differences. There is justice when one's righteous beliefs are never compromised or denied by another. And there is an ever-greater justice whenever a faithful life is rewarded by God's Promise. His justice is what matters above all others, and the most powerful.

2 Samuel 8:15 says that when David reigned over the people of Israel, judgment and justice were equally executed over all of them, meaning that he did what was right for all of his people and not just a select few. Many people these days are going through some of their most troubling of times and view it as being an injustice to them. They see themselves losing their jobs, homes, wealth, health, safety, peace, and others things, while seeing others flourishing who don't appear to be very deserving. Prophet Habakkuk, according to *Habakkuk 1:1-4*, endured some tough times and questioned God as to why it seemed that evil people were still receiving divine blessings while all he was witnessing was injustice. He couldn't understand how God could tolerate all the wrong, destruction, violence, strife, conflicts, unlawfulness, and unrighteousness that were all around him. God answered in *verses 5-11* that the people weren't getting away with anything, and that Habakkuk would see them being punished in ways he wouldn't be able to believe or imagine. God's power would be turning all injustice into justice through their total destruction and domination by the Babylonians.

Justify - To *justify* is when one provides an explanation or rationale for something to make it seem ok or to prove that something is correct or just. One example is when data is given to back up a recommendation that has been made. Another is when a person makes up an excuse to make their bad behavior seem right, and non-believers and believers of the Word may be guilty of that. We all sin and may at times try to justify our actions with all kinds of reasons to make it sound as if there was nothing wrong done at all.

Romans 3:10 says that there is none righteous among us, and in that derives the need for justification. We can always try to justify our sinful behavior through denial or making up excuses. However, it's better to confess the sins to God and receive *justification*, which is the act of divine grace that will restore those that have sinned back to a full relationship with God, and as if no sins had been committed. It is human nature to sin and all fall short of God's glory, but redemption is through Jesus Christ (*Romans 3:34-24)*, who died for our sins and then was resurrected for our justification (*Romans 4:25)*.

Keepsakes - Over the years, I have received a number of certificates, trophies, diplomas, and awards. At home and at work, they have been placed on shelves, desks, and walls for all to see. For myself, looking at those keepsakes brings back many fond memories of my past success, achievement, recognition or glory, and also of the hard work, dedication, sacrifice, and determination it took to earn each one. They will always hold a special significance for me, and during my times of failure or hardships I can look to them for motivation and inspiration, and that has led to some recent mementos that will be treasured too. However, God desires for me to also have some keepsakes that can't be placed on display but in a spiritual nature, and the Bible mentions many things that we all should keep; things that in holding on to will lead to greater accolades and eternal life if we place our efforts, love, worship and trust in God.

Certainly my Bible is a most important keepsake and in it I have read that I should keep the following: the way of the Lord by doing what is right and just (*Genesis 18:19*), the Lord's judgments and do them for my safety (*Leviticus 25:18*), my tongue from evil (*Psalm 34:13*), in perfect peace by trusting in the Lord (*Isaiah 26:3*), the doors closed to neighbors, friends or close ones that I have no trust or confidence (*Micah 7:5*), an honest and good heart in having heard the Word (*Luke 8:15*), a unity of the Spirit in a bond of peace (*Ephesians 4:3*), myself pure by not sharing in the sins of others (*1 Timothy 5:22*), the love of God and His commandments (*1 John 5:3*), the belief in Jesus and be rewarded with eternal life (*John 3:15*), and the words in the Book of *Revelation* prophesying the coming of Jesus for those that are blessed (*Revelation 22:7*).

Keys - *Keys* are instruments to open locks and symbolically may be used to represent a number of things; like people talking about the keys to the future. For Christians the most important keys unlock the doors to God and Jesus, and many of us have some that we need to improve on. One very important key is wisdom and, in *1 Chronicles 28,* David tells his son, Solomon, that there are seven of them. Solomon was told that he should acknowledge God, serve Him wholeheartedly, keep his own motives pure, be faithful, realize that God chose him, be strong, and do God's work. Those are great words for even today. We should all believe and trust in God, and pray to Him for that kind of wisdom to successfully accomplish whatever we are called on to do by Him. Also, in *Luke 11:52,* Jesus tells a Pharisee about how the experts of the law had taken away the key to knowledge. In doing so, they hadn't entered God's Kingdom and were only hindering those that were. And the knowledge of God is a most important key for a Christian life.

In *Deuteronomy 29,* Moses tells of there being four keys to success for Christians: *remembering, obeying, focusing,* and *recalling.* We should remember the times in our lives that God has met our important needs and that He will continue to provide and care for us. Moses tells of how their clothes and sandals never wore out over the forty years of wandering in the desert. In obeying, we follow God's commands by being obedient in avoiding sin and in striving towards holiness. In that we will prosper in all that we do. We must also focus our efforts on God in all that we do and live according to His plan. Those that turn their hearts away from God will face disaster, while those that don't will be safe. Then we must recall by holding on to what we know about God and what He has revealed to us. In keeping our eyes off of worldly things, and placing them on Him, more and more of Himself and His plans will be revealed to our children and us forever. God is the key of life and we must utilize our keys in opening our lives totally to Him.

Kindness - I consider kindness to be one of my good qualities, as I have always had a caring and giving heart for family, friends, strangers, and even some that have been more against me than for me. God desires for us to be kind to each other in serving His purposes and, through generosity, compassion, favors, and acts of good will, I have helped many in different ways and warmed a cold heart or two. I read where the 19th century American novelist Henry James once told one of his nephews that there were three things most important in one's life - *to be kind, be kind, and be kind*. Those are a few very inspiring words to live by and, in living so, one will surely be blessed by God. In being kind to others, even strangers, we are showing our kindness to Him as well (*Matthew 25:40*).

The Bible says that, among other things, kindness should be forgiving, helpful, burden-bearing and inspired by love. We should be kind to one another, tender-hearted, and be forgiving just as God forgives us for the sake of Jesus (*Ephesians 4:32*). The weak should be supported and we are blessed by being more givers than receivers (*Acts 20:35*). Whenever an opportunity presents itself, we should do good for others (*Galatians 6:10*). We should also help to restore the sinful and make sure that we don't fall victim to the same temptations, while carrying the burdens of each other to fulfill the law of Jesus (*Galatians 6:1-2*). Then we are greatly rewarded for loving and helping our enemies, but expecting nothing in return from them (*Luke 6:35*).

Laughter - It has been said that laughter is the best medicine for some things, and I can certainly attest to that. There was a time that I would get really down on myself when things weren't going well. I would find myself overly consumed in thought and worry, while keeping to myself. Being a man of faith, I still hadn't learned to place my concerns before God, rather than always trying to solve problems on my own. However, I now am relying on my faith and laughter to ease my mind. Unlike previously, seldom do I go to bed at night with a frown on my face and losing sleep due to restlessness and stress. When I'm troubled, I first look to God and Jesus in prayer. Then at times, I may think about some of my more happier and funnier times. And before going to sleep at night, I may lie in bed and watch something, like *Seinfeld (*a popular television comedy show from the 1990's), on my laptop computer to enjoy a good laugh. Through prayer and laughter, I feel better about my situation and am more able to enjoy a night of peace and rest. Plus I am apt to awaken in the morning in a better frame of mind, realizing that things often aren't as bad as they may appear and that every new day offers a chance for opportunity, reconciliation and blessings.

Psalm 126:1-3 tells how the Lord brought back the captives to Zion and they were like men who dreamed. Their mouths were filled with laughter, and they sang songs of joy for the great things the Lord had done for them. *Verse 5* goes on to say that those who sow in tears will reap in joy, so there can always be happiness and laughter in spite of one's troubles. Then *Ecclesiastes 3:4* says that there is a time for weeping and a time for laughing, along with a time for mourning and a time for dancing. Taking those words to heart from *Psalms* and *Ecclesiastes*, even in the midst of my greatest storms, I should be able to dance and laugh because of all the great things the Lord continues doing for me. However, *Ecclesiastes 7:3-5* says that for the wise there may come times when sorrow is actually better than laughter, like during times of mourning. A sad face is good for the heart and there is mourning in the hearts of the wise. The hearts of fools and of the vain are consumed by pleasure, and their laughter is as meaningless as the crackling of thorns under a pot; it is also better to heed the words of the wise than to hear their songs. I would simply say that the wise, in their hearts, know there is a right time, place and reason for mourning or laughter, while others may not or even care.

Legacy - A *legacy* is something handed down from an ancestor or a predecessor from the past, good or bad; loyalty, for example, is viewed as a good legacy, while dishonor is not. I want to create a good spiritual/personal legacy for myself and am utilizing the things I've learned and achieved to promote what I'm doing now and still hope to do. My desire is to live a life that may help change the world for the better in at least some way, in serving both present and future generations. As I continue to be blessed, I want to always be able to share the wealth that God has given me with others. In my legacy, I want to leave some of my influence behind through my words, deeds, beliefs, values, hopes, loves, wishes, advice, character... I want to be remembered and missed for being a difference-maker in the lives of many, in having been a good role model and a positive example for any person to learn from and be inspired by. Certainly, my writing will be a legacy of mine, as a number of people, young and old, say that they have been blessed and inspired by the reading of my first book, *Forever A Man With The Lord*, and are looking forward to reading my future efforts.

Acts 10 tells of Cornelius, a Roman army officer, who was a just and devout man that feared God, gave generously to those in need, and prayed regularly. God took notice of his good deeds and they were a reminder to Him of Cornelius' character that set him apart from other men. This was to be a part of his enduring legacy that we all can follow. We should desire to always be looked upon favorably and continually in the eyes of

God, and be remembered and recognized for the good works that we have done. Because of his good character, God used Cornelius to bring about a change of understanding by showing that Gentiles (people outside of Israel) could become Christians, and the acceptance of them into the Church became another important aspect of the legacy of Cornelius. It had been against the law for Jews to associate with Gentiles, but an angel of God had come to Cornelius, in a vision, and requested that he would invite a man named Peter, a Jew, to his home. There it was revealed to Peter that both Jews and Gentiles alike received the gift of the Holy Spirit, and he ordered that all could be baptized together in the name of Jesus.

Life - I read where a miner found a fossil from a shark jawbone, while working 700 feet underground in a central Kentucky mine. It is believed to be from a shark, of the *Edestus genus,* that once swam in the seas over of what is now Kentucky. That certainly was quite a find. However, most amazing to me is that the fossil is estimated to be over about 300 million years old. I'm still not a believer that science can, or will ever be able to, accurately determine the age range of anything thought to be that old. Scientists have had differing opinions about the age of the Earth itself, but I've read too that recent geological evidence indicates that the Earth is approximately 4.6 billion years old. Then a hypothetical unicellular organism or single cell called LUCA (last universal common ancestor) is mentioned for giving rise to all life on Earth between 3.5 to 3.8 billion years ago. Be mindful though that one definition of *hypothetical* is *assuming without proof.* I certainly wonder how many years ago it was that life actually began here, but am a true believer that it was God who created all life, no matter how long ago, and continues to sustain it. Therefore, science aside, I see only God as knowing our true origin and history.

On the day of this writing, I received word that an old neighbor and friend, in her sixties, had died suddenly of an apparent heart attack. That came as quite a shock, considering she had visited our home only a few days earlier. However, while we may know the date, time and place of our births, only God knows when our lives will end here. But life lives on as, while others in the world died too at that moment, others breathed their first breaths of life. *Genesis 1* says that on the 5th day of God's creation, He filled the waters with sea animals and the skies with the winged order. Then on the 6th day, He created beasts and cattle to roam the Earth, followed by man, being created in His own image, to have dominion over all other living things. Yet, there is no mention of the evolution of organisms, cells or apes, as some scientists have theorized and want us to believe. *Man* was created as *man*, and *Job 14:1-2* tells us that in being birthed by women, all of our days are few and full of trouble. Our days are determined, or numbered, *(verse 5)* and we eventually die and are laid low, breathing our last breaths and being no more *(verse 10)*. But God has promised us everlasting life *(Titus 1:2)*, and we can enjoy it in God's Kingdom of Heaven by following His commandments and being saved through Jesus Christ *(Mark 10)*.

Light - We all need the light of God's love to shine on us, and Jesus was sent to bring that light. Jesus was to be the Savior for delivering people out from their spiritual darkness and separation from God. In receiving God's love we never have to worry, fret or fear, but enjoy and experience the peace that can only come through the Lord. I have given myself to Jesus and have been a witness and receiver of God's love many times over. During my blindness from stroke, for example, I saw His light at my fingertips as my eyesight was being restored. Instantly a sense of peace and relief came over me, with my fears subsiding in the feeling of His presence. That light told me who was in control.

As in *Psalm 27:1,* I know that I have nothing to fear or be afraid of, as Jesus is the light of my salvation and strength. Then as *Ephesians 5* instructs me, I am filled by the Spirit and giving thanks to God and Jesus always. I am trying to be an imitator of God, by living a life of love, just as Jesus loves me and gave Himself up for all others and myself. As a child of His light, I have removed myself from the darkness of the immoral, impure and greedy. Now there is a light shining in my life that includes goodness, righteousness and truth. I truly feel myself as having arisen from a spiritual deadness into the light of Jesus, knowing that I have to always be careful and wise in how I live.

Listening - There are times that we all probably could and should be better listeners. A deaf ear may be turned to a person that we really don't care to communicate with, or if we think that another is saying nothing of importance or believable. Then we may not listen attentively because of distractions or thinking about other things. Also, people may have problems understanding, interpreting, evaluating and retaining what they have heard, which is especially of great concern if the communications are with God and Jesus. We surely need to be the most active and effective listeners as possible where they are concerned. If not, it could be much to our disadvantage, or even result in punishment. Just think about Moses. He listened but didn't always understand what God was telling him about how to lead the people of Israel out of sin and into the Promised Land. And over forty years of wandering lost in the desert, it's obvious that many began to totally close their ears to the words of Moses. They refused to listen or take him seriously but continued following his leadership because there were really no other options available for them.

In *Matthew 13:13,* Jesus tells of people listening but not hearing or understanding His words. Therefore, He spoke in parables (stories) for illustrative purposes to make the truths of His messages more intelligible. *Verses 19* and *20* go on to say that the evil one can come and take away what is sown in one's heart, if they hear the message about God's Kingdom and fail to understand it. Those who truly hear the Word understand it with their hearts and receive it with joy. Then according to Isaiah, in *Romans 10:17,* faith comes from hearing the message, and it is heard through the Word of Jesus. Therefore, in that respect, the ability to listen and comprehend Him is most important. *Galatians 3* also tells us the importance of listening and hearing by the faith of Jesus, and that the promises of faith are given to those that believe in what they have heard about the Spirit and God's miracles. The Galatians were questioned about trying to attain their goals through human effort, and suffering for nothing, rather than listening to the promises of God. Through their constraints from the laws of legalized Christianity, they had lost sight of the original truth of Jesus and the freedom given to them by God through Him.

Loneliness - John Cadoppo, a social neuroscientist at the University of Chicago says that every person, even the most popular or extroverted, can experiences feelings of loneliness at times. However, while being lonely isn't a bad thing, staying lonely is. Cadoppo reports that, according to some recent data, nearly a quarter of the people in the United States complain about being lonely, but the rate is lower than in other countries because of our individualist culture. Yet, he expects to see an increase due to people living longer, meaning more widows, and the continued rise in single-person households. Loneliness increases over time and many experience it during key periods like over the holidays, when people usually gather together. Cadoppo, also, says that loneliness can cause problems such as sleep dysfunction, depression, and high blood pressure. I can certainly attest to that. After my divorce, loneliness consumed me with no longer having a wife and children around. A couple of years later, I found myself depressed, sleeping very little, and then battling diabetes, which I never knew that I had. It took a new friendship with a special Christian woman, along with drawing nearer to God and Jesus, for me to finally resolve my issues of loneliness. In that I also discovered that having quality friendships was more important than the number of friendships.

Over *Psalm 102,* there is a prayer of affliction, as a prophet is overwhelmed and makes a grievous complain to God in seeking comfort and mercy. He describes his loneliness, in *verse 7,* as being like a sparrow alone on a housetop while lying awake in watch of his enemies. *John 16:32* then tells of the loneliness that Jesus was expecting to experience. He told His disciples the time had come when they would find themselves scattered, with every man on his own. They were to leave Jesus alone, but He would not be alone because of the Father being with Him. That's a great thing for us to remember, as we never have to be alone if we keep God in our presence. Then even if our sinfulness causes a separation from God, as with the Israelites in the Bible, He will be patient and continue to watch over us, waiting to see if our devotion to Him re-emerges. *Psalm 9:10* says that those knowing the Lord's name will trust in Him, and He has never forsaken any that have sought Him. The children of Israel surely experienced feelings of loneliness, as they became strangers in strange lands, scattered in exile. They just needed to realize the importance of regaining God's favor, while seeing that He had never left them alone and was continuing to provide for them in many ways.

Love - *Love* is a virtue representing human kindness, compassion, and affection. It is a central theme for many religions and for Christians *God is love.* His love is unconditional, and He continues to love us even when we sin, through His forgiveness. He always remains faithful and true, and He never gives up on us, as we may do others or ourselves. During these most difficult times, many people are hurting and may feel that no one cares. Therefore, even more so, God wants us to reach out to others, even strangers, in love. We can do that by giving a nice smile, offering a word of encouragement, or lending a helping hand. Then we should pray for those that mistreat us, as God wants us to love our enemies too. He, also, wants us to love Jesus, and that I truly do. I may desire having a special woman in my life to love, but it is Jesus that places a song in my heart that no other can. I will follow Him anywhere, while loving others in His spirit.

God should be our most important love. Both *Deuteronomy 10-12* and *13-3* tell us that we should love Him with all of our hearts and souls. *Mark 12-30* says the same, but also that we should love Him with all of our minds and strength. Then God inspires love as *1 John 4:19* tells us to love Him because He first loved us. Love is also a proof of being a disciple of Jesus. He tells us that having love for one another just as He loves us provides that, according to *John 13:35.* We should love each other because love is of God, and every person that loves is born of God and knows Him *(1 John 4:7). John 15:13* goes on to praise the greatness of sacrificial love, where a man will lay his life for his friends. Plus there is an assurance of love that we can depend on during our most troubling of times. *Romans 8:28* says that all things work together for the good of those that love God, and those that are called according to His purpose. Therefore, if we love God, along with loving and helping each other, we can always make the world and life better for us all.

Loyalty - I once bought my sons a cat that didn't seem to care much for me. It would hiss and bristle its back at me, probably because it hadn't gotten used to me because, between work and other activities, I wasn't at home as much as usual. Then one night I injured myself playing basketball at the gym and had to have knee surgery. I wound up with a full cast on my left leg, which made it very difficult for me to make it upstairs to the bedroom at night. Therefore, I decided to stay in the downstairs family room over the days that the doctor wanted me off of my feet. On the very next morning after, I am lying there alone and here comes that cat towards me with an evil look in its eyes. But it stopped suddenly and just took a long look at me. Then it jumped up and rested its head on my cast. Much to my surprise, he became my loyal companion and kept me company every day, while the wife was off to work and the boys to school. Plus being very protective of me when anyone came near, hissing and bristling its back at them. That cat really had my back just as we always hope that some people will have for us. Its always a great thing to have a loyal friend that will offer protection, help and comfort during our times of need or distress.

In *Matthew 22*, the Pharisees asked Jesus if it was right to pay taxes to Caesar, the emperor of Rome. In *verse 21*, He tells them to give Caesar what was his and God what was His, meaning that their loyalty could be to one or the other. Of course, God wants us to be loyal to Him above all others, just as He is loyal to us. However, He desires too that His people show some loyalty to each other. The story of Ruth and Naomi is a great story of personal loyalty. *Ruth 1* tells of their being a famine in the land that drove Naomi to the country of Moab with her husband, Elimelech and two sons, Mahlon and Kilion. There the husband died and later the sons married Moabite women, one named Oprah and the other Ruth. Then after about ten years the sons died, leaving Ruth with only her daughters-in-law. It was then said that the Lord had come to the aid of His people and was providing food for them. Ruth told the women that they should go back home to their own mother's home and seek other husbands, and hopefully be dealt with in kindness by the Lord, just as that they had dealt the dead and her. Oprah kissed Naomi goodbye, but Ruth clung to her. She told her mother-in-law that she wouldn't leave or turn her back on her. Where Naomi would go and stay, she would too. They would be of the same people and of the same God, and would die in the same place too. So they went to Bethlehem together to join in on the Lord's barley harvest that was beginning.

Lust - To *lust* is having an eager desire for something, and it is most described as being an unlawful sexual desire, such as wanting to have sex with a person outside of one's marriage. Then Dante (Durante degli Alighieri 1265-1321), a major Italian poet of the Middle Ages, defined lust as being an excessive love of others. It is surely regarded as being a sin in a sexual respect, but Dante viewed any desire that reduced the love that a person could give God as being a lust and sinful too. Therefore things like having an excessive love for money, possessions, power, etc. that take on a higher priority in one's life over all else, including God, would also be unacceptable.

The first instance of lust appearing in the Bible is *Genesis 3:6,* with Eve in God's forbidden garden being tempted by the fruit of a tree. It was good for food and pleasing to her eye, along with being desirable for gaining wisdom. She took some and ate it, then gave Adam some to eat. Then God punished them for their lust of the fruit. *Exodus 20:17* goes on to tell us that coveting anything belonging to a neighbor was forbidden, and that included his house, wife, manservant, maidservant, ox, and donkey. It is also written in the Bible that we should clothe ourselves in Jesus and not think about how to gratify any lusts of the flesh (*Romans 13:14).*

Majesty - *Majesty* means greatness and is derived from the Latin word *maiestas.* It is said that during the Roman Republic it was the legal term for the supreme status and dignity of the state, and to be respected above everything else, which would include God. However, later the meaning of the word turned to being an offence against the dignity of the Emperor, and I can certainly understand that. Roman Emperors demanded to be hailed and served in majesty, but there were still those unwilling to bestow that honor upon anyone other than God.

The Bible tells of the majesty of God and Jesus. *1 Chronicles 29:11-13* says that all our thanks and praise should be in God's name. Everything in Heaven and Earth are His, and in Him are the greatness, power, glory, victory, and the majesty. Wealth and honor come from Him, as He reigns over all, and in His hands are the strength and power to exalt and give strength to all. Then regarding Jesus, *Isaiah 9:6* says that He would be born and have the government upon His shoulders, in taking on the majesty of God. He would be called *Wonderful, Counselor, The mighty God, The everlasting Father,* and *The Prince of Peace.*

Marriage - Even though my marriage ended suddenly and unexpectedly in divorce, after many mostly good years, I truly enjoyed my married life and always tried to be the best husband as possible. I had married the woman I loved and thought surely that only in an earthly death would there be any separation. If I could live my life over, I would again choose being married over single life, and to the same woman, with just doing a few things differently that could have saved my marriage. Then a few years after my divorce, another special woman and myself had contemplated being married. It didn't happen but I still would never rule out the possibility of me being married again. I believe that it is a good thing for those in love taking it seriously. There just seems to be so many people marrying for the wrong reasons, and it doesn't surprise me when I hear about marriages, especially in the entertainment and sports world, ending after even only one or two months. Then the dictionary at my home defines *marriage* as being the legal union of a man and woman as husband and wife. Enough said. I don't judge.

Genesis 2:24 says that a man will leave his father and mother to be united to his wife, as they become one flesh. *Matthew 19:5* says the same, as does *1 Corinthians 6:16*. There are no exceptions. *Marriage*, as defined in the Bible, is a permanent relationship between a *man* and a *woman*, and dissolved only by death (*Romans 7:2-3*), adultery (*Matthew 19-9*), or desertion (*1 Corinthians 7:15*). Also, a man should be monogamous (married to only one woman at a time), and polygamy (married to more than one woman at a time) was greatly discouraged according to *Leviticus 18:18* and *Deuteronomy 17:17*. Marriage is meant to be a divine institution for the propagation (continuance) of life (*Genesis 1:27,28),* as God wants men and women to marry and have children. Then love, over things like looks, wealth, status, etc, should be a top priority in marriage. *Ephesians 5:33* instructs a man to love his wife as he loves himself, and for the wife to respect her husband. A husband's love for his wife should be just as Jesus loved the Church and gave Himself up for it *(Ephesians 5:25)*.

Meekness - *Meekness* is being mild, submissive or compliant and, in today's aggressive and self-centered world, most people don't admire others for being meek. They are thought to be weak and may be called tame, timid, unambitious, repressed, spiritless, wimpish, or mild. Those that usually receive the most recognition and admiration these days are the more competitive, aggressive, and assertive people. Many consider me to be a quite mild mannered person. However, I would never view myself as being weak and have held leadership positions that required me to be strong and authoritative, plus being very outspoken and defensive when a matter warrants it. I would like to be thought of as how Aristotle (384 BC - 322 BC) spoke on the Greek word *prautes*, meaning mildness. According to the Greek philosopher, the prautes person stood in the middle between the two extremes of getting angry without reason and not getting angry at all. They become angry at the right time and for the right reason. The condition of their minds and hearts demonstrate gentleness but in power and not in weakness. Therefore, there is a balance born in strength of character. These are the kind of people I believe Jesus refers to when He says that the meek shall inherit the Earth, for He was described as being meek Himself.

The Bible tells much about the cultivation of meekness, serving in meekness, and the fruits of meekness. *1 Timothy* 6:11 instructs us to live in righteousness, godliness, faith, love, patience and *meekness,* while *2 Timothy 2:24-25* says that we show gentleness towards all men, be apt to teach and show patience, and in *meekness* instruct or correct those that oppose themselves. *Galatians 5:22-23* then tells us that the fruit of the

Spirit includes love, joy, peace, longsuffering, gentleness, goodness, faith, *meekness,* and temperance, for against them is no law, while *verse 26* warns us about becoming conceited or provoking and envying each other. Further back, *Isaiah 29:19-20* says that the *meek* and the poor among men will rejoice in the Lord. The ruthless, scorners, and those having an eye for evil will vanish, disappear or be cut down. In the *Psalms, 25:9* says that the Lord will guide the *meek* in judgment and teach them His way. Then *149:4* says that as the Lord takes pleasure in His people, He will beautify the *meek* with salvation. Also, Jesus set the example for meekness, in that while being oppressed, afflicted, and taken as a lamb to slaughter, He never opened His mouth *(Isaiah 53:7)*. Finally, *Matthew 5:5* assures us that it is the *meek* that shall inherit the Earth, and not the aggressive and self-centered people that are admired a lot today.

Mentors - *Mentors* are teachers or counselors and growing up, outside of my home, church and schools, I had several throughout my neighborhood. Neighbors knew their neighbors well back then and our block was like one big family. A neighbor to our left was my uncle and a mentor. A neighbor to our right was my scout leader and a mentor. A neighbor across the street was my baseball coach and a mentor. Then there were other neighbors I could just enjoy talking to about most anything and some, even on different blocks and streets, that would get on me and/or inform my parents when seeing, or hearing about, me doing anything wrong. I certainly believe that having so many mentors and watchful eyes on me helped greatly in molding me into the person I am today. Nowadays, with so many single parent families and deteriorating neighborhoods, it is difficult for children to find mentors that will help foster their growth and tutor them in keeping on the right track in life, as I had.

2 Kings 2 tells of Elisha becoming Elijah's successor. Elijah had served as Elisha's mentor, though that word wasn't used during Biblical times. However, Elijah is said to have believed in Elisha and wanted him to find success as a prophet. So he willingly offered himself to be a mentor to assure that success, with God having placed him in Elisha's life to prepare, teach and be his friend. In *Chapter 2,* the transition occurs, as Elijah is taken up to Heaven in a fiery chariot, leaving behind his mantle (a sleeveless outer garment) for Elisha and dividing Jordan. Just as Elisha, we all need mentors in our lives that will believe in us and want us to succeed. Unfortunately, because of jealousy or other factors, there are people, even some really close to us, that may not want to witness or help in that success. Then there are others that may just lead one astray or in to trouble. Therefore, we have to be careful in picking our mentors. *Proverbs 27:17* sums up mentoring in saying that as iron sharpens iron, one man sharpens another. Spiritually, it's great if one becomes a trusted confidant and friend for another.

Mercy - A blessing that is an act of divine favor, kindness or compassion is a definition of *mercy*. As I laid in that hospital bed recovering from my stroke, the doctor told me that I *could have* and *should have* suffered more than just temporary blindness. He said that someone from above was surely watching over me on that evening. He even suggested for me to join a church if not already having a membership in one, as I had truly been blessed through the mercy of God. So, he was very pleased to hear that I was already a man of faith and in church. Mercy also implies there being compassion that forbears punishment even though justice may demand it, like where a person will throw himself or herself before the mercy of the court in seeking leniency for their crimes. We all commit sins that should warrant our being punished. However, if we seek the Lord's forgiveness, He will grant it through His mercy, no matter how many times we have sinned and found ourselves standing before Him. I most certainly am truly grateful and blessed in having received His mercy rather than being punished for my many transgressions.

Psalm 103:8 says that the Lord is merciful and gracious, along with being slow to anger and plenteous in mercy. Just as the Heaven is high above the Earth, His mercy is great toward those that fear Him (*Psalm 103:11*). From everlasting to everlasting, the mercy of the Lord is with those that fear Him, as is His righteousness with their children's children (*Psalm 103:17*). *Titus 3:5* then tells us that God saved us not because of any righteous things we had done, but because of His mercy. The Holy Spirit saved us through the washing of rebirth and renewal. That was poured out abundantly on us through Jesus and, in being justified by His grace, we may become heirs having the hope of eternal life (*verses 6* and *7*). In praying for mercy, *Luke 18:13* tells of a publican (a Roman tax collector) standing off, looking away from Heaven as he smote (cut) upon his breast, declaring himself to being a sinner and asking God to be merciful to him. The Bible also tells of the rewards for being a merciful person. *Proverbs 21:21* says that life, righteousness, and honor is found by those that follow after righteousness and mercy. Then the merciful are blessed in that they will obtain mercy (*Matthew 5:7*).

Messengers - I often feel the Lord's presence within me as He directly communicates with me through my thoughts, feelings and experiences, and that presence is said to be the most true and reliable source of His Light. However, He also communicates with us from the world outside through the messages sent by the way of prophets, teachers and other messengers. Among those are simple people, as myself, that spread the Lord's messages through our artistic and creative talents. I've read where some of the most effective messengers are artists as they bring Truth into the world through the creativity found in their union with God. Like prophets, artists are *inspired people,* and all inspiration is derived from God. For years I was a reluctant messenger in not fully realizing or utilizing the talents that I had been blessed with. However, I now view myself as being one of those artists. I truly believe that the Lord has designated me to be a messenger through my inspirational writing and singing, and I am hoping to spread His messages to as many people as possible.

I did this thing on-line, called *Huggy's Inspirational Corner,* where I would share samples of my writing in messages sent to a number of Christian contacts. Often, I would receive responses back from a person saying that what I had written was exactly what they needed to hear. For example, one woman, who really sounded distraught about a number of things, wrote that she found comfort in many of my writings that made her feel more hopeful and better concerning her situation. So to some, I was like it says in *Proverbs 25:13.* Just as the cold of snow during harvest time, so was I being a faithful messenger to those who sent me, as I refreshed the soul of my masters. I was being sent as a messenger to some people that really needed inspiring and uplifting, as many had asked to be on my mailing list that I didn't know at all. They either had been told about my writing by another or saw samples from some Christian writing groups that I had joined. In any event, I have learned that being a good messenger depends on my faithfulness, and bolstered by God's strength and assistance, I hope to be the best possible.

Mind - Most people tend to view the mind in relation to our thoughts. We have many private conversations with ourselves inside our heads from which we may make up or change our minds about certain things. Then there are instances where some may have two minds about something, like when a person will give you equal reasons for attending or not attending church service. However, in any case, most people see themselves as having minds of their own that no one else has access to, and others interpret our thoughts from what we consciously or unconsciously communicate to them. Through my reading though, I have learned that various religious traditions have offered some interesting perspectives on the nature of our minds, especially in terms of spirituality, that many may have little or no knowledge of. There is a *mystical* tradition, for example, that considers the overcoming of one's ego as being a most worthy spiritual goal, and God certainly wants us to focus our minds on Him over ourselves. Another is according to *Judaism,* which teaches that the mind rules the heart, and people are able to approach their spirituality intellectually through learning and behaving accordingly.

My Bible defines the *mind* as being imagination and thoughts, and the content and quality of one's mind is most important to God in gaining His favor. *Isaiah 26:3* says that God brings peace to those whose minds are steadfast because He trusts you. Then *Luke 10:25-28* tells of the mind as being one of the factors for inheriting eternal life. An expert of the law, wanting to test Jesus, asked what he had to do to inherit eternal life. Jesus responded by asking him what was written in the Law. The expert answered that it was to love the Lord his God with all his heart, soul, strength, and *mind,* while loving his neighbors as himself. Jesus then replied that he had answered correctly and would live if he did all those things. Therefore, one of the things we have to do in inheriting eternal life is to love God and always have Him in our foremost thoughts. *1 Corinthians 1:10* goes on to say that, in the name of Jesus, we should speak the same thing and have no divisions among us, especially in the Church. We should be perfectly united in mind and thought. Also, as spiritual people we can make judgments about all things without being subject to any man's judgment because we have the mind of Jesus *(1 Corinthians 2:15-16)*.

Mission - People often ask me if I am on some kind of mission when they see me walking hurriedly throughout my neighborhood and, at times, even miles away. And they are usually right. I often speed walk for exercise. Then presently without the use of a vehicle, I may rely on public transportation and/or my feet to get me to some important engagements or work. In any event, I consider my life to be one continuous journey that sends me out on different missions daily, with some being more important than others and some requiring me to change directions. My speed walking, for instance, takes on another dimension when I do it at one of the public or charity events I participate in concerning things like education, cancer, multiple sclerosis, diabetes, etc. I, also, find things like my spirituality taking on a much higher level of importance now than in the past, and my writing, singing, and volunteer work are some extensions of that. It is certainly likely that I may find myself out and off on one mission or another on this day, following God's will through my dedication and a giving heart, like Paul wrote. He said that no matter what we are doing, we should work at it with all of our hearts, and as if we are working for the Lord, and not for men *(Colossians 3:23)*. In that respect, I try to take advantage of any opportunities to do something good while working or participating in various activities.

Acts 9 tells the story of Saul's conversion. Saul, later known as Paul, had set out on a mission against Jesus but returned as a very influential Christian missionary. Heading to Damascus, he had threatened slaughter against the disciples of Jesus. However, in the midst of his journey, a light from Heaven suddenly shined around him. He fell to the earth and heard the voice of Jesus questioning why he was persecuting Him. Trembling and astonished, Saul asked Jesus what he wanted of him, and was told to arise and go to the city for instruction. All Saul's men could do was stand there speechless in hearing a voice but seeing no man. And Saul saw no man or anything else. He was blinded for three days. In Damascus, Jesus sent a disciple, named Ananias, to see Saul. Ananias questioned Jesus about all the evil he had done, and about his mission to arrest all that called on the name of the Lord. Jesus told him that Saul was to be the chosen vessel to bear His name before the Gentiles, kings, and children of Israel. So, Ananias placed his hands on Saul, restoring his sight, and then baptized him. After that Saul began preaching for Jesus fearlessly and boldly, in Damascus and Jerusalem, proclaiming that Jesus was truly the Son of God. His mission of opposition had turned to him becoming a spokesman for the Lord, just as our missions may take a different direction when we receive and accept our call from Him. As with Saul, there are special missions for us all.

Models - During our developmental years, and even far beyond, we sometimes learn much through imitation. We look for others that we can take as examples to model ourselves after; people doing things that we'd like to in ways that we can admire and respect. That's the kind of person I have always desired to be.

As everyone, I have committed my share of sins but have conducted myself more in a manner that many, especially my children, would like to emulate. My sons were taught in the ways of faith and I have tried to set the best example as possible in teaching and showing them the right ways of life. They've witnessed some of my mistakes but seen how I am able to push my way beyond them in putting God first, and living a life of hope and love in anything I do. In that light, they've also witnessed many of my successes that stem from me being a man of faith and determination. My promise to them is that I will always try to be a father that they can look up to in any way, and hope that my influence will carry over, as they too become models for their own children and others to follow.

I've tried hard to be an example for my sons and others to follow but realize that in my molding there is still some work left to be done. I view myself as like a model airplane in a box full of unattached pieces, waiting on the Lord to glue each one together each day. My greatest desire is to be able to lead others along the path of faith and enjoy a life of hope, love, and promise. However, there are times that my pieces aren't fitted properly together because of my sins and mistakes. Yet, the Lord never gives up on the project and continues to put me together piece by piece in His image. As according to *Ephesians 6:4,* I want to be a model that will not provoke others to wrath, but will show them that the road to a long and joyful life is through the training and instruction of the Lord. In being a model, I should teach that the Lord should be feared while keeping His decrees and commandments (*Deuteronomy 6:2).* Also, I should talk about them whenever and wherever possible (*Deuteronomy 6:7).* As a model, I can continue to do this for my sons and others in showing them that God should be placed above all else, as we are all incorporated into His plan.

Money - A recent newspaper article told of an old man, his late wife, a sister, and a sister-in-law losing over a million dollars through a phony high-interest investment scheme. They were said to have lived very frugally, meaning as cheaply as possible, and the man that bilked them out of their life savings simply said that they didn't need the money anyway. It was a sad story and even sadder that senior citizens and others are cheated out of billions of dollars each year. They say that if something sounds too good to be true it usually is. However, some people just place a much higher priority on things, like money, in their lives than they should and, without proper research or investigation, may only find themselves vulnerable to being taken advantage of or making decisions that they may later regret. In this case, the people were looking to acquire additional money, through investments, that would probably only be tucked away and not used for any really meaningful purposes, as with most that they already possessed. Maybe it was because of wanting not to grow old and on welfare, as the man claimed, or other reasons, but many people just never see themselves as ever having enough money, the root of all evil. The main thing is that many need to find contentment in realizing that money and other things of the world can never really satisfy us. Of course, we need money for the basic necessities of life, but knowing God brings about the true satisfaction and security in our lives.

No person desires to be poor but being rich, or seeking to be, can be a bad thing too, especially if anything illegal or immoral is involved. *1 Timothy 6:10* warns that money is the root of all evil, and those eager for it will wander away from their faith and may only find themselves in grief. The man with the phony investment scheme will surely have plenty of time to grieve and rethink his priorities after he is sent to prison for his crimes. In *1*

Timothy 6:17, Paul tells Timothy to command those that are rich not to be arrogant or place their hopes in wealth, as it can be very uncertain. All hope should be placed in God, who provides us with everything. We should do good unto each other. However, there are just too many people that will rob, cheat and kill to get what they want, especially when it comes to money. Every person should be generous and willing to share, in being rich through good deeds *(1 Timothy 6:18).* Also, there are people who think that money can buy everything, but it surely can't. In *Acts 8,* it is told how Simon offered Peter money after seeing people receiving the Holy Spirit by some apostles laying hands on them. Simon thought that he could pay to be given that ability. Peter told him that his money would only perish with him by his thinking that he could buy the gift of God with money. He went on to tell Simon that he could have no part or share in the ministry because his heart wasn't right before God, and then that he should seek the Lord's forgiveness through repentance and prayer.

Moodiness - We all have our mood swings because of the ups and downs of life. Certainly there is to be much sadness during our troubled times, and often it is very difficult for us to see any reason or purpose for our suffering during those trials. However, as Christians there should be happiness too in understanding that God will never leave or forsake us, especially during our darkest of days. He will provide the light to deliver us from them. Then there is the matter of dealing with the really moody folks. Their moods seem to change like the weather, and you never know what to expect. They may be friendly towards you on one day and then bite your head off on the next. It could be because certain needs aren't being met in their lives, they don't feel appreciated or loved, didn't sleep enough, missed that morning cup of coffee, or maybe not even realize how moody they can be or for whatever reasons. In any event, they can help to make life much harder than need be, as you may have your own problems and don't need theirs too. We all just have to realize that things are usually never as bad as they may seem. Plus there is a safety net to help protect us whenever we feel troubled or falling out of control - Our Faith.

I am usually in a good mood, but there are times that I may find myself in a bad mood for one reason or another. However, I have never been known for bringing others down with me, consciously or unconsciously. I always have a smile and a nice word for all that I encounter, no matter how things are going on in my life, and my outside appearance seldom reveals that there could be things troubling me on the inside. There were times though that I would keep to myself a little when things weren't going well. But nowadays, rather than going into hiding, I concentrate more on the things that are uplifting for me, like my writing and charity work. Then through my faith, I find much peace and joy in knowing that there is always hope and a chance to turn any situation around for the better. *Romans 5* assures me that in being justified by faith, I can have peace through Jesus and rejoice in hope of the glory of God. My sufferings can also produce perseverance, character, and hope. God poured His heart out to us in Jesus, who died for the ungodly. We are justified by His blood, and saved from the wrath of God through Him and saved through Him. Just reading that back has me in a very good mood on this day.

Morals - *Morals* are defined as being ethical, good, and not transgressing with one's behavior in respect to accepted standards of conduct. They imply that there are good things and bad things, and as humans we judge what is good and bad, then try to do more good than bad. We begin learning to live morally at home, as our parents teach us while we are growing up. However, a big problem concerning morals is that, when man chooses what is right or wrong, there is an independence from God. That being, different individuals, leaders, races, countries, cultures, religions, legal systems, etc. may view things totally different in terms of living morally. For example, in some areas of the world, it is a common and accepted practice for men to have more than one wife at the same time. However, in our country, that is called bigamy, which is considered to be a serious crime. With some men not being strict followers of God, it only stands to reason that some will view certain things as being right that He considers as being sin.

In looking up the word *morals,* my Bible refers me to the word *sins,* where God tells us what is *right* and what is *wrong*. Here, though, I am going to make mention of the moral teachings or practical lessons learned in fables, tales, experiences, etc. For instance, as a child I read *Aesop's Fables,* which have been described as being timeless stories with a moral. Aesop, a Greek storyteller, believed to have lived between 620 and 560 BC, wrote fables that were used to teach truths in a simple, understandable way, with his stories ending giving advice to do a thing or not to do it. Even greater, though, were the parables (stories or fables) that Jesus used for the illustration of moral or religious truths. I know that if I pattern my life around His storytelling and teachings, I will ultimately find happiness and true fulfillment all the days of my life on Earth and then in Heaven. So, I try to take the things that He has taught and apply them to my daily life in living morally right.

Moses - The story of Moses is a great example of how one never knows why, how or when God may call them on for a special assignment. After spending 40 years in Midian tending to his father-in-law's sheep, it is said that he was chosen to lead the people of Israel because of his kindness to animals. There was an incident where he was taking the sheep to a river for water, when one lamb didn't come. Moses went after it and carried it to the water for a drink. That showed that, as God, he cared not just about the flock as a whole, but also about each individual in the group, and also that he could be a worthy shepherd for God's flock. Therefore, God chose him to lead the people out of their Egyptian slavery. He appeared to Moses in a burning bush, and being that Moses is said to have died at the age of 120 years, and before reaching the Promised Land after 40 years of wandering in the desert, he was 80 years old at the time. Also, Moses was very reluctant in the beginning. He was to deliver God's message to the Egyptian Pharaoh (king) but worried that he wouldn't be listened to because of his stuttering speech problem. Then in those days too, messengers delivering bad news were usually executed. Moses asked God to send someone else but was given the strength and skills needed for completing his mission, along with his devout faithfulness playing a very important role.

Moses was born in Egypt and his name at birth was Moshe, meaning *the one who draws out,* and is best known as the Hebrew liberator that received the Ten Commandments, with his story starting in *Exodus* and ending in *Deuteronomy.* At the time of his birth, the Hebrew descendants of Abraham, Isaac and Jacob were slaves to the Egypt's Pharaoh, who had ordered that all newborn Hebrew males were to be killed. Moses' mother hid him in a papyrus basket and placed it in the reeds of the Nile River, only for it to be the Pharaoh's own daughter to find it, and then pity and adopt Moses. He fled as a young man, before God appeared to him many years later in a burning bush. Then, with his brother, Aaron, he was sent back to Egypt to demand the Israelite's release from Egyptian slavery. The story goes on to tell of many miracles and Moses' talks with God. Egypt was hit with plaques (punitive afflictions resulting from sin), the people escaped, and the Egyptian army drowned in the Red Sea, as Moses parted it for their safety. Then over a 40-year period, of being lost in the desert, Moses brought the Ten Commandments on stone tablets to his people and, through him, God made a covenant with the Hebrews, laying out the rites of worship and His laws for communal and personal behavior. Moses is said to have died by God's decree (edict or law) just before they entered what is now known as Palestine and Israel.

Mountains - I have watched this old movie several times called *The Mountain* that came out in 1956. It is about a passenger plane that crashes on top of one of the Swiss Alps. Christopher Teller (played by Robert Wagner) wants to climb the mountain to rob the dead, but has no hopes of getting to the crash site unless he receives the help of his older brother Zachary (played by Spencer Tracy), a highly skilled mountain climber. Zachary wants to just leave the dead in peace but agrees to the climb after Christopher kept hounding him about it. The climb up is a very tough one and I think about how difficult it can be to climb the mountains of our lives. It may take a lot of determination, patience, dedication, faith and some help from others. Then just as in most mountain climbing movies I have seen as this one, it seems to be far easier going down than up. And in life, we can be on top of the mountain one day and find ourselves quickly and unexpectedly at the bottom on the next. Another thing I think about is how disastrous the results can be with things like greed and stubbornness in climbing their mountains badly influencing people. In the movie, on their descent, Christopher, with his stolen treasure, ignores Zachary's warnings and falls to his death while trying to cross an unsafe snow bridge.

In the Bible, mountains are spoken of figuratively, like *Jeremiah 13:16* where they are used in denoting things of a difficult or dangerous nature. There it says that glory must be given to God before He causes darkness and makes one's feet stumble upon the dark mountains. They make look for light but only find themselves in the shadow of death and deep gloom. Then there is perpetuity and stability in *Isaiah 54:10*, where the Lord says that His kindness and covenant of peace will remain, as He grants His mercy, even though the mountains will shake and the hills are removed. Likewise, *Habakkuk 3:6* says that even though the ancient mountains may crumble and the age-old hills collapse, God's ways are everlasting and as of old. Also, in *Matthew 21:21-22*, Jesus speaks of mountains as being obstacles that can be removed through prayer. He says that if you have faith without doubts, just as a fig tree had withered away, one can tell a mountain to throw itself into the sea and it will be done. To receive whatever you ask for in prayer, all you have to do is believe. Finally, the Bible tells of the *Mount of Congregation,* a mythical mountain the Babylonians believed to be the home of the gods that I'd love to climb. According to *Isaiah 14:13* it is in the sides of the north, into Heaven and above the stars of God.

Mourning - I was talking with some old *friends* recently after yet another funeral service that we were attending. Among our discussions was how we used to hang out together and go to many parties back in the day, but now, rather than partying and having fun, we are more likely to see each other during times of mourning. That's just one of the sad things about growing older, though we had some friends that also died when we were much younger. As Christians though, we learn that in mourning there should still be much joy in believing that the deceased has moved on to a better life in Heaven. Death is supposed to be a home going where we are united in the presence of God and Jesus for eternity. However, we will never find out who actually made it to Heaven, unless we make it there ourselves. Therefore, as we mourn the death of others, we should realize how suddenly and unexpectedly we might die too. Funerals should indicate to us just how little time there may be to right ourselves before the Lord. If not, we may find ourselves in mourning forever, as the only other destination of permanence for us to reside is in a placed called Hell.

Mourning doesn't have to be a bad thing, as *Matthew 5:4* says that those that mourn are blessed and shall be comforted. Also, righteousness may result when the Lord is glorified in our mourning. In *Isaiah 61:3,* Isaiah says that he was appointed to provide for those that grieved, in bestowing upon the mourners of Zion crowns of beauty for ashes, the oil of joy for mourning, and garments of praise for despair, so that they might then be called trees of righteousness in the planting of the Lord. That is a reason why preachers often open up the doors to the church at the end of a funeral service, as funerals are more for the living than the dead, especially for one that doesn't know God and needs to place his or her life into the hands of the Lord. We all suffer through the loss of a loved one, but God knows our pain and hears our cries, and it is through Him that we can overcome our deepest sorrows. There may be mourning on any given day followed by many new days of God's life-giving and keeping promises, in understanding that life goes on with God and Jesus being the only constants. And that we have to become right with them before the time comes when others will mourn for us.

Moving - United Van Lines, the nation's largest moving company, has been tracking moves since 1977, and it's latest study of January 2012 is based on more than 146,000 interstate moves the company handled in 48 states and Washington, D.C. in 2011. It revealed that Rhode Island, Connecticut, New Hampshire and Maine were among the Northeastern states that had the highest number of people moving out. Also that Illinois led the nation in outbound moves, at nearly 61 percent. Washington, D.C. continued to be the nation's most popular destination, and people moving had a preference for the western United States as well. There was no mention of Michigan. However, statistics report that my birthplace of Detroit had a peak population of around 2,000,000 people during the days of my youth, when the automobile industry was really booming. Recent data released by the Census Bureau though now reports it as being only 713,777, which has the mayor seeking a recount in believing that the number should be closer to 800,000. Ouch! Whatever the true number, either one is really bad. The fact is though that people do move and for different reasons like economics, crime, health, employment, education, marriage, weather, retirement, religion... Surely a combination of several things has resulted in Detroit's population drop to its lowest level since the 1910 census.

In the Bible, individuals and even whole races of people would move at a time, in search of things like safety, prosperity, or freedom, but some would only endure additional hardships when they moved out on their own instead of taking the journey that God had mapped out before them. In being obedient to God, one's moves may be most blessed and rewarded even greater than ever imagined. He may call for people to leave what has been comfortable for them but with the promise of a much better new life. You just have to be willing to leave the old habits, attitudes, sins, and thoughts behind, and allow Him to lead you in the right direction. Unfortunately, many people, even today, have just moved aimlessly from one place to another without ever finding the one that would be most suitable for them. *Genesis 12:1-9* though tells how the Lord told Abram to leave his country, people, and family to go to a land that would be shown to him. He would be made into a great nation and blessed. His name would be great and he would be a blessing. Then those who blessed Abram would also be blessed, and whoever cursed him would be cursed too. And all the peoples on Earth would be blessed through Him. So Abram, seventy-five years old, left with his wife Sarai, his brother's son Lot, all the possessions they had gathered, and the many souls he had gotten in Haran to move into Canaan in seeking the blessings promised.

Multi-tasking - I am one that often may have to concentrate on doing several things at a time, and doing them all well. As a professional worker, for example, I have always been called on to perform duties beyond the scope of the normal job description for a position because of my intelligence, versatility, dedication and ambition. Then along with my jobs, I am usually involved in different personal, family, religious, charitable and community activities as well. It's difficult for me to have a one-track mind and concentrate on one thing fully, but many do even if they find themselves focusing on the wrong things. And they may often tune others out, desiring not to be interrupted or distracted from what they are doing. That includes the Lord too. However, it's great knowing that Jesus is a multi-tasker that we are never an interruption to. He invites us to come to Him no matter what He is doing, or how many people are seeking His attention at the same time. In faith, I know that while the Lord was attending to me during my stroke, many others were calling on Him at the same time and were being attended to as well. My trust is in Him, and there is no telling where I'd be if He ever viewed me as being an interruption or distraction at any time.

A great example of the Lord's multi-tasking abilities is told in *Luke 8:40-44*. Jesus was among a large group of people that had been waiting for Him. A man named Jairus, the ruler of the synagogue there, fell down at His feet pleading for Jesus to come to his house, where his twelve-year old daughter laid dying. Jesus was set to go on His way, when the crowd almost crushed Him. At that time, a woman, which had been bleeding for twelve years, came up from behind Him and touched the border of His garment. The physicians that had been treating her over the years could never stop the bleeding, but just the touching of Jesus, in faith, instantly healed her. *Matthew 9:18-26* then presents an example as to how Jesus was able to look beyond any distractions or interruptions in doing His work. A ruler had a daughter that had just died, and he wanted Jesus to place His hands on her so that she would live. When He went into the ruler's house, there were flute players and people making a lot of noise. He asked them to leave, and they just laughed at Him when He said that the girl was not dead but sleeping. Jesus touched the girl's hand and she arose. The laughing stopped and news of the healing was spread all over.

Murder - The killing of another that is malicious (hostile, evil, intentional) or while committing a crime is called *murder,* and it is very alarming as to how many stories of totally senseless murders appear on television or in the newspaper. Even more disturbing is how often the victims may be forgotten with the focus being placed more on the perpetrator, and how some convicted murderers may not be punished as they should because of legal maneuvering, technicalities, leniency, or outdated laws. I was reading a story on MurderVictims.com, for example, about a serial killer named Coral Eugene Watts, who confessed to the murders of 13 women in the Houston, Texas area, but some believed that he might have murdered up to 100 women in the late 1970's and early 1980's, with some even in the Detroit, Michigan area and Canada. Watts was finally arrested and in 1982 was sentenced to 60 years in prison. But it was for his pleading guilty only to burglary with intent to commit murder, and not murder itself. Then under an old Texas law, he could have been released from prison in 2006 after serving only 24 of those years; there was the possibility of him earning 36 years of *good time credits* (extra time allotted by the prison system for time served). An accumulated total of the 60 years would have meant mandatory parole. Imagine that! A man, that may have murdered as many as 100 women, could have been released back into society to possibly only murder again. However, he never made it out of prison and died of prostate cancer on September 21, 2007. So, maybe a higher authority finally judged and sentenced him.

Genesis 9:5-6 says that God demands from each man an accounting for the life of his fellow man. If one sheds the blood of another, then his own blood should be shed too, as God has made man in the image of Himself. Then not murdering another is listed as being one of God's Ten Commandments (*Exodus 20:13*). *Numbers 35:16-24* goes on to say that killing with malice or hostility is strictly forbidden. Things like striking another with iron, stone or wooden objects is considered to be murder, if the person struck dies. The avenger of blood then has the right to put the murderer to death. However, accidental killings were to be judged by a congregation, since there was no intention to harm and the person wasn't an enemy. *Verse 30* of *Numbers 35* then says that a murderer is to be put to death on the testimony of witnesses, and not on the testimony of just one. However, I am sure that mistakes were made back then just as they were later. Real murderers have been set free or treated leniently, while unfortunately there have been cases over the years where a person accused as being a murderer has been put to death, but later found out to have been innocent of any crime. In *Matthew 19:16-18,* Jesus talks to a man who had asked Him what good had to be done for eternal life. Among other things, Jesus told him that he couldn't be guilty of things like adultery, stealing, giving false testimony, or *murder.* It's sad but true that there will always be killing, but while people may die for things like fighting for their countries or for some unfortunate and unintentional type of accident or circumstance, the intentional killing of another will always be viewed as murder in the eyes of God and man, punishable by a sentencing up to death.

Nature - I am a nature lover and enjoy doing some exercise walking at a few Detroit area parks. My favorite is Belle Isle, the 982-acre island park in the Detroit River between the United States mainland and Canada. The park is surrounded by water and is a habitat for many ducks, birds and small animals. I started walking out there during the summer months in the mid 1990's. However, in 2000, I decided to make it a year-round thing, and can remember one winter walk especially well. It was a very cold day and I was admiring the icy waters and the many ducks sitting by the river. Then suddenly a strange feeling came over me. I sensed my being watched by someone or something. So, I proceeded with caution not knowing what to expect around a short curve, especially since I had heard about some wild dogs running around loose on the island. But much to my surprise, I saw the eyes of well over a hundred deer all focused on me. At first startled, I stopped to take a long look back at them. In my many days of walking there during the warmer months, I had never seen them before (the island was home to a large herd of European *fallow deer* for more than 50 years, and the last 300 were captured and relocated in 2004). It got me to thinking about how even through nature God shows signs of His glory and presence. As I walk and observe the beauty of His creation on full display, I know that through my many walks of life, just as those deer, His eyes are always focused heavily back on me. And I praise God for all the beauty that I see around me, in and out of nature, which keeps me tuned in to His presence.

In *Genesis 9*, it tells about God's covenant (agreement) to man after the rains flooding the world had subsided. He promised Noah that never again would the waters of a flood cut off all life or destroy the Earth. Every living creature for generations to come would be safe from suffering that destruction, and God's promise would be revealed through nature, with a rainbow set in the clouds to be His sign. Whenever He placed clouds over the land and a rainbow appeared in them, it would be in remembrance of the everlasting covenant established between Himself and all life on Earth. *Psalm 19:1* then says that the heavens declare God's glory, while the skies reveal the works of His hands. Therefore, when it rains, we should look up for a rainbow and respond to His glory in seeing the promise of the love and concern He has for all of us and the world He created. Personally, I just see so much beauty in nature, and *Isaiah 35:1* tells of the joyful flourishing of the Lord's Kingdom, as the wilderness and solitary places shall be glad with the deserts rejoicing and blossoming as roses. Then Solomon in his entire splendor was never dressed as beautiful as the lilies of the field that grow *(Matthew 6:28-30)* in terms of being clothed in faith and being able to live a worry-free life. Also, there is a lesson to be learned as God's glory is magnified by His works and His love of man. He cares for us, and while we were made to be a little lower than the angels, He has entrusted us to have dominion over all that He has created, including every living thing throughout nature in the fields, air and seas *(Psalm 8)*.

Nazareth - I learned many years ago that it was believed that Jesus Christ was born in Nazareth, the home of Joseph and Mary, His chosen parents by God. However, I never gave much thought to where that actually was or even if the town had ever appeared on any modern day maps. I have a dictionary that places Nazareth as being a town in Palestine and where Jesus grew to maturity. Then my research indicates that Nazareth is the largest city in the North District of Israel and is known as the *Arab Capital,* with the population made up predominantly of Arab citizens of Israel, of which the majority is Muslim.

My Bible says that Nazareth was a town on an elevation in *Galilee,* north of the plain of *Esdraelon,* about twenty miles southwest of *Capernaum,* and I have never heard of any of those places. *Matthew 2:1* then says that Jesus was born in Bethlehem (a town in Judah and one of the oldest in Palestine located five miles south of Jerusalem) and *verse 2:23* further states that Jesus came and dwelt in the city of Nazareth so that what had been spoken by the prophets would be fulfilled and He would be called a *Nazarene.* However, while some may question His birthplace, it is more important for me in knowing that He did live, gave up His life for us, and continues to live for all that trust and believe in the Lord.

Noah - When I decided to take on the task of totally stripping and remodeling the kitchen in my first house, without any carpentry, electrical or plumbing experience, some thought that I had completely lost my mind and would never complete the project. So, I can imagine what Noah went through as he began building this large vessel on dry land far from the sea. However, we were both on a mission and were successful because we followed our instructions properly. I relied on do-it-yourself manuals and written instructions that came with some of the materials purchased for my project, while Noah received detailed instructions from God on how to build a seaworthy ark. The thing though is that Noah had a lot more time to complete the things God instructed him to do here on Earth, as He lived for nine hundred and fifty years, which included living three hundred and fifty years after the Genesis flood. Therefore, he had plenty of time to start and complete his later projects, while mine is much more limited. It is most important that I make the best use of every day possible, if I am to complete all that I hope to accomplish over the remaining days of my life and what God commands me to do, even if some may not understand my motives or see the importance of me doing certain things.

God, seeing the wickedness of man and grieved by His creation, decided to resolve the issue by sending a great flood to cleanse the Earth of all it's impurity, and *Genesis 6-9* tells the story about God's commanding of Noah to save himself, his family, and the world's animals from the worldwide deluge that would be forthcoming. Noah had found favor in the eyes of God and, because of his righteousness, God desired for him to continue living, while also having His creation of mankind preserved through Noah's family. Noah was given detailed instructions from God for an ark, and he embarked on the building of it, as many people probably just walked by and shook their heads, wondering why any sane man would be building a ship in the middle of nowhere on dry land. After it's completion and with Noah, his family, plus two's and seven's of every living thing, male and female, on Earth safely on board, God sent the flood that covered the mountains and destroyed all remaining life. After forty days and forty nights, the waters receded and dry land appeared, as all onboard the arc would leave to repopulate the Earth. God then placed a symbolic rainbow in the sky and made a covenant with Noah and all living things, by which He vowed to never again send a flood to destroy the Earth.

Obedience - *Obedience* is the act of carrying out demands and differs from *compliance,* which is behavior influenced by peers, and *conformity,* which is behavior meant to duplicate that of the majority. Obedience can also be a good or bad thing. For example, it is a sin if a person willingly kills another innocent person on the orders of another, then it is a virtue if a person willingly kills an enemy, who would have ended a lot of innocent lives, on the orders of another. However, obedience is much more simple with God. We just have to do as we are told, and, being that He will never instruct us to do or consider doing anything wrong, we never have to worry about whether our obedience will be sinful or virtuous. Jesus wants us to believe in Him and be like Him and, when we are being obedient to God, we are doing just that. To know and love Jesus, along with having a personal and intimate relationship with Him, we must be most attentive to God's laws. We must believe, trust and have faith in Him with all of our hearts, and through obedience will be able to receive the fullest of God's favor each and every day of our lives.

The Law of God requires obedience, according to the Bible. *Deuteronomy 27:10* tells us that we should obey the voice of God, while doing His commandments and statutes. Plus in being obedient, we must give Him our full and undivided attention. In serving two masters, as says *Matthew 6:24,* one will either hate one and love the other or hold on to one and despise the other, and we cannot serve both God and mammon (wealth). Then obedience is actuated by love. With *John 14:15,23,* Jesus tells us that in loving Him we should obey what He commands, and that if anyone loves Him they will obey His teachings. In that we are to be loved by God and, along with Jesus, will make our home with Him. It is further told it is for the love of God that we keep His commandments, and they are not grievous in any way (*1 John 5:3*). Finally, Jesus told of His obedience to God, His Father, when He says in *John 8:29* that the Father that sent Him was with Him and had not left Him alone, for He always did what pleased His Father. Jesus, being found in the appearance of a man, humbled Himself and became obedient to death, even death on a cross (*Philippians 2:8*).

Objectivity - The term *objectivity* implies that there is a state or quality of being objective in a person's thinking, and it generally relates to the interaction between a perceiving person and a perceived or unperceived object. The object presumably exists regardless of the person's perception of it, meaning that the object is there whether the person perceives it or not. Therefore, objectivity is typically associated with things like reality, truth and reliability. I may not perceive God being in my presence at a given time, for example, but I still know that He is there. Then I am using objective judgment or belief in that I believe there to be objectively strong supporting evidence that God exists and that it should be easy for others to share that belief. However, there is something called objective reality, as people may perceive things differently, like two people being together outside with one saying that it's cold and the other saying that it's not. In a religious context, there are believers and non-believers, even though the same people may have been given the same supporting evidence that there is a God.

The first words of the Bible start out "In the beginning God", indicating the fact that God exists, with the Bible being the written record of the revelation of God. That revelation is needed, as man cannot, even in searching, know God as He has revealed Himself. Then by no means does the Bible ever reach the conception of God in any way. It is in objectivity that the reality and truths of God become factual. I know that God surely exists and is the source of the world and all other things that followed, with the Bible presenting much to verify His existence and describing His many attributes and perfections. I have an old aunt, living in Florida, that I have never seen. Some could question her existence, when an objective thinker wouldn't, and I have spoken with her on the telephone and heard others speak of her. Likewise, I have read and learned much about God, heard many speak of Him, and have myself felt and seen His presence. Without question, I know that God is the Creator and that there is only one. He is infinite, eternal, omnipotent, all-knowing, omnipresent, wise, morally perfect, holy, merciful, just, faithful, loving, and so many other things.

Observance - The act or instance of following, obeying, or conforming to something is called *observance.* Another definition is the keeping or celebration by appropriate procedure, ceremonies, etc., like the observance of the Sabbath. As a Christian, I should be living a life in observance of Jesus Christ and of God's Law as instructed by the Bible. That may include the observance of religious rituals and holidays, but the observance of God and Jesus themselves are the most important aspect of one's faith. I've read that Jesus often criticized the Pharisees' traditions and rituals because they only burdened man and offered nothing for the promotion of a fellowship with God. True faith in God comes from fellowship and having contact with Him.

As *Proverbs 23:26,* we should give our hearts to the Lord and let our eyes observe His ways. Also, after the Resurrection, according to *Matthew 28:16-20,* the eleven disciples went to

Galilee and the mountain where Jesus had instructed them to go. Upon seeing Him, some worshiped, while some doubted. Jesus then told them that He had been given all authority in Heaven and Earth, and that the disciples were to go and make disciples of all nations. They would baptize people in the name of the Father, Son, and Holy Ghost, while teaching them to observe (obey) all that Jesus had commanded them. Jesus would also be with them always, even unto the end of the world. Therefore, we should be living every day of our lives in observance of whatever the Lord instructs us to do.

Obsession - An *obsession* is when a person allows a thought or action rule their thoughts and actions, and they may have little interest in anything else while focusing on one thing. It is also described as being a compulsive, often unreasonable idea or emotion, even evil, preoccupation with a fixed idea or an unwanted feeling or emotion often accompanied by anxiety. It is certainly true that there are a number of things people may become obsessed with - money, power, sex, food, stalking, cleanliness, health, perfectionism... However, I see God as being one exception to the rule. He desires for us to have a one-track mind concerning Him. So while I may find myself fighting other obsessions, it will be truly great if the only obsession I ever experience is in respect to my faith and the love of God and His Son, Jesus.

While the term *obsession* is not used in the Bible, a description of it may be read in *Mark 7:20-23,* which tells of there being weaknesses of the flesh that can be become obsessions. It says that what comes out of a person is what defiles (makes unclean) him. From within, out of the hearts of men, come things like evil thoughts, adulteries, fornications, murders, thefts, covetousness, wickedness, deceit, lasciviousness, evil eyes, blasphemy, pride, and foolishness. All are evil that come from within and defile the man, and may certainly become obsessive ways of behavior. *Romans 8:1-39* tells us that there is no condemnation for those who are obsessed in Christ Jesus. God sent Jesus so that we could live lives in the Spirit, as He condemned sin in the flesh. We are to walk according to the Spirit and not the flesh. Those living according to the flesh set their minds on the things of the flesh, while those living according to the Spirit set their minds on the things of the Spirit.

Obstruction - The path of one's faith and life will never be a journey without at least some kind of *obstruction,* which is something that obstructs, blocks, interferes, delays, prevents or just makes it very difficult to do something. Just being human, in itself, presents an obstruction as none are perfect and all are subject to sin. We always have to beware of people, desires, circumstances, and other things that may begin to lead us down paths that we may have been trying really hard to steer away from. However, if one calls on God, they may be able to avoid *many* of their obstacles and be led in the right direction. I won't say *all* because that would be too easy. God will test us to see if we are strong enough in faith to be able to work our own way through a few obstructions, and then learning from our experiences as we move forward in life, with our faith, trust, love and knowledge continually increasing in regards to Him. We also have to understand that it's easy to tell others what we are going to do, but only God knows if we will or not.

Whenever one may be trying to move ahead or accomplish some things, a few obstacles can surely be expected. However, the words of *James 4:10-17* are good for one's motivation. It says that a person must humble himself or herself before God and He will lift them up. Then we should not slander another in speech or judge them because there is only one Lawgiver and Judge - God. There certainly have been many that have failed to move ahead or have found obstacles placed before them through the non-supportive words of others and wrongful judgments. Then expressing one's ambitions too loudly may not be a good thing, as some may become jealous and God angered. *James* says that we can't express to others what we are going to do today or tomorrow because we never know what will happen. What needs to be said is that we will live and do this or that according to God's will. We should be more concerned about doing good and allow God to handle the obstructions, for not doing the good that we know we should is a real sin.

Opportunity - Life can be so unpredictable with our days being numbered both few and many. We are born with no idea of how long our journey on Earth will be. That's in the hands of God. So we should live our lives with a sense of urgency and making the most out of each and every day. Far too many people waste far too many days, even when the opportunity to move forward on some really great things is staring them right in the face. *Opportunity* is defined in one way as being a situation or condition that is favorable for the attainment of a goal, and there are doors and windows of opportunity that can be large and small. Therefore, it is very important to grab hold and take advantage of any good opportunity before they close, especially when being God-given. I certainly regret not always doing so.

The Bible tells of there being open doors of opportunity through the Lord. Jesus, for example, commanded John to write to the church of Philadelphia (a city of Lydia in Asia Minor). He was to tell them that their works were known by the Lord, and that an open door had been set before them that no man could shut, and in having little strength they had kept His word and not denied His name (*Revelation 3:8*). Then in *Luke 11:10,* after teaching some people to pray in a certain place, Jesus tells them that every one who asks receives, he that seeks finds, and a door will be open to him that knocks. That means that God's doors of opportunity are universal, and it is expected that they won't be neglected. *James 4:17,* for example, says that a person knowing good but passing up opportunities to do good is committing sin.

Optimism - Even when times get really tough, I try hard to live with a spirit of optimism, in finding it a good to just grin and bear it at times. And to pray on it. As have many, I learned the hard way that things can get the better of you mentally, physically, and even spiritually if you let them. However, *optimism* is a disposition or tendency to look on the more favorable side of events or conditions and to expect the most favorable outcome, which can certainly contribute to longer and happier lives. Staying positive helps improve a person's stress management, productivity, and their overall health. We all face hardships but they never have to lead to things like ulcers, strokes, heart attacks, depression, suicide, divorce, crime, sin, etc., especially if we place our problems in the Lord's hands. There is always the hope for positive outcomes if we believe and trust in Him. We should always look to see the brighter side of things, with a smile and positive thoughts, as our faith holds the promise that tomorrow can be much better than today.

Some may find it difficult in continuing to trust God when things get really bad, especially when loved ones are lost or possessions that have been worked so hard for to attain. However, God never promised that any lives would be free from adversity. We must maintain our persistence and optimism as He promises to be faithful if we maintain our trust in Him. Just think about Job. He lost everything and found himself faced with much hardship, illness and suffering. Yet there was a happy ending to his story because of his continued faith and devotion to God. *Job 42:7-17* tells how the Lord was displeased with Job's friends, Eliphaz and Temanite, as they had not spoken what was right as Job had. They were commanded to offer up a burnt offering and have Job pray for them, which was done. The Lord accepted Job and gave him twice as much as he had before. His life was blessed more in the end than the beginning, with much wealth and also seven sons and three daughters. He lived to be a hundred and forty years old over four generations, when it appeared that he was only headed for death years before. Reading *Job* surely enhances my optimism.

Ownership - We hold ownership over absolutely nothing in life. Everything belongs to God and He is most concerned about what we do with what He gives us. He cares nothing about how much wealth a person has garnered, for example, but what they do with it. A person's heart, and what the money represents, is what He desires. I read where Billy Graham (born William Franklin Graham Jr. on November 7, 1918), the American *evangelical Christian evangelist,* says that God has given us all two hands with one for receiving and the other for giving. We are to be *channels* made for sharing, and it is a divine duty and privilege. In failing to fulfill that obligation, the meaning of Christianity is surely missed. God wants us to appropriately manage what He places in our trust but having no ownership. In giving Him our hearts, He will provide us with all that we need. Greed, selfishness, and the hoarding of possessions or other things will only lead to disappointment as God is only pushed away. We have to always acknowledge that our jobs, money, homes, families, health, etc, along with everything that sustains life, are all gifts from the hands of God.

Jesus taught that we should give our hearts to whatever we treasure the most. However, that leaves our hearts in danger as any treasure may be lost or destroyed. Plus the Lord gives and takes away. In *Matthew 6:21,* Jesus says that our hearts will be wherever our treasure is. We should never store up treasures for ourselves on Earth, where moth and rust can consume, and where thieves can steal *(Matthew 6:19)*. Our treasures should be placed on Heaven where those kinds of things can't happen *(Matthew 6:20)*. Then we should never be possessive as the ownership of any treasure is God's. King David prayed for the gifts that God's people gave to build their temple. However, he understood that the gifts were from the Lord and not the people themselves. He questioned in *1 Chronicles 29:14* as to how the people and him, being who he was, were able to give as generously as they had. His answer was that everything came from the Lord and they had given only what had come from the hands of the Lord. Therefore the people really had no ownership over the gifts that they had given. It was from their hearts with the gifts being provided to each by the Lord.

Pain - Anyone that has ever had the gout knows pain. A big toe or both may swell up making it impossible to wear shoes. There is constant throbbing, and just the slightest breeze hitting a toe will greatly intensify the pain. Then when having it in the knees, the swelling and stiffness makes it near impossible to walk, along with a feeling that someone is warming up your knees with a blowtorch. I can remember having it in my knees when some visitors came to our home. I was sitting in a chair with my legs stretched out and my feet resting across a stool. Hearing about my situation, this mother told her young daughter to steer clear from me. However, that bad little girl with the angelic face just walked right over and whacked me across my knees. Talk about pain! Everyone in the house heard my pain and maybe even a few close neighbors. Yet, I have learned that no pain is as bad as the spiritual pain that results from making unwise choices or unfortunate circumstances beyond one's control, and for which there is no medicine for any relief as there is for gout. Only God can provide the comfort and care needed for that. As we all *will* suffer some kind of pain and trouble, His presence and power *will* always prevail if we turn to Him.

Psalm 38 tells of David experiencing much pain mentally, physically and relationally because of his sins. He had made many unwise choices and faced some things beyond his control that just made life miserable for him. He was suffering great spiritual pain and sought relief. David says that his guilt was overwhelming him and becoming a burden too heavy to bear. He was tired and wounded, with his body sore, injured, diseased and without energy. Then his lovers and friends were avoiding him, while his neighbors distanced themselves far off. Enemies, who had sought his life, were setting traps, and others wanting him hurt were speaking mischievous things and out to deceive him. He described himself as being a deaf man that wasn't hearing and a dumb man that wasn't speaking. Finally, with his back to the wall, he called on God for having his life turned around. David confessed his sins to God and pleaded for His forgiveness. He told God how sorry he was and how he wanted to stop his fall and be delivered from his pain. His enemies were lively and strong, and the number of those that wrongfully hated him was multiplying. God was his only way out and he hoped that God would listen. So he asked that God would not forsake him, be far from him, or take much time in helping him.

Parents - It disturbs me greatly whenever I hear about or see a child disrespecting their parent(s). Then even more so when there are news reports about *patricide,* which is the killing of one's father, and *matricide,* which is the killing of one's mother. It's just very evident that something has gone terribly wrong in the raising of some children. Parents are responsible for the proper nurturing and raising of their children, and that requires years of education, direction and character building. Plus there must be an understanding that a child picks up the behaviors of their parents at a very early age, whether they are good or bad. If parents respect their children through their actions, there is a much greater likelihood that their children, as they grow older, will respect them. Then it's usually even better, if there is the inclusion of some *compaternity,* meaning that there is a spiritual relationship between the parents and their children. The end result of successful parenting is that children will have picked up some good traits and behaviors from their parents that will live on through them, and then even be passed on to their children when they become parents, along with there being more relationships of love and respect between parent and child.

According to *Deuteronomy 6:5-7,* parents should love God with all their hearts, souls and strengths, with that love being taught to their children, as they talk wherever they may be. *1 Timothy 8:4* says that fathers must manage their own families well and see that their children obey them with the proper respect, while *Ephesians 6:4* instructs fathers not to provoke their children to wrath, but to bring them up in the training and instruction of the Lord. Among other things, mothers are expected to be virtuous, as detailed in *Proverbs 31:10-31,* with *verse 28* saying that her children and husband should arise, calling her blessed, while her husband blesses her too. Then *Ephesians 6:1-2* says that children should obey their parents in the Lord because it is right, and to honor their mother and father to receive the promise that things will go well with them in living long lives. The Bible says much more about the duties of being parents and children, and then how bad children may be the products of bad parents. For example, *1Kings 22:51-53* tells of Ahaziah, the son of Ahad, who became king of Israel and reigned for only two years. It says that he did evil in the eyes of the Lord because he walked in the ways of his father and mother, along with in the ways of Jeroboam, son of Nebat, who had caused Israel to sin. He also served and worshipped Baal, in provoking the Lord to anger, just as his father had done. So, it's easy to see that Ahaziah was driven and influenced poorly by his parents and others, just as some children are today.

Passion - *Passion* means having a powerful emotion, strong interest, or boundless enthusiasm in something. Love and joy are passions, for example, but unfortunately hatred and anger are too. However, I will only speak on the word in the positive respect as it pertains to spiritual passion, because it is most important that we are truly passionate about our relationships with God and Jesus. I read a question asking people if they were as passionate now as they were when they first began serving the Lord. That is certainly a very good question because some people may not realize that their spiritual passion has waned in any way. They may be more productive in serving the Lord than before but may not be further cultivating their relationship with Him as they once did. As Christians, we should place the Lord first and then allow our service to follow naturally, as our passions for knowing Him, being with Him, and worshipping Him should now be greater than they were in the beginning.

In *Revelation 2:1-5,* Jesus voices His displeasure with the church of Ephesus, saying that the people should repent and return to doing what they did at first. He recognized their deeds, hard work and patience, while not tolerating evil and testing those that claimed to be apostles that were not, finding them to be liars. Also, that they had persevered and endured hardships in His name without becoming weary. However, He was troubled in seeing that their passion had diminished, as they were forsaking their first love - the Lord. Jesus wanted them to see how far they had fallen from where they once were, just as many of us today should. We may find ourselves serving Him out of duty or habit, and failing to increase our knowledge or build on our relationship as we once did. Jesus warned that they would have to repent, or He would come to them and quickly remove them from being one of the seven churches of God. We too should repent whenever we find ourselves doing the Lord's work more routinely than passionately.

Patience - When times are tough, it's difficult to be patient. We want instant solutions and results for turning our situations back around from bad to good. However, there are usually no quick fixes, especially if we are calling on God for our remedies. Obeying and trusting Him often requires a period of patience. Therefore, we must be willing to trust His timing and answers in obeying Him and waiting on Him, no matter how long the wait. It's useless to be in a hurry, because God isn't. From experience, I have learned to trust God with all my heart and not my understanding. While I may never understand any of my sufferings, I know in my heart that He will eventually make things right, but in His time, and especially if I am patiently obedient. I have endured much over the past few years and have been most patient in my wait for things to turn around for the better. My courage and strength are in God, along with all my confidence and hope, because of His being faithful to me so many times before in keeping His promises.

Patience is commended in the Bible as *Ecclesiastes 7:8,9* states that the end of something is better than it's beginning and that patience is better than pride. Also, it is best not to be quickly angered in spirit, as anger resides in the laps of the foolish. Then we should exercise patience in our relations to God. *Psalm 37:7* instructs us to rest and be patient in the Lord, never fretting when men succeed in their ways, displaying their wickedness. Patience is a great incentive because the sufferings of the present aren't worth comparing to the glory that will be revealed in us *(Romans 8:18)*. We should be running a Christian race as *Hebrews 12:1* tells us to lay aside everything that hinders and any sins that may easily beset us, then patiently run the race that has been marked before us. In running our race, we may fix our eyes on Jesus as our Divine example. He is the author, finisher and perfecter of our faith, having endured the cross for the joy set before Him, despising the shame, and now sitting at the right hand of the throne of God *(Hebrews 12:2)*.

Peace - We all experience times where we just desire to enjoy a little peace and relieve our minds of all our troubles, problems and worries, especially concerning our work, personal and religious lives. Things can surely take their toll on us and we may find ourselves in desperate need of engaging in activities that will provide the freedom for us to distance ourselves from our thoughts, worries, stress, problems and fears. For me it could be things like going out walking, doing some writing, listening to music or watching a good movie, absorbing myself in meditation and prayer, engaging in conversation with some old friends, or taking a short trip. I also find myself having to distance myself from the negative people and their negative conversations, along with limiting the exposure I have to the bad news on television or in the newspaper. Then it is important too for me not to take things, as personally as I am prone to do, in acknowledging that some things can't be changed and that it's best to concentrate on the present and future, while forgetting the past. In being able to recapture or maintain my inner peace, I am able to display an outer peace for others to see and experience, and it often affects them in positive ways.

The Bible says that we should always try to maintain peaceful relations with others. We should depart from evil and do good, while seeking peace and pursuing it *(Psalm 34:14)*. We should also see how good and pleasant it is when brothers live together in unity *(Psalm 133:1)*, and live at peace with all men if it is possible, as far as it depends on you *(Romans 12:18)*. Then there is the peace imparted by Jesus that we can turn to in any circumstances. *John 14:27* tells of the *believers peace,* where Jesus says that He left His peace and has given it to us. He says that He doesn't give as man gives. We can enjoy peace in not letting our hearts be troubled or afraid of anything. It's the peace of God, which transcends all understanding, that will guard our hearts and minds through Jesus *(Philippians 4:7)*. *Romans 5:1-5* goes on to say that we should have peace and joy no matter what the world places before us. In being justified through our faith, we have peace with God through Jesus. We may rejoice in the hope of the glory of God, as well as in our sufferings because it produces patience, experience and hope. And there should be much peace in knowing that hope won't shame us. God has poured out His heart to us through the Holy Spirit, which is given unto us.

Pity - *Pity* is the sympathetic or kindly sorrow evoked by the suffering, distress, or misfortune of another, that often results in one giving relief or aid to another, or showing mercy. It is certainly a good thing to give a person one's heart or a helping hand when they are in need, and at times it may only take something simple, like a warm smile or an engaging conversation, to uplift the person you are showing pity for. However, it's self-pity that can be one's worst enemy if a person yields to it. We all may experience some troubled times where we need a shoulder to lean on rather than always having ours leaned on, but may only find ourselves alone and seeking shelter during some of our worst storms. That can leave some feeling deserted and having no idea of where to turn. It can also lead to things like stress and worry, disassociation from others, health issues, suicide, crime, or making unwise decisions that will only compound matters. The thing is to realize that you only have to be alone if it is of your own choosing, for with God you never have to be. Just call on Him. You'll find that wherever pity dwells, His peace is always there for your asking.

The Bible defines *pity* as being compassion or sympathy. In accordance to that, *Proverbs 19:17* instructs us to be kind to the poor. That is lending to the Lord, and in doing so we are rewarded for what we have given. Also, in the Bible are examples of how we may anger the Lord and be denied His pity. In *Isaiah 63:9,* Isaiah prophesized how Jesus would become the Savior of God's people and bestow His pity over them. It says that in all their afflictions, the Lord was afflicted too, and the angel of His presence would save them. Through His love and mercy, the people would be redeemed, lifted up and carried all the days of old. However, *Isaiah 63:10* tells how the Lord's pity would be denied because of their rebellion. They would grieve the Holy Spirit, so that the Lord would turn and become their enemy, fighting against them. So, we have to be obedient to the Lord in being worthy of His pity. Jeremiah also prophesized how the people of Israel would be denied the compassion and sympathy of the Lord. They were to become evil people, refusing to listen to God, and walking in the stubbornness of their hearts and after other gods, serving them and worshipping them *(Jeremiah 13:10)*. For their actions, the Lord would view them as being like a worthless belt.

Plan - Living a fulfilled life takes proper planning. One can't run off and go wherever there want or do whatever they want without first doing some serious thinking about it. If not, things may not turn out so well. We all have ambitions when growing up and throughout our lives. We want to be doctors, lawyers, construction workers, educators, athletes, entertainers, parents, missionaries, pastors… However, just desiring something won't alone make it so, as a person may have the ambition but not the gift or talent. We have to think more in terms of what God has chosen for our lives, as He gifts us with our special talents, insights, wisdoms, and passions, in creating us to accomplish what He desires us to in His world. He has a plan for all of us, and we have to find out where exactly it is that He wants to lead us, along with His special purpose for us. That can be done through prayer, study, consulting with people we know well and trust, and understanding what it is that drives us most. Then no matter what direction we are lead in, it is important to continue following God's call. In planning our lives according to His plans, they can surely be more meaningful and successful.

Deuteronomy 17:14-20 detailed the proper planning for Israel's choosing of a king, according to God's standards. When entering a land given by the Lord our God, having taken possession of it and settling in it, the king appointed was to be one of the Lord's choosing. He was to be one of their brothers, not a stranger without ties to Israel. He was not to acquire a great number of horses for himself or make his people return to Egypt to gather more of them, as the Lord had instructed them to never return that way again. The king also was not to have many wives to lead his heart astray or accumulate large amounts of silver and gold. Then when the king took the throne of his kingdom, he was to write himself a copy of the law in a book taken from that of the Levite priests. The book was to be with him and read all the days of his life, so that he could learn to fear the Lord, to follow carefully all the words of the law and it's decrees. In that way, he would not consider himself ever as being better than his brothers and turning away from the commandment to the right or to the left. As a result, his days in the kingdom, along with his children, would be prolonged in Israel. Sounded like a great plan. However, we know that some kings in the Bible, like David, turned from the Lord and pretty much did things their own way, making their own laws.

Pleasure - Everyone looks to enjoy some kind of pleasure as escapes and diversions from their everyday lives. However, most are just temporary and will only lead to disappointment if pleasure becomes a false god for them. I certainly did a few things in the past, good and bad, to help keep my mind off of a few things. One was to get in my car and drive out of town somewhere. It was really relaxing and fun being on the road visiting people and seeing different places. But then I would often dread the drive home, knowing that the problems I had left behind would be there waiting for me, and maybe even bigger. So while my travels could bring about a little happiness, it was never very lasting. Nowadays though I have stopped the running. I still may desire to go on a short trip or an extended vacation but am able to enjoy it for the right reasons. I am allowing God to fill the voids in my life and find my ultimate pleasure in Him. In concentrating on things like my volunteer work helping people, continuing my writing, singing and church fellowships, reading and studying my Bible more, and enjoying a few other more pleasurable and meaningful pursuits than before, I find myself resurrected in spirit and don't let things bother me as much as in the past. My life has more meaning than ever and I don't worry about being enticed by any of the bad things that only doom and disappoint in seeking pleasure.

The Bible doesn't forbid pleasure, as there is surely much to be found in the joy of the Lord. It's the love of pleasure that is looked down upon. According to *Proverbs 21:17,* the lover of pleasure will be a poor man, while one that loves wine and oil will never be rich. Then *Ecclesiastes 2* tells how meaningless worldly pleasures can be. The Preacher, the son of David, king of Jerusalem, said in his heart that he would test with pleasure to see what was good. He found that pleasure was just vanity and laughter was mad, with mirth (merriment, hilarity, glee) being questionable. With his mind still guiding him with wisdom, he tried cheering himself with wine and embracing folly (stupidity, thoughtless action, silliness). Then he made great works in building houses, planting vineyards. He also made gardens and orchards (parks), planting trees of all kinds of fruit in them. Reservoirs were made to water the groves of flourishing trees. He bought servants and maids, and had servants born in his house; also possessed more cattle and flocks than anyone in Jerusalem before him. Much silver and gold was acquired by him, and there were men and women singers, musical instruments and many other delights of men for entertainment. He saw himself as being greater than any man ever before him in Jerusalem. Nothing was denied that his eyes desired and he refused his heart no pleasure; for his heart rejoiced in all his labor. Yet, when looking back on all his hands had done, and what he had toiled to achieve, he saw it as being vanity (empty pride). Everything was meaningless, like chasing after the wind, with there being no profit under the sun.

Plentiful - *Plentiful* is being more than enough without being excessive, with synonyms of the word being *abundant, ample, aplenty, bounteous, bountiful, comfortable, generous, extra, surplus, overflowing, rich, adequate, enough, sufficient, wealthy, fruitful, fertile, blessed,* and etc., and all being words that could help describe God's Earth in it's creation. He created a perfect and plentiful world that would be able to sustain itself and all the life on it indefinitely into the future. However, many are now using words like *destruction, depletion, misuse, wasteful, pollution, extinction, global warming, strife, poverty, scarcity, barren, fruitless, needy,* and etc. We surely need to change our direction and priorities as scientists warn that the Earth of the future may not be plentiful enough to sufficiently sustain itself or it's ever-growing population of people.

Genesis tells of God's creation of heaven and earth, and it was to be plentiful with light, water, air, fish, fowl, beasts, cattle, man, food…and it was all very good. Things have surely changed since. The human race in passing from its early state of innocence to a state of sin has caused much damage and alteration to the world and themselves. However, the Bible defines *plentiful* as being enough or sufficient and God will make sure that His children are provided for, as He has the ultimate power of restoration. *Joel 2* presents a great example of that. During a time of peace and prosperity, Joel warned the people of Judah to stop ignoring God. The prophet then described a ravaging plague of locusts and the damage they could cause to remind the people how easy everything enjoyed in life could suddenly disappear. But in returning to the Lord our God, that eaten by the locusts over the years would be restored, with there being plenty of food to eat for their satisfaction, and the people never being ashamed *(Joel 2:25,26).*

Potential - During my second year of college, I ran into my high school track coach on the streets of downtown Detroit. He was quite surprised to see me as he thought that I had gone away to school. Said that he had been asking around but had heard nothing about me running anywhere. When I told him that I was at a city college, and one that had discontinued it's track program, he really let me have it, and many people within shouting distance heard the tirade being directed at me. He was very upset that I wasn't at the college that I had been originally accepted to and had planned on running for. According to him it was just a lot of wasted potential and talent. He had expected me to do well and possibly become even an Olympic runner. However, I missed the opportunity to see how far my running could have taken me. But a good thing is that I made the best of my situation. Instead of becoming a good athlete at another college, I became a good student where I was, by being on the Dean's List most every semester, while earning scholarships for my grades instead of for my participation in sports. The same thing can happen with God when we fail to act on our potential and advantages in making choices against His will and His directions set for our lives. He will grant us other chances to rededicate ourselves to Him and do our best possible for Him.

I may have wasted my potential in track, but God gave me the potential to succeed in other areas that were taken advantage of. And in being a Christian, I am now trying my best to fully utilize the potential given to me through Jesus. That requires me to become dead to sin but alive in Him, as many people allow themselves to be robbed of their potential to serve the Lord by being led astray through the enticement of worldly pleasures and influences. Take Samson, in the Bible, for example. He had never lost a battle because of his might and was a dedicated warrior for God. However, he was tricked and robbed of his strength through the enchantment of a beautiful woman, under the direction of his enemies. As a result he wound up being enslaved by the very people he was supposed to conquer, denying him the potential and opportunity of winning many more battles for God's people. *Romans 6:8-14* tells us that as believers we have died with Jesus and are now living with Him. He died for sin and the life He lives is to God, as we should too. We should view ourselves as being dead to sin but alive to God through Jesus. Therefore, we should not let sin reign in our mortal bodies and find ourselves obeying things like lust, as did Samson. In yielding to God, the members of our bodies should be used in righteousness unto Him. It is God that can help us to ignore our weaknesses and make wise decisions in living up to our greatest potential through His grace and direction.

Power - *Power* is the ability or capacity to perform or act effectively, and political scientists have defined it as being the ability to influence the behavior of others with or without any resistance. There is power in influence, inducement, persuasion, authority, coercion and direct force. Then power may be held through things like politics, social class, wealth, charisma, expertise, knowledge, celebrity, public relations, religion, tradition, domination… Therefore power can be many things and attained by a variety of individuals or groups. Yet it is never real power. Only God has that. Powerful countries have crumbled. Powerful presidents can be voted out of office or serve out their terms. Powerful business leaders may find their organizations facing financial ruin. Powerful athletes grow old and fade away. And even some of the most powerful and influential churches are no longer what they once were. God's power, however, is infinite, eternal and incomprehensible. Plus it can't be checked, restrained, frustrated, limited or reduced in any way or by any circumstance, as it can with men of power.

God blesses us with the ability and capacity to do many things, but not the power to sustain it beyond His will.

God is power: In Him are greatness, *power,* glory, victory and majesty, as all on heaven and earth are His in being the head above all *(1 Chronicles 9:12)*. Plus both riches and honor come from Him as He reigns over all, with it being in His hand to make things great and give us all strength, and power *(verse 13)*. Jesus Christ is power: The Son of man has the *power* on earth to forgive sins *(Matthew 9:6)*. Then in *Matthew 28:18,* Jesus declares that all *power* and authority are given unto Him in heaven and in earth. God's word is power: The word of God is quick and *powerful,* both living and active, and it's sharper than any doubled-edged sword, penetrating even to the dividing soul and spirit, joints and marrow, while judging the thoughts and attitudes of one's heart *(Hebrews 4:12)*. Prayer is power: Jesus told His disciples that they could move mountains if they had faith without doubt, and they would receive whatever they asked for in prayer *(Matthew 21:21,22)*. Then praying for one another is another example of real power. There is healing in confessing our sins to another and praying for another, as the prayer of a righteous man is powerful and effective *(James 5:16)*. Prayers of faith can save the sick and have them raised up by the Lord, along with the forgiveness of sin *(verse 15)*.

Praise - *Praise* is the act of expressing approval, commending, applauding, admiring, magnifying, glorifying, lifting-up, etc., and is often the offering of grateful homage in words or song. For Christians it is an expression of worship as we humble ourselves and focus our attention upon the Lord, in heart-felt love, adoration and thanksgiving. It also places our spirit into an intimate fellowship with God, and should be a part of our daily-prayer life, as praise shouldn't be just something that we do in church along with other Christians. We can praise the Lord anywhere and anytime, be it at work, in the car, lying in bed, or even during an exercise walk, as I often do. Then we should always be able to place our praises above our troubles in entering into God's presence and power. The Bible tells of Paul and Silas being unjustly arrested, then being beaten and thrown into a jail cell. Yet, in spite of their most troubling situation, they were heard praying and singing praises to God. Likewise, through praise and worship, we can always enjoy the presence and peace of God, no matter what is going on in our lives.

There are many reasons for praise and we should give it often. We should give praise for the greatness of God. *Psalm 150:1,2* says that we should praise God in His sanctuary and in His mighty heavens for His mighty acts and according to His excellent greatness. The goodness of God should be praised too, as *Psalm 106:1* offers a great suggestion that we should give thanks to God because He is good and His love endures forever. Also, God is our salvation too, which is much deserving of praise. Isaiah, as we all should, declared that God through mercy was His salvation, and in Him he would trust and not be afraid, for the Lord was his strength and his song, in becoming his salvation *(Isaiah 12:2)*. We should also give praise for our salvation through Jesus; *1 Corinthians 15:57* says that we should give thanks to God, who gave us victory through our Lord Jesus Christ. Then Jesus is worthy of many praises Himself. His peace should rule our hearts and we should be most thankful *(Colossians 3:15)*. In whatever we do, by word or deed, it should be done in the name of Jesus, giving thanks to God the Father through Him *(verse 17)*.

Prayer - We all have a need to connect with someone that can identify with our circumstances and share in our everyday lives, and that can be done through prayer, which is our intimate connection with our Heavenly Father. *Prayer* is a devout petition to God and a spiritual communion in supplication, thanksgiving, adoration, or confession. It is the most direct expression of our religious nature, and man has prayed from the earliest of times and will always continue doing so. I pray daily asking for others and myself to be blessed in the ways we need, while offering my praise and thanks to Him as well. In developing the prayer life that God desires for me to experience, I am most confident in approaching Him, no matter how good or bad things may be going on in my life. I know for sure that if I ask for anything according to His will, He will hear me and act on it in His time. And that includes my prayers for those that I know and love, along with any others personally known or not, needing prayer. However, it is said that if God hears our prayers, we should know that we have what we were asking for from Him, as our prayers are aligned with His purposes.

The objects of prayer are Salvation (We want God to show us His unfailing love and grant us His salvation - *Psalm 85:7* and we want God to have mercy on us because we are sinners - *Luke 18:13)*, Spiritual Establishment (We want God to order our steps according to His word and not allow sin to rule us - *Psalm 119:133* and we want God to know that our ways are steadfast in observing His statutes - *Psalm 119:5)*, Spiritual Revival (We want God to restore us to Himself so that we may return and renew our days as of old - *Lamentations 5:21)*, Divine Vindication (We want God to know that, as the prophet Elijah, we are His servants and do all things at His command - *1 Kings 18:36)*, Preservation and Support (We want God to keep us safe because in Him is our trust - *Psalm 16:1* and we do not want God to hide his face from us but answer us quickly when we are in trouble - *Psalm 69:17)*, Prosperity (We want God to save us and grant us success - *Psalm 118:25)*, and for the Sinful (We want God to forgive us, as Jesus asked of His Father, because we may know not what we do - *Luke 23:34)*. However, if there is sin in our hearts, our prayers may not be heard *(Psalm 66:19)*.

Prejudice - One commonly used definition of prejudice is that of Gordon Willard Allport (1897 - 1967), an American psychologist, considered to be one the founding figures of personality psychology. He defined *prejudice* as being a "feeling, favorable or unfavorable, toward a person or thing, prior to, or not based on, actual experience", and also referring to a negative or hostile attitude toward another social group, usually racially defined. Then others say that the word refers to preconceived judgments toward people or a person because of *race/ethnicity, gender, social class, age, disability, religion, sexuality, nationality* or other personal characteristics. All being said though, prejudice is mostly the end result of unfounded beliefs and unreasonable attitudes that can be very resistant to any rational influence or thinking, and with racial prejudice it is the opinion or attitude where a person automatically assumes superiority and inferiority based on racial differences. Over the course of my life, I have witnessed, read, and heard about many, many cases of just plain outright ignorance and prejudice along different lines, with so much directed against my race. Then I have personally been subjected to some myself, through things like verbal and physical attacks, injustice, zoning, stereotyping, profiling, jealousy, blackballing, targeting and discrimination, for being a Negro (or that other word), a colored person, a black man, an African American, a college graduate, a family man, a company boss, and even for being a Christian.

We are all children of God but, in being human, people just have different attitudes toward one another that may cause barriers between them, whether there is a good reason for it or not, especially when some view themselves as being superior to others. *Proverbs 22:2* says that the rich will meet the poor together because the Lord is the maker of them all. However, we all know that the rich are more likely to distance themselves from the poor than to associate with them on a regular basis. Then when people can't live or get along together in peace, as *Malachi 2:10,* a great question to ask is why we all have one Father and one God that created us but we deal treacherously with every man against his brother, by profaning the covenant of our fathers in breaking faith with one another? It would be wonderful if we could place all of our differences and hostilities aside and treat each other more like in *Matthew 25.* If we see someone hungry, thirsty, a stranger, naked, sick, or in prison, the Lord wants it in our hearts to feed them, offer them a drink, invite them in, clothe them, look after them, or visit them, and no matter who they are or who we are. Only in a perfect world would all be willing to do that though. In an imperfect world of people with varying attitudes and prejudices, one may only find themselves having backs turned away from them or having evil inflicted against them, rather than enjoying the love and care of their fellow man. The best we can do is search our own hearts and do what we can, then pray for the ignorant and the cruel.

Presence - On occasion, beyond thinking about what God looks like, I have thought about what it would be like to stand before Him in His presence face to face. But then on second thought, I think that it wouldn't be that great of an idea, at least right now. I'm sure that He would smile and voice His approval of me at times, then at others He would probably just shake His head and ask "What is wrong with you boy?" like my dad used to. And I must admit that there were some times that just the look of disappointment on my dad's face would hurt much more than the whipping and punishment that followed. So, I can just imagine how difficult it would be for me to stand before God in sin. So maybe just feeling and acknowledging His presence is a better thing. There certainly are times that I sense Him smiling down upon me when I am doing some good things. Then some frowns of disapproval when I sin and stray away from the purpose He has set for my life. However, in prayer I can feel God's presence too, and am able to confess my sins and ask for His forgiveness, if I have done wrong, or give my thanks for the good things that I have been able to do in answering His call.

God is more than just present. He is *omnipresent,* meaning that He is everywhere. David questioned in *Psalms 139:7,8* as to where he could go from God's spirit or to flee from His presence. The answer was that he could ascend to Heaven or make his bed in Hell and God would be there with him. God's presence is surely very near to us, and as Christians He is in us. In that it is possible for us to realize, perceive and be conscious of His presence. His eyes are in every place, keeping watch on the evil and the good *(Proverbs 15:3).* However, even though God is not far us each one of us, we should still seek Him, feel after Him, and find Him, for it is in Him that we live, move and have our being *(Acts 17:27,28).* God reveals Himself to those that seek Him earnestly, and *Deuteronomy 4:29* says that we will find God if we seek Him with all our hearts and all our souls. God desires that we seek to come near Him and will reveal His presence to us when we do. Then it is comforting to know that God's presence is with us no matter the place or the time. In *Genesis 28:16,* Jacob awoke from his sleep and said the Lord was surely in that place, even though he didn't know it. I surely know that God is in my presence whether I know it or not too. His watchful eyes are there for my protection and many other things, including overseeing my sins and my good deeds.

Pride - It is not a good thing to continually ⟨
to others. God desires for us to focus on the ⟨
he has placed before each of us. *Pride* often refer⟨
inflated opinion of one's own dignity, importance, merit, or
superiority that a person may possess, and one thinking too
highly of themselves may think too little of God and others.
Being prideful can breed things like envy, jealousy, and
obsession, and it is especially bad when a person refuses to
acknowledge any of their wrongdoings or shortcomings because
of it. Dante (Durante degli Alighieri, 1265 - 1321), a major
Italian poet of the Middle Ages, viewed *pride* as being vanity,
and he defined it as being "love of self perverted to hatred and
contempt for one's neighbor". It was a desire to be important or
attractive to others with an excessive love of one's self, while
not properly positioning themselves in relation to God or others.
However, there is also a positive connotation of the word,
which refers to the satisfied sense of attachment toward one's
own choices or actions, as well as those of another, or even a
whole group. In that there is a product of praise, independent
self-reflection, or a fulfilled feeling of belonging. Therefore,
being a proud and fellowshipping Christian, according to the
will of God, would be viewed as being a positive thing in that
respect.

Proverbs 16:5 says that the proud in heart are an abomination
(detestable) and won't go unpunished. Many will only find
themselves facing calamity, as pride goes before destruction and
a haughty (arrogant) spirit before a fall *(verse 8)*. Surely some
of us have seen people rise to the top and forget where they
came from, only to come crashing back down and seeking
forgiveness from those that they had deserted or looked down
upon during their success. The things that may accompany pride
include shame *(Proverbs 11:2)* and contention, meaning

struggle (*Proverbs 13:10*), and it is condemned as being a sin of the wicked (*Proverbs 21:4*). *Proverbs 29:23* says that a person's pride will bring them low, and *Acts 12:20-23* presents a good example of the consequences of pride, in telling of the death of Herod (a Palestinian ruler). Herod was highly displeased with the people of Tyre and Sidon, who had asked for peace, because they depended on the king's country for their food supply. On a day set by Herod, he sat on his throne, wearing his royal apparel, to deliver a public address to the people. They began to shout that his was a voice of a god and not of a man. Then when Herod did not give any praise to God, an angel of the Lord stuck him down immediately and he died being eaten by worms. So, be mindful of *James 4:6,* which says that God will oppose the proud but give grace to the humble.

Procrastination - As many people, I have been guilty, from time to time, of putting off or delaying doing something that required my immediate attention or something that I had planned on doing within a certain time frame, which is called *procrastination*. In today's busy and stressful world, there are just so many things that may distract us so that we don't have our minds and attention focused on some things that are more important than others. Then we just get a little tired and lazy. There's always tomorrow, if we don't do it today. There have been different reasons why I have put things off. However, I never worried much about it in the past, as I believed that there was always the luxury of time on my side, even after witnessing some friends and family dying really young. I woke up to reality a bit though in 2010 during my stroke. So many things were going through my mind during the temporary blindness, especially concerning my continued ability to do certain things if there was no full recovery. Then after the doctor informed me that I would be well and about how fortunate and blessed it was for me to not have suffered the more severe consequences of a stroke, including death, I realized the uncertainly of life and how numbered my days could actually be. Therefore, I am now doing a number of things with a much greater sense of urgency than ever before.

An example of procrastination in Bible comes from *Acts 24,* after an orator named Tertullus made some accusations against Paul. There was to be a trial before Felix (a slave that had been liberated by Claudius Caesar and appointed as procurator of Judea). Paul was accused of being a troublemaker and stirring up riots among the Jews all over the world, and a ringleader of the sect of the Nazarenes, the people of Nazareth that were held in low esteem according to *John 1:46*. He was also said to have tried to desecrate the temple. However, after denying the charges and defending himself in the name of God, he was released under the guard of a centurion and given some liberty, with Felix saying that his case would be decided later. After a few days, Felix came with his wife Drusilla, a Jewish woman, and sent for Paul, who was heard concerning his faith in Jesus. Upon hearing Paul talk about righteousness, self-control and the judgment to come, Felix was afraid and told Paul to leave until sent for. Then in hoping that Paul would offer a bribe of money that would satisfy the Jews, there were frequent talks to follow. But after two more years, Porcius Festus succeeded Felix, who still desiring to gain the favor of the Jews left Paul in bounds. So, while Felix had a great sense of urgency for gaining the favor of the Jews, just as I have concerning a few things, He also procrastinated in judging Paul because of the fear of God that had been placed in him.

Promises - Promises are promises, and we all make them to others and ourselves. We make vows concerning many things, and that is very easy to do. The difficult thing to do can be the actual fulfilling of promises, especially when one's heart and mind weren't truly in to it from the beginning. There are times that people may be talked into making commitments to do something that they really don't want to, and in the end they don't. Then there are just some people where making promises seems to be a part of their nature. They will make promise after promise, while never honoring them, to the point that others eventually stop listening or believing them, and then viewed as being liars. It is certainly always better to not make a promise than to make one and not keep your word without a good reason for it. However, many may just find themselves guilty of it from one time to another, and even when making promises to God. A person may commit their time, money, talents and lives to Him but not come through for one reason or another, even though God has always made good on His promises to them. That is surely something to think about whenever you fail God too.

Because of our hectic lives, imperfections, sinful nature or other reasons, we are all prone to making a promise or two that won't be kept, unintentionally or not, and no matter to whom they are made. However, God is a promise keeper and promises abundant life, answers to prayer, blessings, comfort, deliverance, eternal life, forgiveness, guidance, health, mercy, peace, plenty, protection, rest, salvation, security, strength, and more to the afflicted, believers, and penitent (repentant). He also makes promises to the tempted because He is faithful. *1 Corinthians 10:13* says that no temptation will seize us except what is common to man and God will not let us be tempted beyond what we can bear. If we are tempted, He will also provide a way of escape, so that we will be able to bear it, which is a promise in itself. Then *1 Kings 8:56* presents an example of the reliability of God's promises. It says that God gave rest to the people of Israel just as He had promised, and had not failed in one word of all the good promises He had given through His servant Moses. It is written too that every word spoken to Abraham, Isaac and Jacob were verified, clearly revealing the faithfulness of God and His fulfilled promises.

Protection - Parents protect children. Children protect parents. Siblings protect siblings. Friends protect friends. Neighbors protect neighbors. Pastors protect congregations. Police protect communities. Firefighters protect homes. Doctors protect patients. Medicines protect ill. Insurers protect policyholders. Unions protect members. I could go on and on, but a meaning of protection is just that there is someone or something to prevent any injury or harm to be inflicted towards someone. However, the only guaranteed protection is that promised and provided by God. He is the only one that you can always turn to and trust, while all else may fail. Recently, I was watching a documentary on television about the fate of the RMS Titanic, the luxury passenger liner that was supposedly built with so many safeguards for the protection of the ship and all aboard that it was declared as being unsinkable. Yet on April 15, 1912, on it's maiden voyage from Southampton, United Kingdom to New York City, United States, it struck an iceberg and sank in the North Atlantic Ocean, killing 1,514 people. That should be a good lesson for us all to learn from concerning protection.

Joshua, born a slave in Egypt, is thought to have been as old as 80 when he became Moses' successor, and in his leadership God offered the same protection as He had Moses. *Joshua 1:1-5* tells how the Lord talked to Joshua after the death of Moses and told him and his people to get ready to cross the Jordan River into the land that He was giving the Israelites. They would be given every place they set their feet as was promised to Moses.

Then, also, as with Moses, God's protection would be with them as He declared that no one would be able to stand up against Joshua all the days of his life. God would be with him and never forsake him. Joshua was to be strong, courageous and observant of doing according to all the law *(verse 7)* and not to be afraid or dismayed because God would be with him wherever he went *(verse 9)*. Therefore, with God's protection, Joshua would never have to worry about any sinking ships, unless God willed it. God protects us too and all we have to do is ask for it as David did in *Psalm 59*. He asked God to protect him from those rising up against him for no good reason. So when you feel that the world is rising up against you in any way, just pray to God for His direction and protection.

Psalms - *Psalms* is a book of the Bible composed of 150 sacred songs, hymns and prayers, with many finding David on his knees, *pouring out his heart to God in repentance, in thanksgiving, in faith, and asking God for assurance, strength, deliverance, and instruction*, as we all can in our spiritual longings that only God can satisfy. The title, *Psalms*, is the one used for this book in the *Septuagint* (A Greek translation of the Old Testament made for Greek-speaking Jews). However, the Hebrew name is *Tehillim,* signifying "Praises". The earliest Christians used the Psalms in worship, and they have remained an important part of worship in most Christian Churches, while the Eastern Orthodox, Catholic, Presbyterian, Lutheran and Anglican Church have always made systematic use of the Psalms, reciting all or most of them in a cycle over the course of one or more weeks. Then several conservative Protestant denominations sing only the Psalms, along with maybe a small number of hymns found elsewhere in the Bible, and they will not accept the use of any non-Biblical hymns. Also, though it has been a subject of debate, I read where in the early centuries of the Church, it may have been a requirement for any bishop candidates to be able to recite the entire book of Psalms from memory, something they would often learn automatically while they were monks. Certainly, in having written many of my own spiritual songs and poems, the reading of Psalms has been a great inspiration to me. The words have helped to guide me in my search for God and provided me with an outlet of peace and contentment from the many struggles of my life. I have tried hard to pick some personal favorites, but they all seem to motivate and uplift me more than any other books in the Bible, as Psalms truly magnifies God and His Word so greatly.

Most manuscripts of the Septuagint also include a 151st Psalm about David slaying Goliath, the giant Philistine warrior, in single combat. It is in Eastern Orthodox translations of the Bible. For many years scholars believed that it might have been an original Greek composition and that there was no evidence that a Hebrew version ever existed. However the *Dead Sea Scrolls* proved that there was. Between the years of 1947 and 1956 the Scrolls, a collection of 972 texts from the Hebrew Bible and extra-biblical documents, were discovered in eleven caves along the northwest shore of the Dead Sea, in an area 13 miles east of Jerusalem. The Scrolls, dating as early as 200 B.C. included prophecies by Ezekiel, Jeremiah and Daniel not found in the Bible. Then there were also never before seen Psalms attributed to King David and Joshua. Therefore the Scrolls suggest that the collection of 150 psalms in the Bible may have been selected from a wider set than originally thought. Plus the Psalms Scrolls presents them in a different order from that found elsewhere. *Psalm 151* is as follows:

My hands made a harp, my fingers fashioned a lyre.

And who will declare it to my Lord? The Lord himself; it is he who hears.

It was he who sent his messenger and took me from my father's sheep, and anointed me with his anointing oil.

My brothers were handsome and tall, but the Lord was not pleased with them.

I went out to meet the Philistine, and he cursed me with his idols.

But I drew his own sword; I beheaded him, and removed reproach from the people of Israel.

Punishment - None of us are total angels and over the course of our lives we all will do one thing or another to warrant some kind of *punishment*, which is the authoritative imposing of something negative or unpleasant on a person in response to their bad behavior. The authority may be a group or a single person, with the punishment being carried out formally through a system of law or informally in a social setting like that of a family. Then along religious lines we all face punishment from God because we all sin. However, we may also acknowledge our wrongful acts and apply a self-imposed form of punishment. There is *penance*, which is the act of self-mortification or devotion carried out voluntarily to show sorrow for a sin or other wrongdoings. It is a sacrament in some Christian churches that may include attrition, confession, acceptance of punishment, and absolution, which is also called *reconciliation*.

In *Isaiah 13,* it is prophesized about how severe God's punishment could be for the Babylonians. Isaiah saw God exercising His wrath upon them, coming one cruel day in fierce anger to make the land desolate and destroy the sinners within it *(verse 9).* There would be no light as the stars of heaven, constellations, sun, and moon would all be darkened *(verse 10).* The world would be punished for their evil and the wicked for their iniquity, while putting an end to the arrogance of the proud and humbling the pride of the terrible *(verse 11).* The Medes from Media (an ancient Asiatic kingdom in NW Iran) would be risen up against them and have no mercy because they had no regard for silver or gold *(verse 17).* They would be there to kill, rape, destroy and loot homes, with no mercy for infants or sparing any children, and leaving the land in a state that it would never be inhabited again by any people, just desert creatures *(verses 16, 18, 20 and 21).* It is certainly better to live a life deserving of His blessings rather than His punishment.

Purpose - I try to live each day with a sense of purpose, aiming to accomplish at least a little something of importance. Every day should be viewed as being one of opportunity. Life is short and the fewer days we waste the better. Therefore, it is very important to find out what our true purpose in life may be, and then get busy. But that could take some time. While growing up, for example, I began hating my voice because people in school and around would laugh and call me a slow talking hillbilly when I spoke. As a result, I became a little quiet but great at expressing myself through written word. However, I realize now that even though I was being ridiculed, my voice made people stop and listen. Nowadays, people tell me that they enjoy hearing my voice, and look forward to hearing me speak or sing in church, along with reading my inspirational writing, which God always has a hand in. It's easy to see one purpose that He had for me. Another is a giving and caring heart as I do many things for different people, and without any expectations of receiving anything in return. God has that covered too. There was even an article in the Detroit Free Press in October of 2011 detailing some volunteer work that I have been doing to benefit senior citizens in Detroit, which had nothing to do with my purpose or reason for doing such things. Some think that I am crazy working so much for free, while the beneficiaries of my good deeds view me as being a welcome blessing. So, I feel great as I step out each day and demonstrate the purpose that God has placed before me for my life. And very few of my days are wasted.

As mentioned, one purpose of my life, and a very important one, is the glorification of God, in doing everything to make Him look good when others see Him on display in my life. I may face my struggles but people admire my positive attitude as I fight through them, while continuing to do good things for others. The Bible defines *purpose* as design or intention, and *Ecclesiastes 3:1* says that there is a time for every purpose under the heaven. Therefore, God may have a purpose set for me now but another in mind for my future. And it should be noted that things like marriage, success, and happiness are benefits of life and not purposes. *Acts 11-23* tells us that with purpose of heart we will cleave (be faithful) unto the Lord, which is what God desires from us in living according to His design or intention. Then as *2 Corinthians 9:7,* a man should give accordingly to the purpose set in his heart, and not grudgingly or out of necessity, for God loves a cheerful giver. It is from my heart that I am doing all the things I do in church, community and for others. I am inspiring, uplifting and doing good deeds for many people, with the purpose not being for any financial gain or accolades desired. People may not see or understand it, but I am being rewarded through God and it will be through His grace that any additional rewards are forthcoming. He will see to it that I am blessed especially for being a blessing to those that may not have anywhere else to turn for anything. However, the many smiles and thankful words I hear are rewards enough. That lets me now that my efforts are most appreciated and purposeful.

Questioning - When things aren't going very well, it's easy to have a "why me?" attitude or questioning God. During a most problematic, stressful and discouraging period of my life, I lost much that was very important to me and began to question my faith, God and myself. Just couldn't figure out what I was doing so wrong to warrant my suffering. Then there were some that began questioning if maybe I was not the faithful Christian they had thought me to be, and that I had to be doing much wrong in the eyes of God that I was being punished for that they didn't know about. With all the questioning, things just weren't getting any better, but worst day-by-day. It felt like the whole world was against me and at times I felt like I was turning against myself too. However, I finally realized that God wasn't treating me unfairly and was actually doing many good things to help me survive through my struggles, like making sure I had a mother's home to return to after losing my apartment. Rather than questioning His motives, I should have been turning to Him rather than away from Him. In repentance, things are now much better and I am at peace in my self and my situation.

As myself, Job, in spite of losing his family and all of his possessions, had no right to question God's fairness. Things were surely disheartening and he heard all the bad talk about him, just as I had. However, blaming God was unthinkable. He needed to be taught a lesson, and I believe that God had done just that with me in making things all the more unbearable as I failed to maintain my trust and faith in Him. So, God had to show Job just how powerless he actually was in having control over anything. First God told Job to brace himself like a man and that he would be questioned and give answers (*(Job 38:3)*. Then Job was the one barraged with questions, including being asked where he was when God laid the foundations of the Earth (*Job 38:4)*, who marked off the dimensions of the Earth and stretched a measuring line across it (*Job 38:5)*, and if he would discredit God's justice and condemn Him just to justify himself (*Job 40:8)*. God also presented two powerful beasts, a behemoth and a leviathan, before Job to reveal His power. Job couldn't handle the beasts but God could, as everything under Heaven belongs to Him (*Job 41:11)*. Therefore, if Job didn't have God's power he had no right to question His wisdom. Finally, in wonder and awe of God's strength and wisdom, Job says that he despised himself and repented in dust and ashes (*Job 42:6)*.

Rainbows - I sometimes pray that my life be painted by the vibrant colors of a rainbow, rather than by any darkness or gloom. However, I realize that one may have to weather a few storms before they can fully appreciate the sunshine and rainbows of their existence. Then, it is great when something beginning in any kind of sadness ends in joy, which is always possible through the Lord. The bow-shaped display of violet, indigo, blue, green, yellow, orange and red colors, caused by the refraction and reflection of the sun's rays through rain or mist, often causes much excitement and finger pointing. However, I never envision there being any leprechauns (those mischievous dwarfs of Irish folklore) or any pots of gold at the end of any. During the midst of my storms, I look to see the faces of God and Jesus in my rainbows.

In Genesis, Gold told Noah that the rainbow was to be the symbol of the covenant between God, Noah, and every living creature *(Genesis 9:12-17)*. Therefore, the appearance of a rainbow in the clouds should always be an uplifting sight. Then *Revelation 4* describes the throne in Heaven with there being a rainbow, resembling an emerald, encircling it, as God has a reminder of His covenant always within His close view. There are also other examples of God's presence on display above, like the Castor and Pollux, the *Twin Brothers (Acts 28:11)*, of Jupiter and Leda, Greek and Roman divinities, appearing in the heavens as the constellation Gemini and believed to be the protectors of mariners. Another is Arcturus, a bright red star of the northern sky known as the guard or keeper of the Great Bear (Ursa Major), which contains the stars forming the Big Dipper and mentioned in *Job 9:9*.

Reading - I read a countless number of books over many years for educational purposes up until my graduation from college. Then I began reading books of my own personal preferences, even joining a Book-Of-The-Month club, with my selections covering a wide variety of interests. I read Sherlock Holmes detective novels and other writings of mystery and intrigue. I read the autobiographies of famous people that I admired. I read about ancient civilizations, wonders of the world, and the mysteries of the pyramids. I even read scientific books about things like black holes (regions of space-time where the gravity is so strong that nothing entering the region, not even light, can escape); just sounded like a bottomless pit in the middle of outer space to me. Surely didn't understand that and a few other things that I read but still found them to be interesting reading. However, in all of my reading, I hadn't committed myself to fully reading the most important book that I needed to read - the Bible. Then beginning in January of 2007, I began to do so when I read a church's daily plan for reading the Bible over the course of the year. It didn't take me that long though. I became so engrossed that I finished my reading on August 3, 2007, followed by the reading of another Bible, being read in conjunction with it, on August 31, 2007.

Exodus 24:7 tells how after Moses read the Book of the Covenant to the people, they responded that they would obey the Lord and do everything He asked of them. Then in *verse 12,* Moses was told by the Lord to go up to mount before Him and receive tablets of stone, with a law, and commandments for which he was to use in teaching the people. Later Joshua, Moses' successor, read the same words to the people that had been previously heard. He read all the words of the law, with its blessings and curses, just as written in the Book of the Law, and not a word was missed before the Israelite congregation that Moses had commanded (*Joshua 8:34-35*). King Josiah of Judah later renewed the covenant. *2 Kings 23:1-3* tells how he called together all the elders of Judah and Jerusalem. In the house of the Lord before many people, small and great, he read for all to hear from the Book of the Covenant, which had been found in the temple of the Lord. Then, standing by a pillar, he made a covenant before the Lord to walk after Him, and to keep His commandments, testimonies, and statutes with all their heart and soul in confirmation of what was written, and all the people pledged themselves to it. Therefore, from the earliest of times, the reading of the Word was most important for the Lord's teaching and instruction, just as it should be today and always.

Rebellion - A *rebellion* is a resistance against something, like the government, authority, or any other controlling force, and an example is when a large group of people refuses to follow a certain law. Then revolutions are rebellions that succeed in overthrowing governments and establishing new ones, which is how our country became what it is. Our founding fathers built the United States on the foundation of rebellion, as the early American colonists, facing overwhelming odds, fought to free themselves from British rule. Therefore, rebellion can be a good thing. However, it's another matter when children rebel against their parents through insubordination, disobedience, and defiance, or when individuals refuse to conform to the laws or rules of their own society. Then worst yet when people rebel against God. The colonists rebelled and won the Revolutionary War (1775-1783), but rebelling against God never works, and the Bible presents many examples of that. Many have rebelled and ignored His commands only to pay a terrible price for it.

Israel's rebellion against the Lord was predicted and Moses warned his people about the consequences of it. With his death near, the Lord told Moses that after he rested with his fathers, the people would prostitute themselves to the foreign gods of they land they were entering, while forsaking Him and breaking the covenant made with them *(Deuteronomy 31:16)*. As a result, the Lord would forsake them and hide His face from them, as they would be devoured with many evils and troubles befalling them *(Deuteronomy 31:17)*. Moses was then instructed to write down a song to teach to the Israelites and have them sing it in being a witness of the Lord against them *(verse 19)*, which he did *(verse 22)*. Moses goes on to tell the people that he knew of their rebellion against the Lord and questions how much more it would be after his death, saying that they would utterly corrupt themselves and turn away from the way in which he had commanded, resulting in their being subjected to evil for the evil done in the sight of the Lord, provoking Him to anger through the work of their hands *(verses 27 and 29)*.

Reckoning - *Reckoning* is a settling of accounts and we all face that day when we will have to stand before God and give an accounting of the lives that we lived, and face a judgment where we will be rewarded with a grand new life in Heaven or be banished to the pits of Hell. Unfortunately, there are no other choices. So it's best to always live as best of a Godly life as possible in preparing for your day of reckoning, which can come very suddenly and unexpectedly, as only He knows the day and the time beforehand. Therefore, if you aren't living right, today is a great time to start.

The Bible tells of *reckoning* as a settling of accounts but also in terms of calculations or estimations, which are other definitions of the word. *Matthew 18:23-27* describes the Kingdom of Heaven as being like this king that wanted to settle accounts with his servants. One owed him money and he demanded that the servant, along with his wife and children, be sold for payment. However, the debt was forgiven after the servant fell on his knees in worship asking the Lord for patience. Likewise, before entering Heaven, we may have to settle a few debts with God through His forgiveness. Then with *Romans 8:18* there is the reckoning or estimation that the sufferings of our present time aren't worthy of being compared to the glory that will later be revealed to us.

Rejection - I read where the word *rejection* was first used in the year 1415, with the original meaning being *to throw* or *to throw back*, while now it more commonly refers to a refusal, discarding or casting off of something, which is pretty much the same thing. Rejection is something that we are all subjected to at one time or another in our lives concerning things like love, careers, friends, school, etc. and often occurs when an individual is deliberately excluded from something. We are born into a state of happiness and suffer when we think that we have lost something that we need. During my early life, being excluded from a certain group of friends because I didn't do some of the things they did brought about a great sense of rejection. Later it was things like my divorce or a job loss. However, while quite unhappy then, I later learned that at times you just have to move on and not allow any kind of rejection to weigh too heavily on your feelings.

Samuel, the prophet, became the chief religious authority of Israel, and *1 Samuel 8:1-22* tells of his rejection in being asked that he be removed from his position and a king be appointed to replace him. He had become old and made his two sons, Joel and Abiah, judges over Israel. However, they did not walk in the ways of their father, but sought dishonest gain, while accepting bribes and perverting justice. So, Samuel was asked to step down. The people had decided that they wanted a king to judge them that didn't represent the Lord. But Samuel didn't argue against his rejection, as one would have expected him to do. He instead prayed and voiced out his disappointment to the Lord. Samuel was told that it wasn't him that was being rejected. They were rejecting the Lord as being king over them. Samuel was instructed to speak to the people and tell them the disadvantages of having a king that would only take away most of what had been given them by the Lord, who would no longer hear their cries for relief. When they refused to listen, the Lord told Samuel to give them a king just as they wanted, and he did.

Relationships - *Relationships* are viewed as being connections between two individuals or groups of people. There are relationships between parents and their children, church pastors and their congregations, presidents, mayors and other elected officials with their public, nations and other nations, and many other different types of associations. Then many think in terms of their personal friendships and the romantic or intimate relationships between man and woman, which are at their best when there is mutual respect, trust, honesty, support, fairness, equality, separate identities, and a lot of good communication. Therefore building those kinds of strong and lasting relationships requires work and may be a little difficult for some, especially for the more self-centered individuals. The best relationships begin and are maintained when there is a strong relationship established between yourself and God foremost. In developing an intimate relationship with Him all of your other relationships are bound to be successful with His guidance. He provides great instructions for how we should treat each other, plus love each other as we love Him.

The great thing about a relationship with God is that He is not concerned about our looks, size, education, social status, race, wealth, etc. Also, God will still want to have a relationship with us no matter the mistakes that have been made in our lives. Whereas in human relationships there are damaged reputations, ruined friendships, divorces, legal actions, misunderstandings, prejudices, and other things that may cause people to steer away from each other, there are no such occurrences with God. No matter what is going on in our lives or relationships, if we trust in God there is security. *Psalm 91* says that God is our *refuge* and *fortress* if it is in Him that we trust. He will save us from what attacks us with His angels guarding us in all our ways. We have nothing to fear and will observe with our eyes the punishment of the wicked. No harm will befall us and we will be distanced from any disasters. Therefore a relationship with God is the key to a successful and safe life. As we grow in Him, we become more rounded and effective in all that we do, including our personal relationships. With our relationship with

God, we learn to be more forgiving, patient, understanding and considerate of others, plus more loving as we are driven more by our hearts and His love than by our minds.

Reliance - *Reliance* is having the faith, confidence, or trust of something. We have a reliance on our parents to raise and support us properly. We have a reliance on our schools to educate us. We have a reliance on our churches to teach us the ways of the Lord. We have a reliance on our bosses to pay us for our work. We have a reliance on our seatbelts and airbags to provide some protection during a car accident. Even Lebron James, considered by many to be the best basketball player in the world, has a reliance on his teammates to help him win games. Plus he has to have a lot of faith, confidence and trust in himself, as we all should in ourselves. Then above all else, we should have a reliance on God in everything.

My Bible defines *reliance* as being trusting, confiding or reposed (resting), and there surely are times that we should rely on the Lord, rather than on our personal strengths, when going through some things, as Asa discovered. *2 Chronicles 14-16* tells how Asa, the third king of Judah, did what was good and right in the eyes of the Lord his God, whom he placed his reliance upon. In doing so, when his army was to face a much greater Ethiopian army in battle, the Lord came to their rescue. However, years later, Asa would lose the Lord's favor and support as he became increasingly less loyal and began relying upon his own personal strengths in doing many things. Then in relying solely upon his physicians for his health concerns, he would only die from having an incurable disease in his feet.

Relief - During the summer of 2012, I did a lot of walking and bike riding over a stretch of really hot days, while not eating that much. I was losing the weight that I wanted but didn't realize, until it was too late, that the uric acid level in my body had raised sky high. The result was a bad case of the gout in both of my knees. They were so swollen and painful that I was totally unable to walk. Found myself having to scoot around the house on my rear for over four weeks, while waiting for my slow acting gout medicine to end my suffering. It was such a relief when I was finally able to go outside after being confined to the house for such a long period. However, there were some lingering after-effects that prevented me from returning to my exercise routine for even several weeks to follow. *Relief* is the alleviation of something and I certainly experienced that. Just nothing like the relief I have endured since confessing my sins and turning my life over to the Lord. That's the best there is as He offers a relief more effective than any medicine, but he wants us to be a relief for each other in any ways possible too.

We all may face something that we need to be relieved of, in assistance, aid or support, and it's a great thing if we are able to help another in need of some kind of relief. *Leviticus 25:35*, for example, tells us that we should offer relief to a person in our area that has become poor and unable to support themselves, even a stranger or temporary resident. In doing so, they would be able to remain among us. *Isaiah 1:17* encourages us to learn to do well in seeking judgment, defending the cause of the fatherless, pleading the case of widows, and offering relief to the oppressed. In being willing and obedient concerning that, and in other ways, a person will be blessed with the good of the land *(Isaiah 1:19)*. *1 Timothy* 5:10,16 then offers advice to widows that would be great for all of us. Firstly, they should be known for their good deeds. Then among other things, they should show hospitality and help those in trouble. If she is a believer and has widows in her family, she should offer relief to them, so that the burden wouldn't be placed with the church, that could then concentrate more on helping those widows really in need. Widows or not, we all should have a concern for doing good deeds and being a relief for others in some way.

Religion - The definition for *religion*, according to the old *Webster Dictionary*, was that it was the worship of God or gods, or a belief or system of doctrines of faith and worship. They relate humanity to spirituality and may have narratives, symbols, traditions and sacred histories intended to give meaning to life or explain its origin or the Universe. I read that, according to some estimates, there may be around 4,200 religions in the world (that number is high because there are so many people worshipping something other than our God). They have been divided into three broad categories: *world religions* that refer to transcultural or international faiths, *indigenous religions* that refer to the smaller, culture-specific or nation-specific groups, and the *new religious movements* that refer to the recently developed faiths. Then according to a global 2012 poll, it was reported that 59% of the world's population is religious, while 23% are not and 13% are atheists (don't believe in God or a Supreme Being).

Religion is our system of faith, and *James 1:19-27* says that religious people should be listeners and doers. We should be quick to listen, slow to speak, and slow to anger, as anger does not bring about the righteous life that God desires. We should, also, get rid of all the moral filth and the evil that is so prevalent, and humbly accept the word planted in us, which is able to save our souls. Then it is important to be doers of the word and not just listeners because in doing so a person would only be deceiving himself or herself. It is said that a man who listens to the word but doesn't do what it says is like a man that looks at his face in a mirror, then immediately forgets what he looks like when he moves away from it. The man, who looks intently to the perfect law that gives freedom, and continues to do so without forgetting what he has heard but doing it, will be blessed in what he does. Also, a man considering himself to be religious but does not keep a tight rein on his tongue only deceives himself in his heart, and his religion is useless. The religion that God views as being pure and faultless is one where afflicted orphans and widows are visited, and where men keep themselves from being corrupted by the world.

Remembrance - When thinking back, there are a lot of special memories that warm my heart and bring a smile to my face. Then there are the bad ones that continue to sadden me, like the remembrance of the death of my father when I was quite young. That made things very difficult while growing up and even beyond. However, while I had no control over that, I wonder about some of the bad memories that really didn't have to be. My marriage, for example, was one that I expected to last through the good and the bad times. Maybe I could have done something to have made that more possible? I have a lot of joyful memories about what had been and think about what could have been in remembrance of all that was lost.

Your greatest remembrance should be of the Lord your God for all the great things that He has done for you. Plus you should acknowledge those blessings and fond memories in giving thanks on a regular basis, while you are among the living here on Earth. *Psalm 6:5* says that there is no remembrance of Him when a person is dead. Then it asks the question as to who can praise God from the grave. The answer, of course, is nobody. So, we have to appreciate our memories and give Him praise while we are yet alive. And we could do some of the same for each other. We can share our good memories and give thanks to those who helped make them possible. I certainly want to hear praises of myself and be able to praise others while I am still here. A funeral is too late to share any good memories, or to make amends for any bad memories you may have caused.

Repentance - Many people think that *repentance* means to turn away from sin, when actually it is the regret of past sins or actions and the changing of one's mind and behavior because of them. When one repents and turns to God their repentance is proven by their deeds. Therefore, repentance is more than just praying to God and apologizing for your sins. Then in relation to salvation, it is the changing of one's mind from the rejection of Jesus to the faith in Him. That means that we should become more knowledgeable and accept whom He is and what He has done. So while turning away from sin is not the definition of repentance, it is one of the results of your faith-based repentance towards the Lord.

I read that repentance is not a work we do to earn salvation. *John 6:44, Acts 5:31,* and *Acts 11:18* tell us that no one can repent and come to God unless He pulls that person to Him. Repentance is something that God gives, and it is only possible out of His grace. So, no one can repent unless God grants it. Then all of salvation, including repentance and faith, is a result of God drawing us, while opening our eyes and changing our hearts. Also, His longsuffering leads us to repentance, and He is patient, not willing any to perish, but desiring that all should come to repentance (*2 Peter 3:9*) out of His goodness (*Romans 2:4*). Finally, *2 Corinthians 5:17* says that a person truly repenting from the rejection of Jesus to faith in Him will give evidence of a changed life, from the old to the new.

Rescue - We all may find ourselves facings problems that we see no solutions to or any means of escape from. Our backs are to the wall and we don't know which way to turn. Yet, there is never a reason to just throw in the towel and give up, and then there are the times that we can become our own worst enemies in taking inappropriate actions that will only compound our problems. No matter what we are going through, however, all we have to do is hold on and never give up hope in placing our trust in God. He can rescue us from even the most difficult situations. I can remember losing a job during a time that I was really in debt. However, I didn't know that my name would be passed around. The following day I received a call and was interviewed for another job that I landed. That was God! Certainly I was greatly worried when I left the one job, but there was the faith and hope that God would rescue me somehow.

In *Psalm 35*, David seeks a rescue by the Lord, who he wants to oppose those that opposed him, and fight those that fought against him. He wanted the Lord to use His weapons to aid him, while giving the assurance of his salvation. David wanted those that sought his life to be disgraced and put to shame, turned back in dismay for plotting his ruin. They would be like the chaff (grain husks separated from the seed) before the wind, and having the angel of the Lord driving them away, in pursuit and making their path dark and slippery. David wanted that because they had hid their net for him without cause and dug a pit for him without cause. So, he asked for the Lord to turn the tables on them, resulting in their own ruin. Then his soul could rejoice in the Lord and delight in his salvation. Continuing on, he tells how he was being repaid with evil in spite of all the good things he had done. In calling on the Lord, he looked to be rescued from their destruction. Then upon them seeing the error of their ways, he could speak of the Lord's righteousness and praise Him all day long.

Resources - One definition of a *resource* is that it is a supply, support or aid, and especially one that can be readily drawn upon when needed. And that's one pretty good description of God too. He is our greatest resource as He protects, provides, and cares for us. We never have to be overwhelmed by our circumstances or obstacles. We can readily call upon God for anything and everything whenever He is needed. In prayer, just ask Him to remind you of His blessings and resources.

Caleb, was one of twelve spies sent by Moses from Kadesh to Canaan, which was to be given to the Israelites by God (*Numbers 13*). Upon their return, he strongly advised that they should go forward and take the land. However, those with him said that they couldn't attack because the people there were much stronger and powerful. The land did flow with milk and honey, but the cities were fortified and very large, with even some descendants of Anak (a race of giants) there. Yet, with God as their resource, he still believed that they would be victorious. Because of that demonstration of faith, Joshua was allowed to enter the Promised Land (*Numbers 14:24*), along with Joshua, both over twenty years of age, that had found themselves alone in the company of their fellow spies.

Respect - Just listen or observe how some people talk to others or treat others. On occasion, far too many just seem to have little respect for any person or any thing, including them or even the Church. A niece told me of an incident that occurred during the summer of 2012 at her church. Apparently, a young male member and some friends were having issues with another group of young men, who had decided to visit the church one

Sunday morning and settle their differences. There was a very disruptive presence inside during service followed by a fight outside after service. Some concerned members of the congregation, as well as the church pastor, even found themselves being verbally or physically assaulted. That was very sad for me to hear, especially since I have enjoyed attending service and other programs there from time to time. Then it was also saddening that I didn't find what happened to be that unbelievable, but just a sign of the times. *Respect* is to regard with difference and concern, and the respectful are dutiful, civil and obedient. Our youth certainly need to be taught that and have parents or others in their lives that can demonstrate how respectful people behave under different circumstances and towards each other. However, that can be said for some older folks as well.

God looked upon the children of Israel and had respect for them (*Exodus 2:25*). Solomon asked God to respect his prayer and his plea for mercy, to hear his cries and his prayer of dedication (*I Kings 8:28*). Aleph would not be ashamed in having respect for all of the Lord's commandments; as he learned the righteous laws, he would praise the Lord with an upright heart, and obey His statutes in not being forsaken (*Psalm 119:6-8*). The Lord has respect for the lowly, though he only knows the proud from afar (*Psalm 138:6*). *Proverbs 24:23-25* gives advice for the respect of others. For the wise, showing partiality in judging is not a good thing. One considering the guilty as being innocent will find themselves being cursed by others and denounced by nations. However, it will go well for those that convict the guilty, as they will be blessed richly. Further, giving the right answer is like a kiss on the lips for those that respect honesty (*verse 26*). Then *Isaiah 17:7* tells of a day that men will look to their Maker, and have the respect of the Lord in their eyes;

something we all face, whether we are headed for Heaven or Hell. Additionally, *James 2:1* says that the faithful aren't true believers of the Lord if they don't have a respect for others, and that respect should be for the rich and poor alike (*verses 3-4*).

Rest - *Rest* can be the refreshing quiet of sleep or the inactivity after any exertion or labor. The relief or freedom from anything that wearies, troubles, or disturbs is also rest, just as is the period of inactivity or solitude of getting away from it all. We all need some good rest, but at times it can be so hard because of our hectic daily schedules and the worries that go along with living. I am a hard and dedicated worker that will skip taking break periods or giving in to rest when really concentrating on getting an important job done during the day. Then if there is a lot on my mind, I may find myself awake at night, consumed in thought, rather than getting the proper rest and sleep that I so very need. However, I have found that I can rest my mind, body and soul just by taking a few minutes out of each day to communicate with God. Through Him is a mental and spiritual tranquility that re-energizes me in every way possible.

The Bible speaks much about rest. *Genesis 2:2* says that God completed His work on the seventh day, and then rested from all of His work in creating the heavens and the earth. God then declared that there would be a Sabbath (a weekly day of rest and worship) for His children to observe as a holy day; defiling (making filthy or impure) it would result in one's being put to death and those working would be cut off from among their people (*Exodus 31:14*). *Verses 15* and *16* say further that six days could be worked but none on the seventh day that would be the Sabbath to be observed throughout the generations for a lasting covenant. *Leviticus 25:1-4* also tells of there being a Sabbath year, rather than a weekly day. The Lord spoke to

Moses on Mount Sinai, instructing him to speak to the Israelites, telling them that, when they entered the land being given them, the land itself would have to observe a Sabbath to the Lord. For six years they could sow the fields, prune the vineyards, and gather in the fruits, but in the seventh year the land would be rested with there being no sowing or pruning.

Restoration - We all go through some times when we may need a restoration of our faith to get us back on track. Things just may not be going too well. There may be the loss of a job, car or home, financial difficulties, health concerns, stress and worry, a broken marriage… One may find them making one bad decision after another that may affect their own selves and others as well. Then there may become a lot of insensitivity, uncaring attitudes, and just some plain outright giving up, while turning away from God. However, in Him there can always be a happy ending no matter how bad things have developed. God will remain faithful if we place our trust in Him. You can be welcomed back and restored to a good place you were before and even far beyond, if you only have a restoration of your faith in God and yourself. Just remember that God never promised us to have lives without any adversity. His love and help is a promise to the faithful and the trusting though.

Throughout the Bible, there are stories of people turning away from the Lord our God and then returning, with Him standing ready to welcome them back in restoring a relationship with Him. The story of Jehoahaz, who reigned for seventy years on the throne of Israel, is one example, as he spent many years turning away from the Lord before having to seek His favor. *2 Kings 13:1-7* tells how he had done evil in the eyes of the Lord and Israel was delivered into the hands of Syria. However, when he turned back to the Lord, his prayers were listened to and there was a restoration of favor, as the Lord saw the oppression of Israel by the king of Syria. A savior, or an ally joining Jehoahaz's forces, was provided and they were able to escape from the Syrian's power. They began living well as they had once before, but later returned to the sins that had angered the Lord so much. As a result, the Lord's favor was again lost, and the king of Syria destroyed them, leaving Israel with a much smaller army for its defense. The Lord offers restoration for all. However, as in that story, it may not be permanent.

Resurrection - Harry Houdini, the magician, was born as Erik Weisz on March 24, 1874 in Budapest, Hungary. His grand illusions and daring, spectacular escape acts made him one of the most famous ever. He even performed a magic act where he would be buried alive underground without a casket. That almost cost him his life, on one occasion, as he found himself with limited air and totally exhausted while digging up through the dirt to freedom. However, apparently there were some that believed the *Man No Jail Could Hold* could indeed escape or rise from the dead. That's called *resurrection* and only God can perform that kind of magic. Yet, Houdini and his wife, Bess, even made a promise to each other that whoever died first would try to contact the other *from the other side.* Houdini died on October 31, 1926. Bess waited to hear from him for over 10 years but never heard a word. Houdini certainly had no power over his physical death in any way, as none of us do. God does give us the power, though, to resurrect our lives in spirit, faith and in other ways that we probably should do on a daily basis.

It's Jesus, not magic, that can offer life *from the other side,* so maybe Houdini was just hoping that the Lord would allow him to send a message back to his wife. *John 3:15-16* tells us of God's love for the world, and the giving of His one and only son. Then those believing in His son would not perish but have eternal (everlasting) life. Jesus was not sent to condemn the world but to save it through Him (*verse 17*). God is seeking worshippers that will be worthy of a resurrection in Heaven. *John 4:23* says that the time has come (then and now) when true worshippers will worship the Father in spirit and in truth, for they are the kind of worshippers that He seeks. Then *John 5:28-29,* also, tells of a time when all in their graves will hear the Lord's voice and come out. Those that have done good will rise to live (in Heaven) and those that have done evil will rise to be condemned (in Hell). I enjoy the words from a man in *Luke 14:15: Blessed is he that shall eat bread in the kingdom of God.* And, I certainly want my resurrection to be in Heaven.

Revelation - *Revelation* is the act of disclosing or divulging, and for Christians it's the revealing of God's divine truth. *The Revelation,* in the Bible, and said to have been authored by John the Apostle, is a book about *things revealed*. However, the purpose of the book has been greatly debated, as well as its authorship. Yet, as many still do, I stand behind John the Apostle and believe that Benjamin Breckinridge Warfield (Nov 5, 1851 - Feb 16, 1921), a professor of theology at the Princeton Seminary from 1887 to 1921, stated the purpose of the book very well in writing: "As the victory of Christ over the world is evidenced in the triumph of the kingdom of God which He came to establish, the theme of the book comes to be the gradual triumph of the kingdom of God; and as this triumph culminates in the second coming of Christ, it is the return of the Lord in glory to which all the movement of the book advances. It may thus be conceived as the bridge cast over the chasm which divides the first and second advents." Therefore, *The Revelation* is a book of victory, glory, and celebration.

The introduction for *The Revelation* in the Bible I read says the following: *As the book of Genesis gives the Creation story and, at the beginning, the first promise of the world's Savior, so the Revelation at the close of the Bible announces the end of the present order and sets forth the glory and majesty of Christ in His second coming. He came first in humiliation; He will come, the second time, in exaltation* (spiritual delight). *1 Peter 1:13* tells us to prepare our minds for action, be sober, and hope fully on the grace to be given us through the revelation of Jesus Christ. Plus, as it is written, we should be holy just as He is holy (*verse 16*). All nations will come and worship before Him because of His righteous acts being revealed (*Revelation 15:4*). God will wipe away all tears, as there will be no more death, mourning, crying or pain with the old order of things being passed away (*Revelation 21:4*). God will make all things new (*verse 5*), including the Heaven and the Earth but no sea (*verse 1*). Jesus is to be coming soon and he that keeps the prophecy of the *Book of Revelation* will be blessed (*Revelation 22:7*), in being rewarded according to what they have done (*verse 12*).

Revenge - I have always been pretty mild mannered and slow to anger. However, there are just some people that can drive any person beyond their limits of toleration. They can do some really hurtful and uncaring things that may have another seeking *revenge*, which is to repay the injury that has been inflicted upon you. I must admit to having had some physical and verbal confrontations over the years but never to the point of planning any type of retaliation beyond the initial conflicts. Getting even with revenge can be satisfying but it's easy to go overboard and end up doing something that may be later regretted. Far too many find themselves in prison, dead or facing other serious problems because of an act of revenge. The Bible tells us to forgive and forget but at times that is not always such an easy thing to do for some, especially when human emotions and quick tempers are involved, as in the case of road rage.

In *Jeremiah 15:15,* Jeremiah prays for the Lord to know him, remember him, visit him, and avenge him of his persecutors. He doesn't want to be taken away in the Lord's long-suffering and asks that it be known that it was for the Lord's sake that he has suffered rebuke (condemnation, insult, contempt...). *Verse 20* says that Jeremiah had heard the whispering of many, with terror on every side. Even all of his friends were waiting for him to slip, hoping that he could be deceived; so they could prevail over him and take their revenge out on him. However, Jeremiah believed that the Lord would be with him as his warrior. In that his persecutors would only stumble and not prevail, being greatly ashamed and not prospering, and with their dishonor never being forgotten (*verse 11*). Therefore, while Pashur, a priest and also chief governor in the house of the Lord, had sought to punish and destroy Jeremiah for his prophesies (*verses 1-2*), Jeremiah was prayerful that any type of revenge would be in his favor.

Righteousness - I have read that *righteousness* is an attribute implying that a person's actions are justified, and that the person is viewed as living a life pleasing to God. I have, also, read that the word appears in the Hebrew Bible more than five hundred times and in the New Testament over two hundred times. Therefore, it is very apparent that righteousness is a most important word for God and us all. In righteousness there is ethical conduct. Then in a legal sense, the guilty are judged, while the guiltless are viewed as being righteous. Then God's faithfulness to His covenant is viewed as being a large part of His righteousness. He is a righteous savior. I believe that I am living a life of righteousness. However, I do have my moments of weakness. If I find myself behaving badly, it may only be because I am just feeling badly about myself. Yet, as a righteous man, I believe that in God I'll be vindicated (defended).

Righteousness is a moral attribute of God. His work is with honor and glory, with His righteousness enduring forever (*Psalm 111:3*). Then with His righteousness being everlasting, His law is the truth (*Psalm 119:142*). Righteousness is, also, an attribute of Jesus that extends to us. God made Jesus who had no sin to be a sin for us, so that in Him we might become the righteousness of God. In that, there is the distinction of becoming a new person in Jesus. We are made alive in Him, and *Ephesians 22:10* says that we are God's workmanship, created in Christ Jesus to do good works, which God prepared in advance for us to do. We are made new in the attitudes of our minds, with a new self created to be like God in true righteousness and holiness (*Ephesians 4:23-24*). Then in being righteous, one is rewarded for their state of spiritual hunger. It is those who hunger and thirst after righteousness that are blessed and filled (*Matthew 5:6*). And in our righteousness, we should always be careful to obey God's law as He commands us to (*Deuteronomy 6:25*).

Risks - I am a risk taker but wonder what would have happened if I had just taken just a few more risks. Maybe I'd be working in another state now and not having all the worries and problems I have endured since losing my job here. Or had married the woman I had thoughts of moving away with a few years after the sad ending of my first marriage? Things may have worked out really well or maybe not. I just rejoice in all the great things that I am doing here in spite of where my risk taking could have landed me. My mother has certainly been blessed by my continued presence, and the many people I help through my volunteer work and spiritual offerings. Life is always a gamble but I had not heard the word from God that my moves would be blessed. I place my full trust in Him and believe that I will be a winner no matter the circumstances or the place, in spite of it all. He will tell me the right risks to take and those that are not.

Living a Christian life may require some risk taking. *Proverbs 3:5* tells us to trust in the Lord with all our hearts and to not lean on our own understanding. In acknowledging Him in all our ways, He will make our paths straight (*verse 6*). That may be risky thinking for some, but the wise will step out in faith and trust that the Lord will indeed lead them in the right directions. Also, risk takers may be rewarded for their faithfulness. In *Malachi 3:6-10,* God asks the people of Israel to take a risk in Him. He had turned away from them because they had turned away from Him and were not keeping His ordinances. Plus they were robbing God in not giving their tithes and offerings. Therefore, God offered a challenge through the prophet Malachi. If they would bring the whole tithe into a storehouse, so that there would be food in His house, He would throw open the floodgates of Heaven and pour out such a great blessing that they wouldn't have room for receiving it. All they had to do was to accept the risk of testing Him in having His promise fulfilled.

Rivers - When I was in high school, a semester of swimming was mandatory. However, there was some construction going on that cancelled my class. Later, it was on my schedule but the track coach had the school principal exclude me from it. He felt that his fastest runner could better spend his time training rather than in a pool of water. So, I never learned how to swim. Then one day I was at my senior picnic when I heard a lot of my classmates having fun down the side of a hill. Didn't know that there was a small lake below. When I went to take a look a buddy of mine snuck up behind and pushed me over into the water. Didn't know what to do! But I swam out like I had been swimming for years. And that's how God works. You may find yourself drowning in the rivers of life but He will provide you with the ability and strength to swim your way to safety.

Psalm 46:1-4 says that in God there is a river of confidence and safety. He is our refuge and strength, our ever-present help when we are in trouble. The earth may give way and the mountains may fall into the sea, but we have nothing to fear. Though the waters may be roaring and troubled, and the mountains shaking and swelling, there is a river whose streams bring joy to the city of God, the holy place where the Most High dwells. God is within her and she will not fall; He will be her help at the break of day (*verse 5*), just as He can always be for us. He can end all wars, break bows, shatter spears, burn shields with fire (*verse 9*); and certainly calm the raging rivers of our lives. All we have to do is be still and know that He is God; exalted among the nations and in the Earth (*verse 10*). He is among us and is our refuge (*verse 11*); no matter how many rivers we may find ourselves swimming out of.

Roads - After my marriage, our honeymoon was to be spent at the Pocono Resorts in the mountains of Pennsylvania. We hit the road that night, from Detroit, and I figured the trip would take about 12 to 14 hours. I drove and drove thinking that I was headed in the right direction. Even saw a sign that indicated so. Yet, I was so wrong! Hours later I headed down what I thought to be the final stretch of our destination, and did see some mountains, but just not the right ones. I forget the state but there were some houses on the sides of these mountains like those I had only seen on television. Knew then that something was very wrong. Stopped at a gas station and showed an attendant my directions. Found out that I had made a wrong turn somewhere in Ohio and driven many miles out of the way, for a road that had the same name as the one I was looking for. He gave us the right directions and we headed back out, reaching the Pocono's over a day late. Now isn't that a way God works? You may find yourself on the wrong road of life but, if you call on Him, He can provide the directions for you to get back on the right one.

God counsels us and will lead us down the right roads. *Psalm 32:8* says that He will instruct us and tell us which way to go, in counseling and watching over us. We don't have to be like the horse or mule that have no understanding, and must have their mouths controlled by bit and bridle in coming to you (*verse 9*). Then *1 Samuel 27:10* describes a road in terms of invasion, as they were necessary for trade, communication, and military purposes. Roads were, also, built for leading to cities of refuge (*Deuteronomy 19:3*), and we may all find ourselves seeking that kind of road from time to time. The road leads to God for everyone who is godly and prays to Him, as they may not reach Him when the mighty waters rise; He is our hiding place that will protect us from trouble, and surround us with songs of deliverance (*Psalm 32:6-7*). Therefore, while the Bible views roads mostly in terms of commerce, like the ones that helped Egypt carry on their extensive commercial relations with other nations during early times, the most important roads are those that lead to God and the ones that He will lead us down.

Roles - *Roles* are a display of our character and an indication of our duties and responsibilities, and we may become set in one or another based upon different factors. There may be a *societal influence* where a person's role is formed based on the social situations that were chosen; like parents enrolling their children in certain programs at a young age. Then there is *genetic predisposition* where people take on roles that come naturally to them; a person with athletic ability becoming an athlete for example. Next there is *cultural influence* where a different culture may place a different value on certain roles. There was a time, for example, that soccer players weren't highly regarded in the United States because soccer was far less popular here than in other countries. Another thing could be a *situational influence* where a person's role is created or changed based on the situations they are placed in that are outside of their own influence; like the son becoming man of the house when the father has passed away. All said, people might usually have multiple roles for one reason or another. However, the most important are those that are set before us by God.

God chooses each of us for different roles. *Ephesians 4:11-16,* for example, says that He called on some to be apostles, some to be prophets, some to be evangelists, and some to be pastors and teachers, to prepare God's people for works of service as saints. In that, the body of Jesus may be built up until we all come in the unity of the faith and in the knowledge of the Son of God in becoming mature and attaining to the whole measure of the fullness of Jesus. Then we would no longer be children, tossed back and forth by the waves, and blown here and there by every wind of teaching by the tricks and shill of the cunning and crafty men that only lie in wait to deceive others. Instead, in speaking the truth in love, we will in all things grow up into Him, which is the head, even Jesus. Therefore, one of the roles that we have for each other is love, especially in our honesty. Plus through working as a team, from whom the whole body, joined and held together by every supporting ligament, grows and builds itself up in love, as each person does their work. In our roles as Christians, God desires for us to be imitators of Him, as dearly loved children, living lives of love, just as Jesus loved us and gave His life for us (*Ephesians 5:1-2*).

Rules - *Rules* can be established working principals and laws, or guides for moral conduct. The *Ten Commandments* are an example of rules. God knew that His people needed rules to live well, and each commandment reflects an element of our sinful nature that we have trouble controlling. While some of man's rules may seem to have been arbitrarily made to control us and take the fun out of life, God's aren't. Following His rules wholeheartedly, with no questions asked, leads to life.

Psalm 119:33-40 presents a great prayer concerning God's rules. The writer, *He,* asks God to teach him His rules and laws, and he would keep them to the end. He sought understanding and would keep the law and obey it with all his heart. In being directed in the path of God's commands, he would find delight. His heart would be turned towards God's statutes and not toward selfish gain. He, also, wanted to be turned away from the disgrace he dreaded, as he saw God's rules and laws as being good and longed for, to preserve his life in righteousness.

Sacrifice - Life means *sacrifice*. There are times that we may just have to go without something in favor of something more important; like the time I had to give up my basketball playing because the choir I joined had their rehearsals on the same Tuesday nights that we usually played. Then as a parent, I often had to make different sacrifices of myself for the love and benefit of my wife and children. Likewise, we should all be willing to make sacrifices for God and place Him first, serving Him wholeheartedly. No matter the positions we hold at home, work, public or church, God should be represented in any way that He wishes for us to serve Him. We can view our whole lives as being a sacrifice to God, while still enjoying all the great things He offers to us for our love and obedience in Him. No matter what we do, each day we can honor Him with our attitudes, effort, enthusiasm, and through our sacrifices.

Romans 12:1-2 urges us, by the mercies of God, to offer our bodies as living sacrifices, holy and pleasing to Him, as our spiritual acts of worship. We should not fashion ourselves according to the world, but be transformed by the renewing of our minds, in being able to test and approve of the good, acceptable and perfect will of God. Then over the course of our lives we can view ourselves as having been an asset for Him, as did Timothy, the apostle. According to *2 Timothy 4:6,* as he expected to die at the hands of the Roman Empire, Timothy wrote that he was ready to be offered (sacrificed) and that the time of his departure was near. He says that he had fought a good fight and finished his course, in keeping the faith (*verse 7*). On his final day, he expected to receive the crown of righteousness from the Lord, the righteous judge, as would all who love His appearance. So, through our love, good works and sacrifices, we can expect to receive the same even today too.

Salvation - *Salvation* is the act of saving or protecting one from harm, risk, loss, destruction, and etc., and in religion is the saving of one's soul from sin and its consequences, which may also be called *deliverance* or *redemption* from sin and its effects. From my understanding, man was separated from God through sin when Adam and Eve rebelled, and His holiness required punishment and payment for their sin, which was and is eternal death. Then biblical salvation became God's way of providing His people deliverance from sin and spiritual death. While in the *Old Testament* salvation concerned Israel's deliverance from Egypt, the source of salvation in the *New Testament* is in Jesus Christ. We are saved from sin and eternal death by our faith in Him, and that requires each person to map out a road for their salvation. One must admit that they are a sinner, understand that they deserve death for being a sinner, believe that Jesus Christ died on the cross to save them from sin and death, repent by turning to a new life in Jesus from their old life of sin, and then receive the gift of salvation through their faith in Jesus.

In the Bible, I have read a number of verses in *Romans* that have greatly encouraged me in planning my own personal journey to salvation. I understand that no person is righteous, not even one (*3:10*), as all sin and fall short of the glory of God (*3:23*). However, while the wages of sin is death, we can have the gift of eternal life from God through a life in Jesus Christ our Lord (*6:23*). God has demonstrated His love for us, in that while we were (and remain) sinners, Jesus died for us all (*5:8*). All we have to do is confess with our mouths that Jesus is Lord, and believe in our hearts that God raised Him from the dead, to be saved (*10:9*), for it is with one's heart that they are justified and with their mouths that they confess and are saved (*10:10*). And there is no difference or distinction between people, as all who call upon the Lord will be saved, in having the same Lord that richly blesses us all (*10:12-13*). There is life through the Spirit, as there is no condemnation for those in Christ Jesus, who walk after the Spirit and not after the flesh (*8:1*). And I believe whole-heartedly that through Christ Jesus, the law of the Spirit of life will set me free from the law of sin and death (*8:2*).

Satisfaction - Mick Jagger and the Rolling Stones have a song called *I Can't Get No Satisfaction,* and I must admit that there are times that I don't feel much satisfied at all. There are just so many things that I want to do before my life here on Earth is over. I surely have a few struggles to be worked out. However, God is still blessing me, as He gives us what we need and deserve most. He frowns upon the selfish and the greedy, and there are certainly some people that desire to acquire far too much beyond what they really need. I may find myself struggling from time to time, but God always provides me with enough to sustain myself until things get better, which He won't do for those that have lost His favor. Surely God wants us all to accomplish and acquire more than we could ever imagine, but only through His grace and will. He expects us to be totally satisfied with the blessings that He grants us. So while I may feel unsatisfied, in my mind, at any given time, I am also satisfied, in my heart, because I am receiving all that God has for me at that time. Then by being obedient and serving, through my faith and deeds, I know that all I do and receive will become totally satisfying for God, myself, and those I bless.

With *Psalm 17:15,* David, son of Jesse and one of the greatest men in the Bible, tells God, that in righteousness, he would see His face, when he awoke, and would be satisfied in seeing God's likeness, as I feel so strongly in the same way. Then *Psalm 22:26* says that the poor will eat and be satisfied: they who seek the Lord and praise Him, as their hearts live forever. But, even as I am not doing as well as I once was, I still feel that I am rich in the Spirit of the Lord. No matter what I am going through, I know that the Lord will always feed me and satisfy me with the bread of Heaven (*Psalm 105:40*). However, there are just so many that speak wrongly in their labor, with eyes not satisfied with seeing or their ears being filled with hearing (*Ecclesiastes 1:8*). For me, I desire a long life to satisfy God and show Him my salvation as *Psalm 91:16,* in my desire to do so much to His satisfaction. I want to be satisfied each morning with His unfailing love, that I may sing for joy and be glad all of my days (*Psalm 90:14*). Most of all, I am most confident and satisfied in knowing that God will always go before me and be with me, never leaving me or forsaking me and, in that respect, I will have no good reason for ever feeling afraid or discouraged, (*Deuteronomy 31:8*); or even dissatisfied.

Seasons - Many view seasons as being spring, summer, fall and winter. However, they are also defined as being any kind of time period. As such, each person may experience a varying number of seasons over the course of his or her lives, beyond those that just divide each year up. For example, on this day in the winter of 2011, I am enduring a season of much uncertainty, worries and unhappiness, along with the cold and snow. With the continued poor job market and economy in our country, I like many others have really been struggling to get by. And there are times that I feel so alone as I fight my battles. We have our good and bad seasons and through them all we have to maintain our trust and faith in God. *Luke* tells how the devil departed for a season when he was unable to tempt the Lord with power and glory. We need to always be strong like Jesus during our times of adversity. Too many just give up or do some things that they could never be tempted to do in the past. I continue to be patient and obedient, as I know that there are some great seasons ahead. God has a plan and I'm sure that I'll be celebrating soon as things turn around for the better. I am most confident that, through God's love, care and guidance, many seasons of joy, contentment and success are forthcoming.

My desire is to be as the man described according to *Psalm 1:3*. I would be like a tree planted by the rivers of water, bringing forth my fruit of the season, with my leaves never withering and whatever I do prospering. And I'd have joy from the answers of my mouth, with my words spoken in due season, for the good of it all, for others and myself (*Proverbs 15:23*). I certainly believe that I could be a burning and shining light, and being most willing for a season to rejoice in the light, as with *John 5:35*. Then distancing myself from man's world, as *Hebrews 11:25* encourages me to suffer with the people of God, rather than enjoying the pleasures of sin for a season. Therefore, it is most important for a person to be with God, and not stray away for any season for any reason. God designated that there would be seasons for days and for years (*Genesis 1:14*), and declared to Noah that the Earth would remain, through seedtime, harvest, cold, heat, summer, winter, day, and the night (*8:22*). However, it's a great thing that the devil was not included in that plan, and even had to depart for a season. *Luke 4:12-13* says that he went away upon finding the Lord could not be tempted by him in any way. So, in spite of the devil's evil intentions, Jesus returned to Galilee, in the power of the Spirit, as the news about Him spread across the whole countryside (*verse 14*).

Security - We all may find ourselves being victims of misplaced trust, in believing that our security is there when it isn't. The only real security is in God, and it is in Him that we should place our trust. Our cars get stolen with burglar alarms installed in them. Our homes get broken in to no matter how much we pay for steel bars and security systems. Our bank accounts become overdrawn even with overdraft protection. Our best investments result in no profitable returns. Our great jobs end in company layoffs. Our marriages end in divorce. Our good health fades with age. Our peace of mind becomes stress and worry. I could just go on and on. Security? There is no such thing unless it is with God. He can make even the most insecure situations secure if you place your confidence and faith in Him. People often assume that they have security but are often wrong in thinking in the ways of man, rather than in the ways of true believers. God is my security and has come to my rescue on many occasions, in answering my prayers.

Security means not being exposed to danger, and there is indeed security in God. *2 Chronicles 16:9* says that the eyes of the Lord range throughout the world in providing strength (security) for those whose hearts are perfect towards Him. David said that the Lord was a shield for him (security); his glory and the lifter of his head (*Psalm 3:3*). The angel of the Lord encamps around those that fear Him, and He delivers them, as one can taste that the Lord is good, with those being blessed that trust in Him (*Psalm 34:8-9*). That most certainly is security. *Psalm 91:11-12* says that the Lord will command His angels concerning us, and they will guard us in all our ways, lifting us up in their hands, making sure that we will not strike our feet against any stones (security). Also, *Psalm 125:2* says that just as the mountains surrounded Jerusalem, the Lord would surround His people both then and forevermore (security). Then *Proverbs 3:6* says that in acknowledging the Lord in all our ways, He will direct our paths (security).

Self-Destruction - I read somewhere that *self-destruction* (sabotaging, punishing, or harming one's self) was one of seven basic flaws of character or negative personality traits. The others are: *self-depreciation* (belittling, diminishing, or undervaluing one's self), *martyrdom* (reacting as being persecuted, victimized, or oppressed), *stubbornness* (resisting change in one's life), *greed* (selfish overindulgence or over-consumption), *arrogance* (inflating, exalting, or overvaluing one's self), and *impatience* (excessive eagerness or restless anticipation), with all seven of the listed flaws being much displeasing to God. We all have the potential for behaving in a self-destructive manner, but it can become quite a dangerous thing when it begins to dominate a person's personality. Self-destructive people can be really self-serving, demanding, and very quick tempered, to the point that they may hurt themselves and others, if they blow up and lose it all, or have their own agendas placed before a group of misguided and unsuspecting followers. Also, in considering themselves as being in charge, even over God, they are only cut off from Him. We must walk humbly and obediently with God to receive our blessings and proper direction.

Korah, a son of Esah, found himself being a victim of his own self-destruction. He, along with Abiram, Dathan, and On, had conspired against Moses and Aaron. With them were also two hundred-fifty Israelite men, well-known community leaders who had been appointed members of the council (*Numbers 16:1-2*). Moses and Aaron were told that they had gone too far, and that they had set themselves above the Lord's assembly. The whole community was holy and the Lord was with those that were opposed to Moses and Aaron (*verse 3*). However, Korah was wrong. Moses ordered the people to leave the area where Korah and his followers had their tents. Then at that spot the earth opened and swallowed up the conspirators, with the two hundred-fifty men being devoured by fire (*Numbers 26:10*). The problem was that Moses focused on God and His people, but Korah placed everyone at risk in only being out to get what he thought he deserved, and in wanting more recognition. He had gone against God's explicit directives and paid the price for it. In being self-seeking, insolent, and arrogant, Korah headed down the path of self-destruction, as he had attempted to place himself in charge over God.

Selfishness - *Selfishness* may be seen as the harming of someone else in order to help oneself, while God desires for us to be the opposite, or *altruistic,* which is the harming of oneself in order to help someone else. He wants us to be givers more than receivers, and especially when it comes to the church. However, I read something quite interesting about selfishness that appeared in an article for *Christianity Today* on September 2, 1988. A non-profit research and service organization in Champaign, Illinois did a survey of 31 denominations to contrast changes in per-member giving patterns with changes in U.S. per-capita disposable income from 1968 to 1985. Their finding was that 24 of the denominations showed a decrease in giving of 8.5 percent as a percentage of disposable income, even though income after taxes and inflation had increased 31 percent over the time period studied. Therefore, people were richer but selfishly giving less to their churches. I wonder what a new study today would reveal?

The Bible says much about selfishness. It is one of the works of the flesh *(Galatians 5:20),* leads to disorder and every evil practice *(James 3:16),* caused the children of Israel to willfully put God to the test in demanding the food they craved *(Psalm 78:18)*, caused a rich young ruler to turn his back on Jesus *(Matthew 19:21-22)*, ruins friendships *(Proverbs 18:1)*, hinders prayer *(James 4:3)*, a product of earthly wisdom *(James 3:13-14)*... When God asked Cain about the whereabouts of his brother Abel, who he had slain, Cain responded that he knew not and asked the question, *Am I my brother's keeper?* He most certainly could have been, as God desires for us not to be selfish towards one another. *Matthew 5:42* instructs us to give to those that ask us, and to not turn away from those that want to borrow from us. We should unselfishly do good, and carry each other's burdens in fulfilling the law of Jesus *(Galatians 6:2)*. Our hearts should also be turned to His statutes and not toward selfish gain (*Psalm 119:36*), and that would include the giving of tithes and greater offerings when blessed with additional income.

Self-reliance - I hear people say that they don't have to rely on any one for any thing, which I don't think is ever possible. Just think of a time, for example, when your car broke down and you had no choice but to call on a mechanic. Many think that they are now living in a do-it-yourself world, and I have often heard that if you want to have something done right it's best to do it yourself. However, that kind of attitude doesn't work for everything, especially when it concerns God, Trying to be overly self-reliant may only cause a separation from Him. We just can't call on God in our own way and in our own time, and only when the need arises. He must be a constant in our lives, as we may behave as if we are God, but surely we aren't. Self-reliant people may also even create their own gods, ones that they can control, like their pocketbooks when they are doing well, which may only lead to the sins of greed, selfishness, or other things. God doesn't frown upon some self-reliance and independence though, as long as it doesn't exclude Him.

Exodus 32:7-10 tells how God was going to destroy the people of Israel because they had corrupted themselves and turned away from what He had commanded them. They had even made a molten cow that they were worshipping and sacrificing to as their god. God described them as being *stiffnecked people*, which self-reliant people often are. He planned to dispose of them and create a great nation. *Jeremiah 32:33* tells of the people turning their backs to God and not their faces. Though He had taught them again and again, they would not listen or respond to instruction, in going their own way. The story of *Ezekiel* tells how we may need help on the battlefield, whether we want to admit it or not. God placed him on guard to stand watch over Israel, just as we need friends who care about us to stand watch in our lives. True friends won't tell us just what we want to hear, but also what we need to hear. They can be counted on to offer words of hope when things aren't going too well, and even fight alongside a person during their battles. Then, more importantly, if you try to go it too alone in your self-reliance, they will help guide you back to God rather than away from Him.

Separation - There was a time when things just weren't going very well for me. Just had a number of financial and emotional problems that I was trying to overcome, that I really didn't want anyone to know much about. I began keeping a lot to myself, from my family, friends, and even my church. Plus, in feeling that my prayers weren't being answered, I stopped praying. So, my attitude was causing a separation from people and God, when I should have been drawing nearer to them. With people, it was just my pride in not wanting others to know how things had gone from good to bad for me. With God, I just needed a renewal of my faith. I knew that He hadn't really turned His back on me but was too stubborn to turn to Him as I had in the past. Just seemed determined to try winning the battles on my own. However, my separation from the world and God only led to loneliness, additional stress and worry, health issues, and thoughts of just completely giving up, as things weren't getting any better or moving too slowly. Knew then that it was time to especially renew my relationship with God, before it was too late, and mend a few fences with some people that wouldn't give up on me, as I appeared to have done.

Joshua was appointed to succeed Moses, after his death, and in *Joshua 1:5-7,* God assures him that there would be no separation between the people of Israel and Him caused by the change of leadership. They would still be able to cross the Jordan River into the land He was giving the Israelites, every place where they set their feet, as He had promised Moses. Plus He would protect the people against all that stood up against them for all the days of their life. God would be with them, never fail them, and never forsake them. In being prosperous and successful wherever they were, they just had to be strong and courageous, in being careful to obey the law that Moses had given them, with no turning from it to the right or to the left (*verse 7*). *James 4:7-8* tells us to submit ourselves to God and resist the devil, who will separate himself from you by flight. Us sinners and double-minded should cleanse our hands and purify our hearts, for in drawing near to Him, He will draw near to us (*verse 9*). Also, *1Peter 5:8* tells us to be self-controlled and alert in keeping our separation from the devil. He prowls around, as a roaring lion, seeking to devour any person he can. In being steadfast in our faith, we can maintain our separation from him, as can our brothers throughout the world (*verse 9*).

Servants - As I began this writing, on the afternoon of December 14, 2012, I decided to turn on the television next to my computer for a few minutes, only to see a news alert that, at an elementary school in Connecticut, 26 people had been killed by a 20 year-old gunman, including 20 children between the ages of five and ten years old, after already having killed his own mother, who owned the guns used, in their family home. Unbelievable! As are all reports of that nature. Just seems that there are a lot of people out there with some serious issues, to the point that they would even want to end their lives, and take others along with them. It appears that the devil is still out there actively recruiting servants that would do such horrendous things, as reports indicate that church rolls continue to decrease.

Then in many cases, there is only speculation as to *why* a person did what they did, upon that person having taken their own life or having been killed by law enforcement officials. The dead surely can't speak and explain their actions, and the devil can be most wise in choosing his servants, recruiting those that may be really down on themselves and the world for one reason or another, and living without God. Of course, it could be attributed to a mental illness, although some are still able to devise some really elaborate plans for their destruction and evilness, but only God could know for sure, beyond even the greatest of psychologists. I think of the killers that have lived, only to claim of hearing voices instructing them to kill, which certainly are not the words of my God to any of His servants.

True servants of God do as He instructs them to do, as Elijah the prophet attested of himself, according to *1 Kings 18:36*, and God never instructs His servants to do anything of a wrongful nature. Certainly, He has sent servants off to war, where many have died, but for a worthy cause, and never for senseless murder. Elijah proclaimed that he was a servant of God and had done all things according to His word. In *Ezra 5:11,* it was declared that the people were servants of the God of Heaven and Earth. They were rebuilding a temple that had been built many years before, that a great king of Israel had built and set up. However, because their fathers had provoked God to wrath, they were delivered into the hands of enemies, who destroyed the temple (*verse 12*). Therefore, it is not enough for a person to just say that they are servants of God. They must prove that they are *true* servants to be deserving of His blessings. Nebuchadnezzar, a king of Babylon, had three of God's servants thrown into a blazing furnace, in being angered with Shadrach, Meshach, and Abednego, because they worshipped God and not Him. However, when he looked into the furnace he saw a fourth man with them, with his form being like the Son of God (*Daniel 3:25*). He then called for the servants of the most high God to come out, which they did, showing no signs of the fires having harmed their bodies, singed the hair on their heads, scorched their robes, or even the smell of fire upon them (*verses 26-27*). So, they were surely true servants of God and He rescued them because of that.

Shelter - Many think of shelter as only being a roof over one's head. However, having shelter can mean a number of other things, like feeling secure and confident when the storms of your life rage on. There are times that just an encouraging word may provide us with a bit of shelter when things aren't going very well, or a broken heart needs mending and reassurance. The greatest shelters aren't built of wood, brick and other construction materials, but upon a strong foundation of faith. A tornado may destroy your home but doesn't have to destroy your hope or spirit, if you trust God for your shelter. Just when things seem to be at their darkest, He can let the light shine in.

Isaiah 4:2-6 tells of a day that the Lord's kingdom would become the people of Jerusalem's sanctuary. On that day, the branch of the Lord would be beautiful and glorious, and the fruit of the land would be the pride and glory for the survivors in Israel. It would come to pass that those left in Zion, and those remaining in Jerusalem, would be called holy, all who were recorded among the living in Jerusalem. The Lord was to wash away the filth from the daughters of Zion, and wash away the bloodstains from Jerusalem, by the spirit of judgment and burning. Then upon every residence of mount Zion, there was to be created clouds and smoke by the day, and a shining, flaming fire by night, to act as a canopy of glory. The people would have shelter and shade from the heat of day, and a refuge and hiding place from storm and rain.

Sin - *Sin* is the violation of an accepted moral, religious, or social code, and Christianity says that there are sins that are worse to commit than others, with seven considered to be the most deadly. Those sins, called the *seven deadly sins,* aren't recorded in a list or referred to as such in the Bible, but the Scripture validates the concept. Pope Gregory I is named to have first compiled the list around the year 600. So, there was no such list anywhere before the *Ten Commandments*, which were given at Mt. Sinai around 1450 B.C. However, it has been said and probably true that they were used to teach the principles of God back then, when the Bible was not available for the common man to read and study. Gregory listed the sins as being *pride, covetousness* (greed), *lust, anger* (wrath), *gluttony, envy,* and *sloth.* At the same time, he also compiled a list of seven virtues: *faith, hope, charity, justice, prudence, temperance,* and *fortitude.*

All unrighteousness is considered as being *sin (1 John 5:17)*, and whoever sins breaks the law because sin is the transgression of the law *(1 John 3:4)*. There is no man that doesn't sin *(1 Kings 8:46)*, as all have sinned and fallen short of the glory of God *(Romans 3:23)*. In saying that we don't sin is just the deceiving of one's self, with no truth being in us *(1 John 1:8)*. *Ezekiel 18:4* then says that in all souls belonging to the Lord, the souls of sinners shall die, for out of the hearts of sinners come things like *evil thoughts, murders, adulteries, fornications, thefts, false witness,* and *blasphemies (Matthew 15:19)*. However, in confessing our sins, God, being faithful and just, will forgive us of our sins, cleansing us from all unrighteousness *(1 John 1:9)*. Therefore, we must repent and change our lives to be saved from our sins (*Acts 3:19*). The only unpardonable sin, according to the Bible with *Matthew 12:31*, is the blasphemy (cursing, swearing, abusing, denouncing...) against the Holy Ghost (Spirit).

Skies - I love walking out to a bright blue sunny sky, and it feels as if a few clouds are just smiling down on me at times. However, it doesn't bother me much if it's really cloudy, with thunder and lightning, and the rains just pouring down heavily on me, for I know that God has a good reason for both. Nature requires our skies to behave in different ways for our survival. Just think about how the unusually warm winters and record setting hot dry summers, in some states recently, have affected many crops. Sun and rain are surely equally important in God's creation. But, no matter what I see in the skies, I often gaze faithfully upward and envision my new life and my new home up in God's Heaven, where we never have to worry or have any concerns about what the skies here may have in store for us.

In the Bible, the *skies* are referred to as a *firmament,* the expanse of space surrounding the Earth, which includes everything between the Earth and the stars. *Psalm 104:2* and *Isaiah 40:22* compare it to a tent being spread out above the Earth with God being clothed in splendor and majesty, while *Job 37:18* describes the skies as being like a mirror. Then the skies were spoken of as having doors and windows. *Genesis 7:11* says that in the six hundredth year of Noah's life, in the second month, on the seventeenth day of the month, the windows of Heaven were opened. In *2 Kings 7:2,* the possibilities were questioned for if God was to make windows in Heaven. *Psalm 78:22-23* tells of there not being a belief in God or a trust in His salvation by the Israelites, even though

God had commanded the clouds from above and opened the doors of Heaven.

Sloth - *Sloth* is defined as laziness, idleness, and the wastefulness of time that a person has. It's hated because others may have to work harder and it delays what God wants a person to do or finding them not doing it at all. Then it makes life harder for the person as an individual because useful work fails to be done. Like gluttony, sloth is considered as being a sin of waste, mostly time, and it may be because of one's pride. However, while that person may not produce much, they may not need much either. Also, in the theology of Dante (Durante degli Alighieri 1265 - 1321) *sloth* was said to be the *failure to love God with all one's heart, all one's mind, and all one's soul,* with examples including *being lazy, being scared, lack of imagination, complacency,* and *not doing what the person should do.*

Proverbs 18:19 describes a slothful person as being a brother to one who destroys in great waste. *Proverbs 24:30-34* then provides words of wisdom concerning slothfulness. Solomon, the writer, tells of passing by the field of the slothful and the vineyard of a man with no understanding. Thorns and weeds covered the land, with a stone wall broken down. Upon his observation, he learned a lesson from what he saw. With just a little sleep, a little slumber, and a little folding of the hands for rest, poverty may come on you like a robber and in wanting like an armed man. *Romans 12:11* says that we should never be slothful in business, but always be fervent in our spirit in serving the Lord. We should rejoice in hope, be patient in tribulation, pray steadfastly, distribute to the necessity of saints, and be given to hospitality (*verses 12-13*), which requires a person to be active and have a willingness to do some work.

Smiles - The world may be crumbling around me but I still usually have the strength to return any smile that is given me, though some may not return mine. I won't list them, but I read that there were 19 variations of the smile, with 16 being produced by enjoyable emotions, meaning that people mostly smile when they are feeling good, which is most understandable. Then I read many claims that it takes more muscles to produce a frown than a smile, with a 1931 book claiming there were 50 muscles for a frown and only 13 for a smile. So smiling may also be a much easier and healthier task. Another most interesting thing I read was that some biologists believe the smile originated as a sign of fear, with Primalogist Signe Preushoft (a woman whose studies go back to the mid 1990's), tracing the smile back over 30 million years and telling of a *fear grin* that monkeys and apes used, with barely clinched teeth, in portraying to their predators that they were harmless. However, a smile or not for whatever reason, I always try my best to give genuine smiles rather than fake ones, along with distancing myself from those that seem to enjoy making others frown, in their own misery.

All said, and just plain unpleasant personalities aside, most smile when they are happy with their lives, while it can be a most difficult task to muster up a few smiles when things aren't going as well as one would like. Happiness is having God by you, with His help and His hope (*Psalm 146:5*), as well as the finding of wisdom and understanding (*Proverbs 3:13)* from his relationship with God. Then in being blessed by God, He will correct us, and we should never despise the discipline of the Almighty (*Job 5:17*). Therefore if you are feeling a bit down, don't be surprised if God encourages you towards a much happier disposition. As *Acts 26:2,* I consider myself happy, and most fortunate to have a God that will always listen to me, as I answer for anything that has been troubling me. And I am all the more happier if I am suffering for righteousness, without being afraid of anyone's terror, or the least bit troubled, as with *1 Peter 3:14*. *James 5:11* counts them as being happy and blessed for their endurance, through all that confronts them. Just as with the patience of Job, we may find ourselves being able to smile beyond any situation because of God's compassion and mercy. So, the best smiles are those that He delivers.

Soldiers - I was never a member of any U.S. Military service, as I was not drafted heading into the end of the Vietnam War. However, I did pursue some career opportunities with the Navy after my graduation from college. Then, I am most proud that my oldest son, Raymond, did enter into the Navy, and was onboard the USS John C. Stennis, a nuclear-powered aircraft carrier, during the early years of the Afghanistan War, beginning in 2001. He served admirably and in honor of his country, just as his father would have. But our wars don't just extend beyond our shores or are limited to the Army, Navy, Air Force, or Marines. With all the crime, murder, drugs, poverty, unemployment, broken homes, hopelessness, and more that we see so often these days, we need many dedicated soldiers right here too, especially God-serving warriors that can be sent out on missions of leadership, encouragement, witnessing, mentoring, charity, and other things.

We should be in the grace that is in Jesus Christ (*2 Timothy 2:1*) and endure our hardships in being His good soldiers (*verse 3*). Then in being chosen as His soldiers, we should do what is pleasing to Him (*verse 4*) under His command. As Christian soldiers we should be strong in the Lord and in the power of His might, putting on our whole armor of God in taking a stand against the wiles (trickery) of the devil (*Ephesians 6:10-11*), as we wrestle against not flesh and blood, but against the rulers, authorities, and powers causing darkness in our world (*verse 12),* including our enemies from overseas and those right here at home, along with being against the spiritual forces of evil in heavenly places (*verse 12*). In being fully armored by God, when the days of evil come, us soldiers are able to stand our ground, upon having done everything to stand (*verse 13*), with our belts of truth buckled around our waists and our breastplates of righteousness in place (*verse 14*), among our other pieces of important spiritual armor.

Songs - I have written a number of songs that I have sung at different churches, with or without being accompanied by any musicians. Many times, I am asked to sing during a program and just get up and sing from my heart, prepared or not. When I first overcame my fear and began singing some of my own songs acappella, it would really impress my oldest son because he said that I was the only one brave enough to get up and do what I did. Raymond said that the music could cover up the mistakes that other singers made but everyone would hear mine. My answer was that no one would know mine because I wrote the words. Plus in relying on my heart more than my memory, the Spirit often leads me. However, I wasn't always that brave. My confidence in singing grew right along with the growth in my spiritual faith. I once told my choir that I would never sing by myself in front of anyone. Hard to believe that now when I am up singing my songs and others. Plus there was little purpose in writing songs of praise that weren't being heard, as I had done for quite some time.

Just as many in the Bible, peculiar circumstances have provided the motivation for most of my songs, so there is a great amount of significance in each one. A great example is Moses and the children of Israel singing a song of deliverance (*Exodus 15:1-19*). They had been caught between the pursuing Egyptian chariots and the Red Sea, before they were miraculously saved with the Egyptians perishing in the waters, and them being sent off on dry land in the midst of the sea. In the song they sing of their triumph in being rescued by the Lord. He was their strength, their song, their God, and they were exalting Him for His greatness. In another song, (*Deuteronomy 32:1-43*), Moses describes God as the *Rock,* after they were delivered from the forty years of wandering in the wilderness. God's work was perfect and in all His ways were judgment, in being a God of truth and righteousness, without iniquity. In being their *Rock,* he was being compared with the rock of their enemies, whom they had trusted as their gods in vain. Then an example of mine is a song about my struggles and how, in spite of them and what others may say or think, I am *still a black man with the Lord*, will always be, and exalt Him for my deliverance from many things and paving the road for my salvation.

Sorrow - *Sorrow* is defined as being sadness or grief, and in first thinking back over the year, on this last day of 2012, it was with a bit of sorrow. They say that the economy is becoming a little better, but it remains a difficult task for many of us older Americans to find suitable employment, as in my case. So, I still have my financial concerns. Then it was a fairly lonely year for me in many ways, without enjoying the steady companionship of a woman in my life, not seeing my grandchildren as much, rarely communicating with some of my old friends, and having lost some loved ones in death. However, when I think further, it is without sorrow. I can see the many ways that God was blessing me and I myself was a blessing to quite a number of people through my volunteer and Christian work. Then in experiencing good health presently, maybe my year wasn't that bad after all. With a few prospects already, along with my continued work benefiting others, I am most optimistic about 2013 being a year of much joy and success, with little sorrow, beyond the unexpected.

Just as with the people of Israel, when they were held hostage in Egypt, God has seen my affliction, heard my cries, and knows my sorrow (*Exodus 3:7*). He promised that He would come down and deliver them out of the hand of Egypt and to a better land filled with blessings (*verse 8*), and I know that He will do the same for me in delivering me away from my troubles to the peace, love and security that I have been seeking. I know that God will preserve me, if it is in Him that I place my trust (*Psalm 16:2*), and know that my sorrows will only be multiplied in placing my trust in something other than Him (*verse 4*). Therefore, I praise Him that counsels me, as even at night my heart instructs me (*verse 7*). He is always set before me as my right hand of security (*verse 9*), with there being no sorrow in my heart because I can rejoice with my body resting in hope and dwelling in safety (*verse 9*), knowing that He will never abandon me during my times of trouble (*verse 10*). Further, I know that a merry heart shows on my face, while sorrow will only break my spirit (*Proverbs 15:13*).

Soul - The *soul* is the animating and vital principal in us, which are evident in our thoughts, actions, and emotions, and also conceived as being our spiritual being. It is regarded as being immortal, separable from our bodies at death, and susceptible to happiness or misery in a future state, that us Christians view as Heaven or Hell. The soul is the central part of our nature and includes our feelings, morals, and desires. I wrote a poem, *My Soul Cries Out,* telling of my desire for my soul to be heard and understood by others. I want to be known as being a man of great soul, character and courage through my actions, along with having an honest, inspiring, caring, and giving soul. Then as a Black person, our *soul* has been defined as being a sense of ethnic pride, which we express in areas such as our language, social customs, religion, and music. Therefore, I would like to be known as a black man that personified the soul of his race in a great way too.

In the Bible, both the *Old* and *New Testaments* say that without a doubt our souls are immortal. *Psalm 22:26* - Our hearts (souls) shall live forever. *Ecclesiastes 12:7* - Our spirit (soul), upon our deaths, will return to God who gave it. *Daniel 12:2* - The dead shall awake, some to everlasting life and some to shame and everlasting contempt. *Matthew 25:46* - Some will go away to eternal punishment but the righteous to eternal life. *James 5:20* - The souls of converted sinners are saved from death. *1 Corinthians 15:12-19* - The hope of our bodily resurrection is at the very heart of our Christian faith. Our lives, true or spiritual, do not end in death. Our souls will exist eternally, whether it's in Heaven or Hell. And the promise of the Bible is that not only our souls will live forever, but also that our bodies will be resurrected as well. It's just a matter of where you would like to spend your eternity, and our souls, good or bad, are our guiding force.

Spirit - The dictionary defines soul and *spirit* as being the same as our life force; the immaterial part of us believed to survive after our deaths. However, the spirit, for me, may also be defined as being something delivered out from one's heart and soul that can be seen, heard or felt by others: love, joy, respect, ambition, optimism, determination, thoughtfulness, enthusiasm, caring, generosity, consideration, praise, honesty, sincerity, loyalty, commitment, wisdom, hope, peace, righteousness...and unfortunately a lot of bad things that are opposites of the good things I have written here. Likewise, the soul and spirit are distinguished as being different according to some others, as well. *Dichotomists*, for example, are defined as being believers that man is of body and soul, while *trichotomists* are believers of body, soul, and spirit. Then the scriptures speak usually of man as being body and soul, or of body and spirit. I'm a believer in there being a separation of soul and spirit, and a great thing I once read said that the soul is there to make decisions, while the spirit is there to fellowship with God.

Concerning the return of Jesus, the apostle Paul wrote that he wanted God himself, the God of peace, to sanctify the people wholly, and he prayed that their whole *spirit*, soul and body be held blameless at the coming of the Lord (*1 Thessalonians 5:23*). *Hebrews 4:12* then says that the Word of God is quick, powerful, living and active. It is sharper than any two-edged sword and penetrates even to the dividing soul and *spirit*. As David, in *Psalms 31:5*, I commit myself to the God of truth for my redemption in knowing that while I may see all my ways as being clean through my own eyes but knowing that God will weigh my spirit (*Proverbs 16:2*). Also, while my soul may be restless at times, I know that it is better to be patient in spirit rather than being proud in spirit (*Ecclesiastes 7:8*). One's pride and impatience may only doom them, while in patience the end of something will be better than the beginning. In turning my life over to the Lord, as with *Ezekiel 11:19,* a new spirit has been placed within me. That spirit has given me a new life (*2 Corinthians 3:6*) and I will always walk in the Spirit (*Galatians 5:16)* for others to see, hear, and feel.

Standing - I have been through so much that I may not understand but I'm never giving up. So just hit me with your best shot. My knees may buckle but you'll never drop me all the way to the ground. I'm most strong and ever determined. With the Lord as my strength and guidance, there is nothing to fear, and I can always end up standing tall, no matter what it is that is trying to bring me down. My faith has been tested on several occasions, and I believe that I have fared well through most, for even in losing a few battles it has only made me wiser, stronger, and better prepared in moving on to the next. Standing tall, I am doing what's right and persevering despite all the odds and my foes, and defending what I know is true.

As Moses told the people of Israel, I should have no fear but need to stand still and see the salvation of the Lord (*Exodus 14:13*). Therefore, I am standing with all before the Lord on this day (*Deuteronomy 29:10*). As David, I am standing up for the Lord's help (*Psalm 35:2*). Then in my stand, it is never in any evil thing (*Ecclesiastes 8:3*). I'm justified in faith and there is grace where I stand, as I rejoice in hope of the glory of the Lord (*Romans 5:2*). In my battles, all I have to do is stand fast in faith and be strong (*1 Corinthians 16:13*). Plus, wearing the whole armour of God, I am doing all that I can in the face of evil (*Ephesians 6:13*). I stand fast in the Lord (*Philippians 4:1*) and, as a servant of Jesus, my stand can be perfect and complete, fully assured, in all the will of God (*Colossians 4:12*), who gives life to those that stand tall in Him (*1 Thessalonians 3:8*).

Storms - The storms of life may rain down upon you in what may feel like a never-ending deluge of trouble, pain, misery, and hopelessness. And as all, I have certainly weathered a few. However, in faith, I discovered that there was no need for me to ever live my life in fear of any to come, as they surely will. My security and confidence are in God, whose love can be seen in the center of even our greatest storms. He can provide the hope and shelter for any cloudbursts of misfortune and bring light to the darkness of any situation confronting us. All we have to do is trust Him first no matter how overwhelming our storms may appear. His favor rests upon the faithful. We all may face some sudden and most powerful storms beyond our reasoning, but in God they can be diminished into only slight drizzles of concern.

I praise the Lord for His presence and support, as did the prophet Isaiah. He praised the Lord, his God, for being a strength to the poor and needy in his distress, plus a refuge from the *storm* and a shadow from the heat, when the breath of the ruthless are as the *storm* against the wall (*Isaiah 25:4*). *Matthew 6:25-34* tells us not to worry. Life is more important than things like clothes and food, which God will supply. He knows our needs but it is in faith that they will be given. We are to first seek His kingdom and His righteousness. In doing so, we don't have to worry about tomorrow as tomorrow will worry about itself. Each day certainly has enough trouble and evil of its own. So, while we may have our needs and find ourselves weathering a few storms, all we have to do is be faithful and trust God. Worrying about your needs and problems will not add a single hour to your life (*verse 27*), will it? May cause you to only lose a few as you become lost in a storm of hopelessness.

Strangers - In seeking a new job, I had begun to consider the employment opportunities out of state from my hometown of Detroit, Michigan. However, I found myself passing on some because of the fear of moving and being a stranger, away from my family and friends. Things could have surely worked out for the better, but thoughts of loneliness and some other things worried me, like crime or people trying to take advantage of my being a stranger. Of course, I could certainly have felt safe and welcomed with open arms wherever I went, just as God wants me to do with any strangers I encounter here, but didn't have enough faith or trust in myself, or others, to give it a chance then. Maybe I will though the next time a worthwhile opportunity presents itself that requires relocation. After all, with all of today's travel and communication options, we are never that far away from home. Plus, in meeting people on the Internet, as I have through my Christian writing groups, I could find myself not being a total stranger in moving away after all. Then too, one doesn't have to go away to feel like a stranger. During the troubled times a person may feel like no one cares, like a stranger in a strange land. I certainly have experienced that but know that I am not alone. God's people have been alienated throughout history for one reason or another. We just have to do as God says and love others, especially strangers, as we love ourselves, here or in another place, in spite of our circumstances or the reasons for a move.

The Bible defines *strangers* as being *sojourners* (visitors), and under Mosaic Law, they were considered as those living among the Hebrew people but not of their nationality. *Leviticus 16:29* and *17:8* relates to the visitors of the land as being the strangers that sojourn among you. *Deuteronomy 10:18-19* tells of strangers having claims upon the kind treatment of the Hebrews. God loved strangers and would give them food and clothing. He wanted the people to love the strangers too, as they themselves had been strangers in Egypt and knew how it felt. The rights of strangers were safeguarded according to *Exodus 22:21* and *23:9.* They were not to be mistreated or oppressed, as God's people were as strangers in Egypt. Then *Leviticus 17:10, 20:2* and *24:16* say that strangers were required to refrain from the things prohibited to the Israelites or be subject to the same penalties as the people of the land. All said, I shouldn't be that afraid of moving away and becoming a stranger in a new place. Just as in the Bible, I should look to be treated kindly, welcome, and able to live like the people there do, while having the same rights and laws. Also, *Ecclesiastes 3:11* says that God has set eternity in my heart, so that my soul can always look beyond what I see here and toward a better future, without any fears or second guessing.

Strength - When my father died before I was even a teenager, I was surely going to have to be stronger and more independent than my friends, who all lived with both a mother and a father at home. Things were going to be especially tough for a widow, five children, and no breadwinner in our home. So at an early age I learned the value of getting out and earning a dollar, with no weekly allowances coming my way. Started doing a lot of odd jobs for our neighbors and local businesses. However, a more important need than any money was the guidance that my father would have provided. Found myself making many life decisions on my own. The end result was that as I grew older I developed a "do it all myself" attitude in believing that there was no reason to look to any one for any thing. It was only after a few setbacks later in life that I realized that we all have to depend on some one or some thing, at one time or another, no matter how independent we think we are. Therefore, it was truly great when I learned to look to God who knew my heart and potential, for my strength and guidance. He could guide me through the worst of times and offer the direction and strength I needed in reaching my goals.

The Bible speaks much about strength in being a support and security for us through the Lord our God, which was something that I really needed without having a father to provide that for me. *Exodus 15:2* says that the Lord is my *strength* and my salvation. *Job 12:13* says that wisdom and strength are God's, along with counsel and understanding. As *Psalm 27:1,* the Lord is the light, salvation and strength of my life. In that there is nothing for me to fear concerning anyone or my circumstances. God is my refuge and my strength, while being an ever-present help when I am in trouble *(Psalm 46:1)*. In being righteous, the way of the Lord is my strength, while being evil would only cause my ruin *(Proverbs 10:29)*. Then *Ecclesiastes 9:16* says that wisdom is better than strength, and it was a wise decision for me to seek the Lord's strength rather than continuing to rely on my own, with mixed results. I now turn to Him for my strength to do all things. However, I may also turn to others for help who have been given their strength from the Lord, who may want us to work as a team in certain situations. Moses, for example, considered to be a workaholic, is said to have strengthened his position among the people by using trusted individuals to work for him and with him, in realizing that the more he tried to do on his own the less effective he was.

Stress - Everyone is familiar with stress and experience it in varying forms and degrees every day. A little can actually be beneficial for us. It motivates me, for example, and makes me all the more determined to accomplish what I've set out to do. Stress, however, becomes a real problem if it becomes too great, affecting one physically or mentally. I found myself passing out from diabetes, which I never knew that I had, and then suffered a stroke over a really tough period. My growing stress had taken such a toll on me mentally, spiritually, and physically. As a result, there were times that I just felt like giving up which, believe it or not, was actually the right thing to do. I had begun to really take it personally, as it felt like the whole world was fighting against me, and I was losing the will and strength to fight back. Finally decided that the best thing was to just "give up" and place everything in the hands of God, which I should have done from the very beginning, especially with little else working. Had to realize that I am never in control of anything. God is though. I still have a few battles left to be fought but have been winning a few through His care and direction. Surely God can't pay any of my bills or give me a job back. However, in placing things in His hands, positive things are happening not because of the actions I have been taking but from the results of what I expect my actions to effect. In willing my mind to be still, I am much more at peace in dealing with my concerns. God is in control and will remain there, as the pressures of my life are greatly diminishing.

Many people become stressed because they don't trust God to provide the basic necessities of life. However, *Matthew 6:25, 27* tells us not to stress over such things as it will not add a single hour to any life. Jesus offers encouragement in saying that we should not let our hearts be troubled and believe in God and Him (*John 14:1*). That does not mean that our lives will be without stress but a life without Him makes coping with stress an impossible task. In handling stress, *Philippians 4:6-7* advises us not to be anxious about anything. We should turn everything over to God in prayer. Lifting our burdens and concerns to Him on a daily basis will help to lessen or eliminate the stress in our lives. We can cast all our cares to Him because He will sustain us and never fail us (*Psalm 55:22*). Jesus offers peace if we come to Him with our worries and concerns. He says that our hearts should not be troubled and there should be no fear, as He leaves and gives His peace to us, not as the world does (*John 14:27*). He doesn't promise that we will never be without stress though. Stress of any kind is just a natural part of life, as say *Job 5:7* and *14:1* (Man is born to trouble), *1 Peter 4:12* (We shouldn't be surprised by the fiery trials we suffer, as though strange things are happening to us), and *1 Corinthians 10:13* (The temptations we suffer are common to man). So, there will always be stress, even for the most faithful. How we deal with it is up to us. Trying to do it on our own will result in a long uphill battle of failure. The only way to deal with it successfully is with Jesus, with first having a belief in Him. Then we must trust and obey Him. We can then look to reap the blessing of true contentment from a loving God. Through, and only through, His grace, mercy and love can the stress in our lives can be managed.

Stroke - On October 20, 2010, I suffered a stroke. Thought that I was in pretty good health but had been really stressed and had a lot on my mind that evening. In reading about strokes, I found out that it is a medical emergency that can cause permanent neurological damage and death resulting from the rapid loss of brain function due to a disturbance in the blood supply to the brain. With a stroke, the affected area of the brain cannot function, which may result in an inability to move one or more limbs on one side of the body, inability to understand or formulate speech, or an inability to see one side of the visual field (I was blind in my left eye). High blood pressure is the number one risk factor for strokes, followed by atrial fibrillation (an irregular heartbeat), diabetes, family history of stroke, high cholesterol, increasing age (especially after age 55), and race (black people are more likely to die of a stroke). On that evening, I had 5 of the 7 risk factors listed, though normally my blood pressure is normal and returned to being normal a few days after the stroke.

Of course there is nothing specifically written about strokes in the Bible, but in many ways there is a great deal written about it. As I laid in the hospital bed on that evening, there was a group of medical technicians tending to me and asking me a number of questions because the tests they were taking hadn't revealed much. However, I was totally blind in my left eye and greatly worried. As they continued their tests, I told them what had happened, while beginning to see a flickering of light at the end of my fingertips. A sudden feeling of calmness then came over me. I felt God's presence, and was at peace, with my eyesight returning. Later, a specialist took some tests and couldn't initially figure out what had happened either. He took some additional tests and came back later with an explanation. I was told then that it was a stroke. However, there was more. He asked me if I had a church and told me that I should find one when I left the hospital if I didn't. He explained that he hadn't seen a case such as mine before and that the consequences of my stroke should have been much more severe than just a temporary blindness. Whatever blockage it was that caused the stroke had moved far to the back of my eye, rather than to my brain, where it couldn't do any greater damage. He said that someone from above was surely looking down on me on that evening. I certainly believe that I saw the light of God's love and care, which is most certainly written throughout the Bible, as the great physician did His work. It's no wonder why a few tears came to my eyes as I was writing this.

Stubborn - *Stubborn* people are defined as being unreasonably or perversely unyielding, and they can be most difficult to handle, manage, or treat. At times they only hear, see, and do what they want. However, being stubborn is only a part of human nature, which makes us all susceptible to it. I know that I can be when feeling really strongly about something, but it's not a bad thing because there is never any evil intent or denying God in any way. God frowns upon stubborn pride and the stubborn people that refuse to listen and obey His instructions, doing as they please and worshipping their own created gods. The Bible presents many examples of how God punished the stubborn like that. Then there are the stubborn children who don't listen to their parents or obey them, as they should. They anger God as well, and the Bible tells of how severely they were dealt with during the Old Testament days, in ways that would never be allowed in today's world. A lot of stubborn children would certainly clean up their acts pretty quickly.

Judges 2:19 basically tells that some stubborn people may change their ways for a time but will only return to their old evil ways and even more so when the opportunity presents itself. Therefore, an unrighteous and stubborn person must really commit themselves to change and maintaining it. Then *Deuteronomy 21:18-21* tells of the stubborn and rebellious son who did not obey his father or mother, and refused to listen when his parents disciplined him. He would be brought before the elders to have his behavior reported. After that, all the men of the town would stone him to death, in putting evil away and being made an example for others to hear of and be afraid. Quite a punishment! Of course, that wouldn't happen today and a lot of the evil and stubborn children remain that way because of there being no strict discipline for them to fear. Teachers can't punish them as they once could and some parents don't believe in any kind of physical punishment, like a good and well-deserved spanking. Finally, *Proverbs 7:11* tells of a loud and stubborn woman. Do you know of any women like that?

Success - *Success* is the favorable or prosperous results of certain attempts or endeavors, like the attainment of wealth, position, honors, or etc. In striving for success, one must first begin with goals, and it should be made sure that they are things you can realistically do if you put a lot of hard work and effort into it. Just remember that how someone would become successful is dependent upon what his or her idea of success is. Some, for example, may view success in terms of being wealthy while others may view it in terms of the good that they do in sharing their wealth. Personally, I have been successful over the course of my life in a number of ways. Then there are some goals that I have yet to reach and may never. Plus I have had my share of struggles and still face a few battles. However, my view of success has changed greatly from years ago when they mostly concerned things like college, employment, marriage, wealth, etc. My idea of success now is having lived a life that will land me a place in Heaven after my days here on Earth are over. No other success is as important as that. True success is in God. He offers it in abundance to the faithful and righteous but for the unrighteous success may be short lived or ever achieved. The great thing for me is that even during the most troubling of times or my various pursuits, in being a man of faith, I can see where God has continually blessed me through His love, guidance, provision, protection, and care, which is nothing but success at its greatest.

As *Joshua 1:8,* I know that in meditating day and night, along with observing and doing according to all that is written in the Bible, I can become prosperous and enjoy good success, as God promised Joshua, who succeeded Moses. In being faithful, the words of God will never depart from my mouth, as I know where my success begins and ends. Also, I know that walking with others that are successful in the Lord will be beneficial for me. *Psalm 1:1-3* says that a man is blessed who does not walk in the counsel of the wicked, stand in the way of sinners, or sit in the seat of mockers. The successful man has his delight in the Law of the Lord and whatever he does prospers as he continually meditates on it. Plus, I believe in sharing my success as God blesses those that practice generosity. Sharing the bounty of one's success will only cause them to reap even more success (*2 Corinthians 9:6*). Then even during the most troubling times, I don't have to have the worries or stress that used to consume me in trying to win a few battles and make ends meet. I should be strong and courageous, plus live without fear or dismay, in knowing that God is always with me (*Joshua 1:9*). Also, in first seeking God's Kingdom and His righteousness, I will be given all the things that I truly need (*Matthew 6:33*). There is no need to worry about tomorrow because it will worry about itself, as each day has enough trouble of its own (*Matthew 6:34*).

Suffering - The fact is that there are times that life hurts and sometimes a lot. One's suffering can be physical or mental and due to a number of things, like the loss of a job or loved one, poverty, crime, injustice, oppression, racism, divorce, abuse, illness, financial losses, the effects of natural disasters... We just have to face the fact that there may be suffering in our lives and there may be reasons that can be identified or some that we may never know the reasons why, or even if there were reasons. The 'why' of suffering can surely be a mystery, and some may question where God was during their suffering. However, suffering is no more of a mystery than love when it comes to Him. Just remember that Jesus was executed for having spoken and lived the truth. The whole point of it was for Him to go through things that no one else would want to go through in completing the task at hand for our salvation. Just as there may be a great plan behind God's motives for some of our suffering. The terrorist attacks of September 11, 2001 (World Trade Center in New York City), for example, certainly had many turning back to Him and, in the midst of all the suffering, it just brought out the good in so many people.

Acts 17:2-3 tells how John reasoned with some Jews in a synagogue through the Scriptures explaining and proving that Jesus had to suffer and rise from the dead. He proclaimed that our Jesus was indeed the Christ foretold about, and the 'why' of His suffering was for us. Then *1 Peter 4:12-19* tells of our suffering for being Christians. Peter, an apostle of Jesus, in exhorting the Christians of Asia Minor to cease from sin by the example of Jesus, who had suffered in the flesh and ceased from sin, wrote that they should not have been surprised by the painful trials that they were suffering as though something strange was happening to them. They should have rejoiced that they participated in the sufferings of Jesus, so that they would be overjoyed when His glory was revealed. If they were to suffer, it should not be as murderers, thieves, other criminals, or even meddlers. In suffering as Christians, they were not to be ashamed but praise God for bearing that name. Plus in suffering according to God's will they should have committed themselves to Him and continued to do good, just as we should do today. In Jesus' suffering, God expects to see our best even during ours.

Suicide - Most certainly, I knew that s*uicide* was the act of intentionally causing one's own death and that it was often committed out of despair, the cause of which is frequently attributed to mental disorders like depression, bipolar disorder, schizophrenia, alcoholism, drug abuse, etc., or the stress from things like financial difficulties, troubled relationships, and other problems. A terminal illness may also have a person considering suicide as being a better alternative than living a life of constant pain. Then the most common methods of suicide include hanging, pesticide poisoning, and firearms. However, it was the additional information I read about suicide that was most alarming for me and not known previously. Suicide is the 10th leading cause of death worldwide with there being around 800,000 to a million people dying from it each year. Males are three to four times more likely to kill themselves than women. Then there are an estimated 10 to 20 million non-fatal attempted suicides every year, with the attempts being more common with the young and females. Those are just huge numbers of people seeking to end their lives rather than battling the things troubling them! A final note is that views on suicide have been influenced by things such as religion, where the Abrahamic religions, for example, consider it as being as offense towards God due to the belief in the sanctity of life.

According to *Job 7:15,* Joel says that his soul chose strangling and death over the life he was living, which is a choice that many make in just plain giving up on life and choosing suicide, which is a sin. Then in reference to suicide, *Proverbs 8:36* says that people sinning against God have wronged their souls and in hating themselves hate God in loving death over the life He has given. Essentially, those committing suicide have given up on themselves and on God. They have come to despise their lives and feel there is no longer any meaning, while not turning to God for other answers. Sadly, we often hear about suicides and ask ourselves what would cause a person to choose that route rather than fighting on. Some may leave notes explaining themselves while others don't, leaving their suicides as total mysteries. In the Bible a number of suicides are cited, usually connected with some kind of lost battle. Ahithophel, counselor of David, deserted David but committed suicide when he saw that the rebellion he was involved in would be crushed. Judas, fourth son of Jacob, betrayed Jesus and hung himself. Saul, a king of Edom, committed suicide after he lost his army and his sons were slain. Zimri, grandson of Judah and the fifth king of Israel, set fire to the palace and perished in the flames when his city was taken over. However, Job, contemplated suicide but turned to God rather than completely giving up, as all should.

Sun - Finally back writing on September 21, 2013, after a few months off, for a number of reasons. Especially concerning the summer. Never seem to have much motivation to get home from work, or not working, and do any writing. Just want to be outside enjoying the sun and warm weather, since the season seems to go by so fast. And this summer has really speeded along quickly by me taking on a position with the postal service and working six days a week. Certainly, there have been some days that were so hot that I asked myself "why?". But I love the sun and view it as one of God's everlasting blessings. It's the fire of life that never burns out. And during even the most dreariest of days, I know that the sun of His glory will soon brighten and uplift my spirits. For I view the sun as being the light, heat, and sustenance of my existance. Scientsists report that our sun, 70% hydrogen, 28% helium, and 2% metals, is one of more than 100 billion in our galaxy. What they fail to mention though is that it is 100% God in so many different ways. Plus the sun, often called just an "ordinary" star, has been burning for over an estimated 4.5 billon years. However, nothing is "ordinary" with God, only "great and beyond".

Even on the cloudiest or raineist of days, your life can be brightened by the *sun* of the Lord. *Revelation 21:23* tells of a city needing either the moon or the sun to shine in it. The Glory of God lit it, and the Lamb (Jesus) was the light. Then *Malachi 4:2* says that the promised Messiah, Jesus, was called the "Sun of righteousness" with healing in His wings. He was to come before us with plenty of energy for ruling, leaping like calves released from a stall. Therefore, our sun, being the heavenly body around which the Earth and other planets revolve, is certainly much more that just a source of light as defined. As the descendants of Israel were encouraged to do, we need to acknowledge the greatness of God in maintaining a covenant with Him. He makes the sun shine during the day, the moon and stars to shine at night, and stirs up the seas to make the waves roar (*Jeremiah 31:35*). He, also, causes His sun to shine on the evil and the good, and makes it rain on the righteous and the unrighteous, be it physically, mentally, or spiritually. I view the rain and the sun to be blessings, as we all should. We surely wish that all of our days could be filled with nothing but sunshine and happiness. But that would be too easy in God's eyes. How could we survive with dry lands and dry spirits?

Supplication - During church sermons, I listen very attentively and like to have an understanding of all the words being heard. So on this one Sunday, a visiting minister, at my church, was preaching and used the word *supplication* a few times. From his words, I really couldn't place a definition with the word. Then by the reaction of many, I felt like I was the only person there that didn't know what he was talking about. Later that evening, I called a church friend and asked him if he knew the meaning of the word. He gave me his thoughts but wasn't that confident about his answer. I then looked to my dictionary and found out that one definition of the work is to make a *request,* which is something we may do in many or most of our prayers. After that, I turned to my Bible to see where the word was used.

Job 8:5 tells of making a *supplication* to the Almighty (God). In *Psalm 6:9,* David tells of the Lord hearing his *supplication* and receiving his prayers. Jeremiah prayed to God that his *supplication* would be accepted so he would not have to return to the house of Jonathan, where he would face death (*Jeremiah 37:20*). *Acts 1:14* tells how people, all in one accord, can give themselves to prayer and *supplication,* just as Mary, the mother of Jesus, the women, and the brethren of Jesus did. *Ephesians 6:18* instructs us to pray with all of our prayers and *supplication* in the Spirit, while watching with perseverance and *supplication* for all saints. Then *Ephesians 6:19* goes on further in saying that we should open our mouths boldly in making the mystery of the gospel known. Therefore, it is a good thing to voice our *supplications* in sermons and prayers.

Symbols - A number of years ago, I had my left ear pierced and began wearing an assortment of different earrings, strictly as a fashion statement. These days, however, I usually just wear a gold cross as a *symbol* (sign) of my being a Christian, and I proudly provide that answer when asked why I am still wearing an earring at my age. In my reading, it appears that the most commonly seen Christian symbols are the *Christian Cross* symbolizing the resurrection of Jesus after His crucifixion and also as a symbol of salvation and triumph, the *Ichthys (fish)* used as a mark for meeting places and tombs, the *Six Pointed Star* representing the six attributes of God (love, power, wisdom, mercy, majesty and justice), the *Alpha and Omega* of God being eternal as *the beginning and the end,* and the *Agnus Dei* describing Jesus as a lamb who makes the ultimate sacrifice in atoning for our sins.

In *The Old Testament*, the most prominent symbol was the *altar*. They were built for worship in showing allegiance to God, and there were acts of sacrifice performed there. It was a place of slaughter that required the blood of animals in atoning for the sins of the people. However, these days a person can just set aside a time and a place to be their altar where they can communicate with God each day in prayer. As far as something that a person wears or possesses as a symbol, the Bible tells of *Aaron's Rod*, which was a staff (rod) Aaron, the older brother of Moses, carried that would turn into a serpent when cast before the Pharaoh (*Exodus 7:9-12,15*). Then during a tough period in the wilderness, it budded, bloomed blossoms, and yielded almonds as a sign of the divine approval of Aaron and Moses. (*Numbers 17:1-10*). Later it was preserved in the *Ark of the Covenant (Hebrews 9:4)*.

Teaching - We all learn through teaching and we all can be teachers in sharing what we have learned and experienced with others. My parents taught me a great deal about life while I was growing up. Then there were my teachers from grade school to college, along with the ministers at the various churches I have attended over the years. Along with that were the many things I learned from relatives, neighbors, friends, and others. Likewise, I have done a lot of teaching myself, from the workplace, to my home, to many others. Believe that my best teaching comes from trying to set a good example in all that I do for others to observe and learn from. For there are many people out there teaching far more bad things than good, from their words to their actions.

Of course, the ultimate teacher was Jesus and His teachings are spread throughout the Four Gospels. One may read quite a number of things that He taught on various subjects. *John 3:1-2* tells how Nicodemus, a man of the Pharisees, went to Jesus and told Him that they knew that He was a teacher from God because no person could do the miraculous things Jesus was doing were God not with him. Also, the Bible describes a teacher as being an instructor and, as Solomon says in *Proverbs 5:1*, it is a good thing to pay attention to wisdom and listen well to words of insight. In that your lips may preserve knowledge (*verse 2*) concerning many things. However, we must beware of the false teachers among us that will only lead us in the wrong direction and to our quick destruction (*2 Peter 2:1*).

Temptation - *Temptation* is the enticement or lure of something. There is that overwhelming desire that we just have to have something and want it now. That may cause us to make hasty choices, like buying that new car that we really can't afford. Then in the Bible, Esau gave up his birthright for some bread and stew. Therefore, we can surely make some decisions that will only be deeply regretted later on. At times, we just need to pray and take our time in giving some things a lot more thought to resist our temptations. Surely, I have fallen victim to temptation but find myself having much better control these days in trying my best to be obedient in the Lord. With His help and Word, I have developed much wisdom, maturity, and endurance.

As with *James 1:12,* I want to wear what some call *The Victor's Crown.* It says that blessed is the person that endures temptation. Once they have been tried and stood their test, they will receive the crown of life that God has promised to those who love Him. A Divine Example for resisting temptation can be read in *Matthew 4:1-4.* Jesus was led by the Spirit into the desert to be tempted by the devil. There He fasted forty days and forty nights, while becoming hungry. The tempter then came to Him and said that, being the Son of God, some stones could be commanded into bread. Jesus answered by saying that it was written that no man could live by bread alone, but on every word that came from the mouth of God (*Matthew 4:10*).

Terrorism - The word *terrorism* isn't listed in my *Grosset Webster Dictionary* (1966 Edition). Could definitely use a more updated version but this was the only one that I could find around the house presently. That aside, while being a more modern day word, terrorism has been used since the beginning of recorded history. For example, I read where the Babylonian invasion of Jerusalem in 586 B.C. is said to have been an act of terrorism. Terrorism has been defined as the *systematic use of violence as a means of coercion for political purposes*. However, it has been increasingly common for those pursuing extremist goals throughout the world, like the attacks of September 11, 2001 in New York City. All considered, terrorism might be described as being a tactic or strategy, a crime or holy duty, a justified rebellion against oppression, or an inexcusable act, among other things.

Terrorism is certainly something that we have to have great concerns about these days, with all the senseless acts and killing all over the world. However, in God there is hope and relief. I still think about all the baseball games that I watched following the New York City attacks where they were singing *God Bless America,* with even many non-believers joining in. It reminded me of *Psalm 30* where David praised God for his deliverance. He had been lifted up and the terrorists were not able to have any rejoice over him. He had cried to God and was healed, while being kept alive or condemned to a pit. Surely there was anger but it would not endure. There would be crying through the night but joy in the morning. David's sadness turned into dancing, as he was filled with gladness. He declared that his heart would sing to God and not be silent, while giving thanks forever. And just think about it. The terrorists caused a lot of destruction and lost lives on September 11, 2011 but it brought us closer together singing, dancing, and giving praise. Where are they? Their joy wasn't very lasting.

Tests - Throughout our lives we face many tests, be they physical, financial, emotional, or vocational, and the results reveal a great deal about our values, commitments, and beliefs. I certainly learned a lot about the confidence I had in myself after taking a Financial Accounting test in college. I believed that I had done well but my attitude changed when our professor wrote down the much disappointing results on the chalkboard. Only one student had received an "A" grade. Then he started calling off names. I was sitting in the back with my buddies as we all wondered who that one bright student was. And as their names and low scores were called off, he suggested that maybe they would do better if they sat closer up front and paid more attention to his lectures. Finally, my name was called and he immediately looked up front for me. I called out and he looked to the back with a much-surprised expression and asked, "What are you doing back there?" Then as the front roomers looked back, and my greatly surprised lower achieving friends, he announced that I was that bright student. I surely hope that I have been passing a few tests like that in God's classroom.

In thinking about tests, Job comes to mind. According to *Job 1,* he was blameless, upright, feared God, and shunned evil. He, also, had seven sons, three daughters, seven thousand sheep, three thousand camels, five hundred oxen, five hundred donkeys, a large number of servants, and was considered to be the greatest man of the East. Then he was tested as Satan suggested to the Lord that Job would curse His name if everything were taken away from him. Job passed that first test as he had everything taken away but didn't sin in blaming God for his troubles. In a second test, *Job 2,* Satan declared that Job, as any man, would give all that he had for his own life. Job would surely curse God to His face if his hands and flesh were struck by the outstretched hands of God. So Job was then afflicted with painful sores from the soles of his feet to the top of his head. He was surely in bad shape, and his wife told him to forget about his integrity. He should have just cursed God and accepted death. However, Job just called her a foolish woman. To him, we should be willing to accept the good, as well as the trouble, when it comes to God. Another test passed.

Thanksgiving - On Thursday, November 28, 2013, we will be celebrating another Thanksgiving Day. For me, it will be a day of rest from work while giving thanks to God for His goodness, plus enjoying it with a few family members and friends, and maybe watching a couple of football games on television. And I'll thank goodness that the Detroit Lions aren't the only game on anymore! The Pilgrims celebrated the first Thanksgiving, after their first harvest in our country, in 1621. It lasted three days and by accounts was attended by 53 Pilgrims and 90 Native Americans. It became an official Federal holiday in 1863. During the Civil War, President Abraham Lincoln proclaimed it to be a national day of *Thanksgiving and Praise* for our Father in Heaven and it was celebrated on that November 26th, and now on every fourth Thursday in November. However, for all that love the Lord and appreciate all the good things that He does, a Thanksgiving celebration should be an every day event.

According to the Bible, Solomon may have been the first to celebrate Thanksgiving. *2 Chronicles* tells how he felt God's presence while praying outside the temple after beginning his reign in Israel. He was so overwhelmed with thankfulness and joy that he called for a 15-day festival to be celebrated all over the country dedicated to God. There were sacrifices offered before the Lord, with much music, praise, and giving thanks. Afterwards the people went to their homes, with a lot of joy and gladness in their hearts because of the Lord's goodness. *Psalm 100,* also, says a lot about thanksgiving. We should shout for joy and sing our praises, as we know that the Lord is God. He made us and we are His. When entering His courts, it should be with thanksgiving and praise, for He is good and His love and faithfulness for us endures forever. Then as *Psalm 126:3* says, we are filled with joy because of the great things the Lord does for us. That should be celebrated with much thanksgiving.

Theory - A *theory* is a proposed explanation, conclusion, analysis, or even guesswork.

God and Jesus are real. I believe it and know it. That is all that matters to me. Enough said. They are with me daily. I care not about what the theorist and non-believers think.

Time - One definition for *time* is that it is the duration regarded as belonging to the present life as distinct from the life to come or from eternity. Never thought much about it during my earlier years. However, after my stroke, I began to wonder how much time I have left to complete my life's journey before moving on to another in Heaven. Too bad this is Earth and not Mars. I read a literary piece saying that Martians could live to be three hundred years old and nearer to a thousand were it not for the various means leading to a violent death there. Our present life expectancy rate is something more like 78.7 years, and that is affected by such factors as sex, race, heredity, physical condition, nutrition, and occupation. In any event, there are a number of things that I still want to accomplish, and time is now a much greater concern than it was in the past.

Ecclesiastes 3:1-8 says that for every thing there is a season, and a time for every purpose under the Heaven. There is a time to be born, a time to die, a time to plant, a time to pick, a time to kill, a time to heal, a time to break down, a time to build up, a time to weep, a time to laugh, a time to mourn, a time to dance, a time to cast away stones, a time to gather stones, a time to embrace, a time to refrain from embracing, a time to receive, a time to lose, a time to keep, a time to cast away, a time to rend, a time to sew, a time to be silent, a time to speak, a time to love, a time to hate, a time of war, and a time of peace. *Verse 11* goes on to say that God made everything beautiful in its time and set eternity in the hearts of men, but we can't comprehend what He has done from the beginning to end. Also, God judges the righteous and the evil, as there is a time for every activity and deed. Then *Hosea 10:12* tells of it being the time to seek the Lord before He comes and showers you with righteousness.

Tithes - A tithe is the payment of a tenth of one's income to God. I must say that I was pretty negligent in doing that in the past, but always tried to give an offering of as much as possible. Then finding myself out of work for over a couple of years, I had no income whatever. However, I still gave monetarily, while giving as much of myself as possible in other ways, like with all the volunteer work I did during my extended layoff, along with being an inspiration to others through my writing, singing, and never giving up attitude. Presently, I am back in a paying position and trying to put the pieces back together from a most difficult period in my life. That includes getting my spiritual life even more back in order, which would include the payment of my tithes.

Our blessings come from giving and we should not question whether we have enough to give or not. Instead of worrying about whether we can make ends meet, we should give freely and generously back to God, as we can trust Him to provide all that we need. *Malachi 3:6-12* tells of a challenge issued through the prophet Malachi to the people of Israel, who repeatedly were failing to give their tithe offerings to God. They were to bring their tithe of produce and livestock into a warehouse in demonstrating their trust. They could continue to hold on to what they had and be cursed for robbing God. Or they could accept His promise of throwing open the floodgates of Heaven and pouring out such a great blessing that they wouldn't have room for it *(verse 10)*. Through the payment of their tithes, they would have a delightful land and all the nations would call them blessed *(verse 12)*.

Transformation - Life is all about change and hopefully for the better. We have to exercise patience and be dedicated to transforming ourselves into who we desire to be and God. It may be a tough task but we should never become discouraged and give up. Some habits aren't so easy to break and in growing as Christians we have to concentrate on casting away some of our olds ways and bringing forth the new. I wrote in my first book that I was a new man wearing new clothes after giving myself to the Lord. The old me was cast away and most of my old clothes thrown away. However, I will never be a finished product. Change is a never-ending process. Even at my present age, I am still learning more about myself and trying to do more. Surely, I have had some failures and still need to change a few things in my life. All I have to do is call on the Lord though when needing a little help and encouragement. My transformation was for Him and He can help me to keep those old clothes from coming back into style.

As says *Ephesians 4:23-24,* we have to cast away our old ways of life that corrupted us with deceitful desires. We need to be renewed in the spirit of our minds. Then in putting on a new self, we are transformed to be like God in true righteousness and holiness. *Ephesians 5:1-2* adds that in our transformation we should be imitators of God as dearly loved children. We should live a life of love, just as Jesus loved us so much that He gave His life for us as an offering and a sacrifice to God. Also, the body of the Lord builds itself up in love *(Ephesians 4:16)* and continually strives for maturity *(Ephesians 4:13).* Therefore, our transformations are never complete. Paul the apostle wrote that in receiving Jesus as Lord we should live in Him *(Colossians 2:6)* and we are complete in Him, being the head of all principality and power *(verse 10).* We may be dead in our sins because of our sinful natures, but God will forgive us and make us new in Jesus *(verse 13).* In our transformations, we should set our hearts and our minds on things above and not on earthly things *(Colossians 3:1-2).*

Trust - There are times that we have to place a great deal of trust in ourselves and in God, who never fails us. In that, we can accomplish many great things, even some first thought to have been impossible, and survive through some most difficult and stressful situations. We never know what God has planned for us. However, in our trust, we can be confident that He will lead us to where we desire to be, and that He has many positive things in store for us as we deal with the negatives. I'm living in the present, knowing where my past has led me. Still have some goals but don't wonder or worry about my future that much. I trust that God already has things worked out. Through divorce, death of loved ones, illness, unemployment, loss of possessions, financial problems, and a few other tough times, I have maintained my faith. In placing my trust in God, I have been restored and blessed, as Job, even in the face of hardship, along with being able to move forward and accomplish many things I could have never imagined previously, like the writing of this book and my first.

The story of Joseph is a good example of one placing their trust in God. He was the eleventh son of Jacob and loved the most by his father, who made him a coat of many colors and ornaments. *Genesis 37* tells how his brothers hated him and even more so after he told them about his dreams of being in a high position with people bowing down to him. At the age of seventeen, he was sent to help his brothers tend to their father's flocks in Shechem. There they plotted to kill him. His coat was removed and he was thrown into a pit. Then it was decided that he would be taken out and sold to the Ishmeelites, who went on to sell him to Potiphar, an officer of the Pharaoh and captain of the guard, in Egypt. As a slave, then prisoner, there was virtually no hope for a good future, but Joseph held onto his faith. Later, after being able to interpret the Pharaoh's dreams, he was placed in that high position dreamed of for him. *Genesis 41:41* says that Joseph was placed in charge over the whole land of Egypt, where he would go on to save many Israelites from famine. Therefore, in looking back, he could see that God had a great plan for him, no matter the path, just as he had trusted.

Truth - I was watching one of my favorite television programs, *Seinfeld,* and there was an episode where one of the characters, George, was seeking the *best possible lie* to tell his fiancé in seeking to have a meeting with another woman without her knowing it. Of course, he was caught in the end, as most lies will. But we are human. We all sin and tell lies, be they intentionally or not. I just try to always be as honest of a person that I possibly can be. However, I must admit to having told a few lies to save face, gain an advantage in certain situations, and even to myself. There are just times that the *truth* is more of a beneficial or convenient thing for us, rather than being an absolute truth, as it is with God. It's just a great blessing that with Him, as Christians, our lies and other sins can be forgiven through repentance and worship.

While there may be lies in our words, God's Word is truth, and Jesus prayed for His disciples to be sanctified by the truth *(John 17:17)*, and in that truth all that believe in Jesus may be one, just as God and Himself are one *(verse 21)*. God sent a Son and loves us just as He does Him *(verse 23)*. Also, *Proverbs 23:23* tells us that to be secured and retained we should buy the truth and not sell it, along with gathering wisdom, discipline, and understanding. Therefore, along with God's truth, there has to be some effort on our parts in building upon it in being righteous, as there is obedience in the truth *(1 Peter 1:22)*. Further, E*phesians 6:14* says that, as a part of our Christian Armor, the truth should be worn as a belt buckled around our waists, meaning that it should a regular part of our daily makeup, in God's truth and our own.

Understanding - *Understanding* comes along with wisdom, which is learning or judgment. Therefore, as I have aged, I have a much greater understanding of many things that I did not have before. However, I must admit to at times still questioning why there continues to be so many hateful things going on in this world while God still continues to bless us. He is certainly not taking a blind eye to all the tragedies that continually occur and will punish those that are guilty. We must all just learn and understand that in God's plan there is much happiness along with suffering, and we grow in Him through both. Therefore, I have quit questioning Him, as I understand that all of my understanding is through Him. Whatever He wills it to be is to be, whether we question it or not. In the end the results are very rewarding for those that worship Him in all His understanding beyond theirs. So, while a newspaper report may down my spirits, they are uplifted in my understanding that through God a better tomorrow is always ahead of us if we abide in Him and praise Him in the face of anything that may be beyond our own understanding.

Solomon asked God for understanding for the discernment of justice (*1 Kings 3:11*), rather than for a long life, riches, or the life of his enemies. He answer was to be then given a wise and discerning heart, while there would never have been anyone like him before or in the future, plus he would be given riches and honor, while having no equal among other kings and live a long life, through walking in God's ways and obeying His statutes and commands as did his father David (*verses 12 – 14*). As such, I can see where understanding can be most rewarding for me as I walk in the ways of God through His will and understanding. On the other hand, *Isaiah 27:11* tells of people having very little or no understanding about anything. God has no compassion for them and will show them no favor. Also, *Mark 12:33* instructs me to love God with all of my heart, understanding and strength, no matter what happens, while loving my neighbor as myself is more important than anything they may have to offer in return. So, while I may not understand the things that they may do, their understanding is with God and not with me. In being loving and understanding, I will not be far from the kingdom of God, as was Mark (*verse 34*). Therefore, while I may have to control my feelings from time to time, I will always listen and obey God's instructions, as through His understanding my life will be better here and in the future beyond any questions.

Unemployment - After many years of work, I found myself becoming a victim of the tragedies of unemployment upon losing my job due to the economic crisis that occurred in our country at the time, entailing financial problems, the worries of a very uncertain future, and other issues, which lead to much stress and finally a stroke. However, while recovering in the hospital, I decided that it was time to get back to work in one way or another, and I knew that with God there is always work for those that are willing. I began singing at a few churches and giving testimony about how much I was still being blessed in spite of my many concerns, especially with my return to good health with no visible signs of my having had a stroke. Then I took on a volunteer job that would help many people around my city, and as a result, even in not seeing a paycheck for over a two-year period, my unemployment experience turned out to be quite rewarding for many others, and myself, with the outreach part of my work involving me in a number of community events and speaking at some area churches. The following is a portion of an article that appeared in the Detroit Free Press on October 11, 2011 concerning one of my activities:

Here's how to spot Medicare Fraud

While looking for a job, Ronald Huggins is using his free time to help Detroit senior citizens learn how to spot Medicare fraud.

He tells them to find a safe place for their Medicare card and to tuck it away. And he wants them -- or a trusted friend or family member -- to review all statements from the program to be sure they haven't been billed for care they never got.

"I tell people if they don't understand it, get someone else to read it," he said of the billing statements.

Huggins, of Detroit, is a laid-off human resources administrator for an automotive supplier. He was trained as a Senior Medicare Patrol volunteer in May by Detroit's Area Agency on Aging, a nonprofit group that is part of a national network that helps seniors with Medicare issues.

The Bible tells how Joshua, the commander of the forces of Israel, could have also joined the ranks of the unemployed by resting, retiring, or being cast aside for a younger replacement, with things like company downsizing not being an issue then. However, probably nearing the age of one hundred years old, God called him to work in leading the Israelites after the death of Moses. A successor was needed and Moses, recognizing in him the qualities of courage and efficient leadership that were needed for the position, had placed him before the high priest and publicly ordained him. In his new job, he would go far beyond having just an article being written about his deeds. An entire book in the Bible was written in devotion to him. The main thing is that with God there is always work that can result in different accolades and honors. He doesn't lay people off from their jobs. They do it to themselves through laziness, sin, disobedience, lack of desire, selfishness, and other reasons. As with many, it was quite difficult dealing with my sudden and unexpected unemployment but I wound up doing work that felt much more meaningful, rewarding, and appreciated in many ways than in any of my past paying jobs, which is the kind of work that God offers. Plus, I began feeling most confident that God would reward me with a nice paying job as well in His time, and one better than the one that I lost. Then, too, in working for God, there are no concerns about your age or abilities. He knows my heart and potential, plus He has a much better perspective on what I can become in answering His call. Therefore, as with *1 Samuel 3:10,* I listen for God's voice in my life as a servant and will hear what is best for me. And it was His that I heard during my hospital stay and many times over the course of my unemployment.

Unity - *Unity* is a whole composed of individual parts, and I can remember growing up when block clubs were common, with neighbors on streets banding together and working towards established goals. Nowadays, however, many people don't even know or associate with some of their neighbors or have any desire to do so. Then there are some that you would just love to have moved away from your neighborhood, be it willingly, forcefully, or legally. Therefore, rather than in unity, many are living as individual parts without ever achieving or even working towards the wholeness of unity. A lack of unity may been seen within the church, as well, with some members appearing most content with occupying their individual spots during weekly Sunday morning services, while seldom or never participating in any other church activities as a whole, like Bible study, prayer groups, congregational and religious celebrations, fund raising, fellowship and outreach events, etc. Unfortunately, these days there are just so many going their own ways in our neighborhoods and even in our churches, where different factions, splits, and leadership conflicts may drive people away from God and the church. Therefore, I believe that we need to encourage and concentrate our efforts on building unity in our churches, which should bring many back and also lead to a resurgence of unity in our neighborhoods, with people knowing and caring for each other, along with working together as a whole for the good of all.

Jesus prayed for unity in desiring that all believers would be as one, just as God, the Father, and Him were in each other. Then with us being in God and Jesus, the world would believe that He was sent by God *(John 17:20-21)*. Jesus had given us the glory that God gave Him, so that we may be as one, just as the Father and Son. With Jesus in us, and God in Him, we could be brought to complete unity and let the world know that God sent Him and loves us just as He has loved Jesus *(verses 22-23)*. The apostle Paul, also, stressed the importance of unity in the church. We should make every effort to keep the unity of the Spirit through a bond of peace, and there is *one* body, *one* Spirit, *one* hope, *one* Lord, *one* faith, *one* baptism, *one* God and Father of all *(Ephesians 4:4-6)*. He said that each church member has received a portion of grace from the Lord to perform a specific task *(verse 7),* with the leaders of the church (apostles, prophets, evangelists, pastors, and teachers) being gifts for saints, given in preparation for their works of service *(verses 11-12)*. Then the church grows as the body of the Lord builds itself up in love and continually strives towards maturity, with each member doing their work in unity *(verse 16)*. Therefore, we should pray for unity in our churches and for our leaders. Without unity, church membership will only continue to fall as people view the church and the Lord negatively. In unity, many may witness the power and glory of the Lord shining through the faithful and desire to see the same in them.

Victory - Over the course of my life, I have surely had my share of problems, failures and a number of unavoidable or unexpected battles. However, I know that I never have to succumb to defeat or give up, and have often found myself being more wiser, stronger, and determined, as a result, in battling back to victory, while better preparing myself to deal with any future negative circumstances. I am most confident that there can and will be success and victory no matter what confronts me, and it all started with my faith and trust in God, upon realizing that some things were just too much for me to handle on my own. I look to Him in prayer and have had so many answered in my favor. Never again will I try to go it alone, as I sometimes did in the past, for I know that in God is my victory.

Through God and Jesus we can witness and enjoy much victory. *Romans 8:28* tells us that God works for the good of those who love Him, and have been called according to His purpose. We can be more than conquerors through them and, as with *Romans 8:38-39,* I too am convinced that death, life, angels, devils, the present, the future, powers, height, depth, or anything else in creation can separate us from the love of God that is in Jesus our Lord. That is our victory and in that God works good in all situations. There is also much victory in the future to be witnessed by all that love God and Jesus. *Romans 8:18* adds that none of our present sufferings are worth comparing with the glory that will be revealed to us, according to Paul. In believing that, there can be much expectation and hope that many good things are always before us.

Virtue - *Virtue* is behavior showing high moral standards and some synonyms of the word are goodness, righteousness, morality, integrity, dignity, rectitude, honor, decency, respectability, nobility, worthiness, and purity, which are great qualities for Christians and non-Christians alike to exhibit. It would surely be a much better world if more people did. Just so sad to hear all the bad things that people are doing to each other these days from things like terrorism, murder, theft, rape, selfishness, hate, greed, fraud, infidelity... Also, when looking up the word, I found it to be number seven on the *Celestial Hierarchy,* which is a traditional hierarchy of angels ranked from lowest to highest into the following nine orders: *angels, archangels, principalities, powers, virtues, dominions, thrones, cherubim,* and *seraphim.*

My Bible defines *virtue* as being a natural good or power, while being *virtuous* represents purity. *Luke 6:19* tells of a whole multitude of people seeking to touch Jesus because virtue (power) was coming from Him and healing them all. Then *Philippians 4:8-9* encourages us to be virtuous people. We should think about things that are honest, honorable, just, pure, lovely, good report, and things of praise. We should put into practice whatever we have learned, received, heard, or seen from the Lord and the God of peace will be with us. Also, *2 Peter 1:3* is a reminder that His divine power has given us everything that we need for life and godliness through our knowledge of Him in calling us by His own glory and virtue. *Verse 4* adds that, in being virtuous people, we may participate in the divine nature and escape the corruption in the world caused by evil desires.

Waiting - I recently took my mother to her doctor's office for her checkup. Her appointment was scheduled for 11:00 A.M. but after over an hour we were still sitting there waiting for her name to be called. Finally we were called back only to sit in another room waiting until the doctor finally arrived to do his work. Then, I had to take my mother to her eye doctor's appointment where even more waiting was in store for us. Seems that there can just so much time spent waiting when our time could be put to much better use than being wasted. And then there are those really tough times that we may go through and find ourselves waiting most impatiently for things to get better soon. Those are the times that we need to call on God. In Him we can be confident and patient in knowing that our waiting will not be a waste of any time. When He delivers on His promises, we are able to sit back and reflect on how it was well worth the wait. Therefore, while there may be times that we may find ourselves being impatient, there are also times when waiting can be a real blessing.

It is told that Abraham had to endure some waiting. God had promised him that he would be blessed with many descendants (*Hebrews 6:14*). So Abraham waited patiently day after day, year after year. Finally his patience was rewarded as he received what he had been promised (*verse 15*). Abraham became the father of the Jewish nation, and, as in his case, God proves Himself to be faithful to us again and again. An important thing too is to remember that, while we may not enjoy waiting, what God does within us while we are waiting is as important as the things we are waiting for. So we have to be disciplined and confident in giving God time. As in *Psalms 130,* we should call on the Lord to hear our voices and have His ears attentive to our cries for mercy (*verse 2*). Plus, we should remember that in Him there is forgiveness for our sins (*verse 4*). Our souls must wait on the Lord and in His words our hopes must be placed (*verse 5*). Then through His unfailing love, our waiting can result in full redemption (*verse 7*).

Walking - Over the years, I have done a lot of walking for exercise and health reasons. I have, also, done a lot of walking in special events concerning things like Education, Breast Cancer Awareness, Multiple Sclerosis, Crime Prevention, Religion, Political and Community Concerns, Aid for Seniors and the Disabled, and etc. Then after becoming a mail carrier for the United States Postal Service, I walk many miles daily for my employment (purchased a measuring device and found that on average I may walk anywhere from 8 to 10 miles and over 22,000 steps), However, nothing compares to my walk with God that is far beyond any of my other walks and has no end. Yet, it only took a few steps to get me started. That was the day that I decided to give myself to the Lord and walked up before the congregation at my church to declare it to my pastor and all else that could hear. Now, even though my past walks were for some very good reasons, this walk means so much more as it will take me to my true destiny, which is an eternity of walking in the goodness and everlasting life of God.

As David, God has delivered me from many things and kept me from stumbling, in that I may walk before Him in the light of life *(Psalm 56:13),* along with walking before Him in the land of the living *(Psalm 116:9).* With the walk at my church, I was making a declaration to fulfill my vows to the Lord in the presence of all His people *(verse 14).* I am His servant as He frees me from all that binds me *(verse 16).* Then through my baptism, I was buried with Jesus in death, in that just as Jesus was raised from the dead through the glory of God, I too am able to live a new life *(Romans 6:4).* Now as a prisoner of the Lord, I am trying to live a life worthy of the calling that I have received in being completely humble, gentle, patient, and bearing with others in love, while making every effort to keep the unity of the Spirit through a bond of peace (*Ephesians 4:1 to*

3). I must be an imitator of God, as a dearly loved child, and live a life of love, just as Jesus loved us and gave Himself up as an offering and sacrifice to God *(Ephesians 5:1-2)*. Also, once living in darkness, I am now the light of the Lord and trying hard to live of a life of goodness, righteousness, and truth, and determined to find out what is most pleasing to the Lord as I live on through Him *(verses 8 to 10)*. And in walking in the light, I can be cleansed of all my sins through the blood of Jesus *(1 John 1:7)*.

Walls - The Great Wall of China is really amazing. With a continued series of fortifications beginning some two thousand years ago and made of stone, brick, earth, and other materials, it was originally constructed to protect the Chinese states and empires against the raids and invasions of various nomadic groups, like the Huns from the north. Spanning from east to west of China and winding up and down deserts, grasslands, mountains, and plateaus, it is approximately 12,170 miles. Nowadays it serves as a monument of the Chinese nation throughout history with maybe only 30% of it remaining in good condition because of the forces of nature and destruction by mankind resulting in it's decline. However, as great as that wall is, it may be nothing compared to the walls that we may build ourselves that at times can appear to be pretty indestructible. People may just place walls between themselves and others for a number of reasons, like grudges, jealousy, prejudice, hatred, insecurity, criminal associations, and etc. And they can place a wall between themselves and the Lord for various reasons as well. Then we may have those seemingly insurmountable walls in our lives that we need to conquer for our happiness, success, well-being, health, spirituality, and other things too.

The Bible describes walls even greater than the Great Wall of China. Before the Israelites could enter the Promised Land they would have to pass over Jordan and topple the walls that surrounded Jericho, which were described as being "fenced up to heaven" (*Deuteronomy 9:1*). The cities were great and the people, the Anakims, were great, tall, and most difficult to stand against (*verse 2*). However, no walls or obstacles can stand in the way of what God wants us to accomplish for Him. Facing a most humanly impossible challenge, the people were victorious in being obedient to God's directives. He would go before them, as a *consuming fire* in destroying the enemy, bringing them down, and driving them out quickly (*verse 3*). Just as then, if we stake claim to God's promises and are faithful, we can always topple our walls of any kind and walk in victory. The *Proverbs,* in a description of wisdom, tells of Solomon going by the field of a slothful man and the vineyard of a man lacking understanding, where he was to see the land covered with thorns and weeds, along with a broken down wall (*24:30-31*). He observed what he saw, considered it, and learned a valuable lesson from it (*verse 32*) in seeing how poverty and other things can come before us if we aren't careful, just as they can for robbers and armed men (*verse 34*). As *Psalms 122:7,* I want there to always be peace and prosperity within my walls.

War --I read where a scholar calculated that if you went back and chose any century at random in the past 5,000 years, about 96 out of 100 would indicate there having been a war of some kind in one part of the world or another. Yes, it is sad but true that war and violence appear to be an unavoidable part of life and there has seldom, if ever, been an extended period of time, where there was total peace on earth, or ever will. I, read where in 2014 the United States was declared to have been at war in Afghanistan and Iraq. However, if you take into consideration the number of countries where there were special operational forces involved in combat, special missions, or advising, and training foreign forces, it could actually be said that we were involved in 134 wars. Then it was also reported that there were 10 major ongoing wars at that time, with the war in Syria being the most deadly, and with no solution in sight.

As with *Psalm 120:6,* we may always find ourselves living among those that hate peace. And even if a man speaks of peace, many will still be for war (*verse 7*). *James 4* says that we should submit to God in ending war. We fight and quarrel because of our desires that battle within us (*verse 1*). We want something and don't get it, so we kill and covet, while still not receiving what we want, no matter the quarrel or fight, because of God not being asked (*verse 2*). Then when we do ask God for something, it is not received because it was asked for with the wrong motives (*verse 3*). As with *Psalm 68:30,* I just wish that those that delight in war will find themselves scattered, along with having no will, power, or desire to be involved in any type of future wars. Then I delight in what Jesus prophesized concerning the wars of our time. He said that there would be wars and rumors of wars but we should not be alarmed for, even with nation against nation and kingdom against kingdom, it will all come to pass, though just not yet (*Matthew 24:6-7*). And I hope and pray that there will soon be that day, as with *Isaiah 2:4,* where there will be no warring among the nations and no learning of war either.

***Warnings*—** For me, the stroke that I suffered on October 20, 2010 was a warning and wakeup call, as I realized that some lifestyle changes had to be made for me to continue on in this life and not face any additional health issues that possibly could be avoided through just taking better care of myself. Warnings promote caution and give notice of approaching danger. Continuing on in the direction that I was headed in could cause me to suffer additional strokes or even beyond, including death, was what my doctor warned. However, in changing, my diet, exercising, losing weight, not allowing the little things to stress me, and continuing on in my spiritual journey, I feel great now in mind, body, and soul with a much more positive outlook on my health and future.

As children of faith, we should heed the warnings that God gives us. He can guide us through all things. Plus the advice from others that we trust can be a valuable tool for us too in making the right decisions in our lives. In dealing with my stroke, I prayed and looked to God for answers. Then I obeyed the instructions of my doctor concerning medicine, healthy eating, exercise, and etc. So the main thing is that I didn't ignore my warning, as some may do and only hope for things to get better. I acted on it, or I could have suffered a fate as the people of Judah once did. *Jeremiah* tells a story of how Jeremiah had prophesized the fall of Jerusalem. God has issued a warning that Jeremiah delivered to the people. However, they ignored him and continued living in sin beyond the demands and wishes of God. The end result was their defeat at the hands of the Babylonians.

Wealth - Many think of wealth in terms of money or material possessions, however, in definition, it can include anything of abundance, affluence, riches, utility, natural resources, labor, or more. Then there are many different views concerning wealth. I read a very interesting thing by one man, named Tim Hartford. He says that a small child is wealthier than the 2 billion poorest people in the world because a child has no debt. And for me the most important thing about wealth is how it is utilized once attained. On January 13, 2016, there would be instant wealth for those picking the winning numbers for a Michigan Lottery Game with a record prize of 1.5 Billion dollars. I heard this morning, on January 14, 2016, that there were three winners. My hope and prayer is that those extremely blessed winners put their newly found wealth to good use benefiting themselves and as many others as possible.

It is true that wealth can be a good or bad thing and, as *Psalm 49:6,* it may be a wise thing to steer away from those that trust in their wealth and are boastful of it; certainly something that God does not approve of. Rich or poor, the main thing that we have in common is that the Lord is the maker of us all (*Proverbs 22:2*), and I truly believe that having a good name for myself is more important than any great wealth that I may acquire, as says *verse 1*. Humility and a fear of the Lord will bring me wealth, honor, and life (*verse 4*). And in being a generous man, I know that my sharing with others will be greatly blessed (*verse 9*). As *1Timothy 6:17* commands, I will never be arrogant in wealth or place my hope in wealth because of its uncertainty. My hope will always be placed in God, and I believe in being rich in good deeds and having the generosity and willingness to share with others as *verse 18*. Therefore, it is without question that if I had been one of those lottery winners, my wealth would surely be put to very good use as a blessing for many others and myself.

Weariness - At times, we may all be subjected to just feeling really physically and mentally tired from our work, family friends, uncertainty, exertion, strain, stress, bills, impatience, dissatisfaction, travel, bad news... Therefore, we need things to uplift us in spirit and energy. Taking a day off from work or vacation to get away from it all may help. Then there are other things like my walking to get things off of my mind and then taking time out for prayer as often as possible, especially in the morning to get me started out on the right foot and then at bedtime after the Lord has guided me safely through my day. And of course, there may just be times that you have to steer yourself away from those individuals or things that may be responsible for some of the weariness you are experiencing.

In *Genesis 27:46,* Rebekah tells Isaac of being weary from life because of the daughters of Heth, which is an early example in the Bible of the weariness that others may cause a person. Then Job (*Job 10:1*) tells of his soul being weary of his life and would offer no complaint upon himself while speaking in the bitterness of his soul. He, also, tells of the weary being at rest (*Job 3:17*); something that he greatly needed as we all may from time to time. In my reading, I find *Isaiah 40:29-31* to be an inspiration and directive for me concerning weariness. It says that the Lord gives strength to the weary regardless of our age and even when we stumble and fall. With our hope placed in Him, we can have our strength renewed. And in that, we can run and not be weary, plus walk and not be faint because of the weariness of our lives.

Will-- In definition, *will* may be one's mind, determination, purpose, desire, wish, request, joy, delight, pleasure, intention, choice, longing, or etc.

In Biblical terms, *will* is simply the desire to do something, and in our relation to Jesus, we should do God's will (*Mark 3:35*). Is that too much to ask for?

Windows - I had sent a text message from my cell phone to my friend, Brenda Morgan, and told her that I was working on some writing and was in thought concerning the word *windows*. She texted me back writing; *Windows are like eyes to the soul. You can look in and out. You can look for the windows of Heaven to from which your blessings are poured out. Without windows, you feel locked in, boxed in with no way to escape, etc.* Found those words to be quite interesting and insightful.

In respect to the words of my friend, I read *Malachi 3:10* where it tells of how the people would be blessed through bringing their whole tithe into their storehouse. The Lord would open up the windows of Heaven and there would not be enough room in their storehouses to receive the blessings that would be poured out to them. Therefore, the windows of Heaven are always open to those that are obedient in their tithe giving and worship. And they may be also opened for the passing of judgment for the sinful as in *Genesis 7:11-12* where the windows of Heaven were opened and it rained over the earth for forty days and forty nights.

Wisdom— *Wisdom* is the ability to think and act using knowledge, experience, understanding, common sense, and insight, plus it is said that people generally recognize it when they encounter it, like having to make a wise decision and actually doing it. Also, wise people are said to share optimism that all of their life's problems can be solved and may always exhibit calmness in facing difficult decisions. Further, wisdom may not come from your experiences but rather from the reflection on the lessons learned from the experience. Plus, I, also, read that age and intelligence aren't a guarantee for wisdom as cultivating it may be a deliberate choice, possibly meaning that some may never be that wise because they will never work at it in spite of their age or their intelligence level. Additionally, wise people are said to have the ability to balance self-interest and the common good, challenge the status quo, aim to understand rather than judge, focus on purpose over pleasure, and learn from everyone.

The Bible speaks much about wisdom. *Proverbs 4:7* says that wisdom is supreme and we should get it. It may cost all that we have but it is in understanding that we must get. For wisdom is excellence (*Ecclesiastes 2:13*) with fear of the Lord being the starting point of wisdom and the knowledge of Him is in understanding (*Proverbs 9:10*). Then we must be mindful of sinning against wisdom. Whoever finds the Lord finds life and receives favor from Him, while those failing to find Him harms themselves and all that hate Him love death (*Proverbs 8:35-36*). To him that pleases God receives wisdom, knowledge, and happiness but given to the sinner is the task of gathering and storing up wealth to only hand over to those that please God (*Ecclesiastes 2:26*). Solomon once asked for wisdom and, in showing his love for the Lord and by walking according to the statutes of his father David (*1 Kings 3:3*), was given wisdom, a very great insight, and a measureless understanding of things, with his wisdom being greater than all the men of the east and of Egypt (*1 Kings 4:29-30*). Then for those wishing to read more about wisdom, *Ecclesiastes 7 thru 12* tells much with the conclusion being that in wisdom we should fear God and keep His commandments as our whole duty, as God will bring our works into judgment, with every secret thing, whether good or evil (*Ecclesiastes 12:13-14*).

Witnessing - *Witnessing* is giving a firsthand account of something seen, heard, or experienced and for Christians it is the sharing of our heartfelt faith in Jesus revealing to others what He has personally done in our lives. I told many that I was a witness during my stroke, with the calmness settling over me and the light of the Lord sparkling at my fingertips assuring me that I would be okay. And even my doctor told me that someone from above had to have been looking down upon me on that night. I gave much testimony detailing the events of what the doctor said could have and should have been much worst for me concerning the stroke, with it being very well received by most. I just heard from one doubter, a man without faith that summed it all up to good luck. However, we are not called to be lawyers or judges. We are only called to be witnesses and, when it comes to the Lord, I do not believe in luck.

1 Corinthians 2:1-5 presents a great example of witnessing through the apostle Paul. On a missionary journey, he landed in Corinth where he spoke amid reports concerning the moral and spiritual state of things in the Corinthian church. On this occasion, he told his brethren that he had not come to them with excellency of speech or wisdom in declaring his testimony of God. He was determined to know not anything among them, except for Jesus and His crucifixion. He had come in weakness and fear, with much trembling. And his message and preaching were not to be of wise and persuasive words, but with a demonstration of the Spirit's power, which is witnessing, and he wanted them to have their faith not resting on the wisdom of men but on God's power.

Words - I seem to have always been a man of words and enjoy reading and hearing the especially inspiring ones. Of course, there are the many great ones from Aristotle, Socrates, John F. Kennedy, Martin Luther King Jr., and etc. However, through my love of all kinds of music, I have found a few personal favorites there as well. For example, Mick Jagger of the Rolling Stones sings that you can't always get what you want but if you try some time you just might find that you get what you need.

With the Lord, trying is through praying. Another is Donald Fagen of Steely Dan singing that they have a name for the winners in the world, like the Crimson Tide for Alabama's college football team, but he wants people to call him Deacon Blues when he is a loser. With the Lord, you can always have a good name in winning or losing through faith. Then there was Philppe Wynn of the Spinners singing that he could never repay another's love. With the Lord, what more could you say?

Paul spoke of the wisdom of words. He said that Jesus did not send him to Baptize but to preach the Gospel without the wisdom of words in which the cross of Jesus would have no effect (*1 Corinthians 1:17*). Concerning the message of the cross, it was only foolishness to the perished but the power of God for those being saved, for it was written that the wisdom of the wise would be destroyed and would bring nothing to the wise (*verses 18-19*). In spite of our sins against God and Jesus, God has committed us to the message or words of reconciliation (*2 Corinthians 5:19*). And through Jesus are the words of eternal life (*John 6:68*). There are words of faith in the good teachings that we should follow through the Lord (*1 Timothy 4:6*), and the Word should be preached in preparedness, in or out of season, and with correctness, patience, and careful instruction (*2 Timothy 4:2*), along with encouragement, which is what I greatly desire in writing words that are not only approving, educational, and inspirational for my readers, but also viewed favorably in the eyes of God and Jesus.

Works - In the workplace I have always been considered to be an efficient, intelligent, ambitious, and hard worker, and it has resulted in much praise, awards, bonuses, and promotions being bestowed upon me over the years. Likewise, I am trying hard to be the best worker that I can possibly be for God and Jesus.

I want my light to continue to shine in whatever work that I am doing but, as *Matthew5:16,* want people to see my good work and give the praise to God in Heaven. And as *Titus 2:7,* I want to always be an example of doing good works while exhibiting integrity and sincerity.

Worship - *Worship* is the reverent honor and homage paid to God, a sacred personage, or to any object regarded as being sacred. It also means giving God the best that He has given us and we have to be careful with what we do with the best that we have. However, many have and still worship things that are not of God or sacred in any way, like idols, money, material possessions, success, family, lust, greed, power, jobs, race, automobiles, homes... Then many can be very selfish and arrogant with what they have been blessed with. While others, some even in the Church, may express an outward worship of God but not a true inward love of Him. And I must admit that there was a time during my youth that I went to church only because my parents demanded it. On the outside it may have appeared that I enjoyed being there but on the inside was not there for worship and couldn't wait to get home and enjoy the things that I really wanted to be doing on my days off from school and other things. However, I am now very much a worshipper on the outside and on the inside, while trying hard to do the best that I can with my blessings and being a blessing to others, plus offering my heart in love and adoration to God and Jesus.

With *Exodus 20:3, The Ten Commandments,* God tells us that we should have no other gods before Him, meaning that our worship should be focused on Him above all those other things that I mentioned. Then *Matthew 4:10* reinforces that as Jesus told the devil that worship is for the Lord our God and that He be served only. As *Psalm 95:6-7* says, we have a call to bow down in worship, to kneel before the Lord our Maker. For He is our God and we are the people of His pasture and the flock under His care. Our church pastors and ministers have the task of preparing us for worship jus as the Lord instructed Moses (*Exodus 19:10-11*). And there is nothing wrong with private worship and is a great thing as *Matthew 6:6* encourages prayer and says that we can go into our rooms, close our doors, and pray to our unseen Father, who will see what was done in secret and reward us openly. We may also worship as a family, like *Deuteronomy 16:11* where the person and their sons, daughters, menservants, maidservants, Levites, strangers, fatherless, and widows were to rejoice before the Lord our God in a place that He had chosen for them to dwell in His name. Further, our worship should be joyful and instructive. In making a joyful noise before the Lord, we should serve Him in gladness and come before His presence with singing (*Psalm 100:1-2*). We should hear His instruction, be wise, and never ignore it, for those listening, watching daily at His doors and waiting at His doorway, will be blessed (*Proverbs 8:33-34*).

Wrath - *Wrath* is extreme anger with synonyms of rage, fury, outrage, spleen, vexation, crossness, displeasure, annoyance, irritation... It is also retributory punishment for an offense or a crime, and divine chastisement. Then it is listed as one of the *seven deadly sins,* also known as the capital vices or cardinal sins, along with *pride, greed, lust, envy, gluttony,* and *sloth,* with Dante Alighieri, the Italian poet and moral philosopher (1265 to 1321) seeing it as being the root of murder and assault. He believed that this sin led to other sins and transgressions including violence, along with a desire to seek revenge and a failure to forgive. In vengeance there was a love of justice perverted to revenge and spite. Yet, I read too that it was extreme anger that was chiefly used for humorous or rhetorical effect. Humorous? I view wrath as Noah did when he saw the great flood as being a sign of the wrath of God. Nothing humorous about that! God saw a need to punish the people on Earth and did so, just as He may do today with all the sin and craziness going on all over.

The Bible defines *wrath* as simply being *anger,* which is feeling indignation. In *Genesis 18:30,* Abraham asked the Lord not to be angry. *Deuteronomy 1:37* tells of the Lord being angry with Moses. *Psalm 2:12* says that we should kiss the Lord so that He will not be angry and destroy us in His way. His wrath can flare up suddenly and those that trust in Him are blessed. God is a righteous judge and expresses His wrath every day (*Psalm 7:11*). And, as *Psalm 79:5* asks, can He be angry forever? As *Exodus 32:22,* we should ask the Lord not to be angry with us even though we may be prone to evil. The Lord is compassionate and we may not face His wrath as He causes His goodness to pass before us (*Exodus 33:19*). He can proclaim His name in our presence and have mercy on whom He chooses to have mercy on and compassion for whom He has compassion, which could be the reason why we have not faced His wrath though we may be greatly deserving of it during these times when the world can be a really hateful and ungodly place. This is just a world where a harsh word can stir up anger where a gentle answer would turn away wrath as says *Proverbs 15:1.* Rather than facing the wrath of God, it would be great if, as *Ephesians 4:31,* we could get rid of all bitterness, rage, anger, brawling, slander, and every form of malice. Just be kind and compassionate to one another, plus forgiving, just as the Lord forgives us (*verse 32*) and spares us from His wrath even when we are not that deserving.

Writing - Upon viewing my first book of 334 pages, *Forever A Man With The Lord: Huggy's Journey Of Faith,* a visiting minister at church asked me if I would be writing any additional books. My answer was that I wasn't sure if I had much left to place in another book. He then responded that not only was there another book in me but maybe even more beyond that. Now at 323 pages into this book, I can agree with him and am thinking about what my next journey will be with my writing beyond this second effort. Have been thinking about a novel and some story lines. But maybe the Spirit will direct me again, just hopefully not from a hospital bed. However, any direction will be viewed favorably and have me back writing in whatever direction I am spiritually or individually led. I believe that writing is one of my God-given gifts and should be utilized as much as possible in being a blessing and inspiration to others. I see so many gifts and talents being wasted and was most guilty of that myself. Hopefully, my writing will be a testament of my continued journey of faith.

My Men's Devotional Bible says that *different authors, with different writing styles, wrote the Bible in different eras of history, with different purposes in mind as they wrote.* Made up of 66 individual books, the Bible contains the very Words of God written through different men over a long period of time, just as the writing of my books has taken a considerable amount of time in me wanting to write words worthy and in much worship, honor, and praise of God and Jesus. Then with my first writings being centered on my spiritual journey and written more in terms of my worship and devotion, these writings were to be educational as well. Also, it is hoped that my writing style may be viewed as being a bit different from other writers in church and with a different purpose just as the writers of old. *Jeremiah 30:2* tells of Jeremiah being told by the Lord to write in a book all the words that had been spoken to him, and I hope that the Lord continues to be my encourager in my writings of Him in my books. However, while some may consider me to be an author because of my writing, the Lord is my author as *Hebrews 5:9* says that He is the author of our salvation, while *Hebrews 12:2* says too that He is the author of our faith.

Year - My hope and prayer for this year is that we communicate and keep in touch more. We should always do that because we never know if our last communication will ultimately be our last. I have a number of family members, old friends, and others that I may communicate with from time to time concerning birthdays, holidays, and other matters. Then heading into the 2015 holiday season I got to thinking? Normally it is myself in many situations initiating the communications. So, I decided that I would not initiate any contacts over the holidays in seeing whom I would hear from. The result was pretty disappointing. Out of the many that I usually communicate with, I heard from so few. I know that our lives can be really busy and hectic from time to time. However, a phone call, text message, email, Internet association, or any other form of communication should never be beyond reason. Hopefully, even if not with me, you do find the time to communicate with the Lord each and every day throughout 2016 and beyond. And please accept my sincere apologies for any of my failures of communication as I may find myself being as negligent as anyone else. In sadness, I am writing this as only a few weeks into this new year of 2016, some that I know have already passed away.

Yoke - One definition of the word is in cause with two people or things to be joined together in a close relationship, and I have truly been yoked in my relationships with God and Jesus.

There have certainly been many times in my life that I have felt being yoked by so many unpleasant things being cast upon me, however *Galatians 5:1* tells me that it is for freedom that Jesus has set me free and, in standing firm, I never have to let myself be burdened against the yoke of slavery or any other things that I desire not to.

What Next? More poems, more songs, more inspirational messages, more words, more about myself, more about current events, more about things that I see and feel, more about family, friends and others, more about my feelings, more about my victories, more about my failures, more about my ambitions, more about my past, present, and my future, more about my love and concern for others, more about my education, more about my past, present, and future employment, more about my worries and community concerns, more about you and yours, just more about anything and everything that I am encouraged and inspired to write about? At this point, I have no answer. However, I am sure that any of my future efforts will be through the love and direction of God and Jesus. They direct me in all that I do and always will. And I don't worry about the non-believers. Just hope that many may become believers when they find themselves in situations where they can't help but believe that there is a God looking down upon them. My stroke was a great example. Luck? The medical staff that attended to me when I was taken to the hospital had no clue for what was really going on with me, even though their education and experience should have given them some. However, the doctor had a different view and told me that there was definitely someone looking down upon me on that evening. And he believed as I did that it was the voice of the Lord encouraging me that all would be well. Just as he said, many that don't have a church should find one as our ultimate physician resides in Heaven.

My first book, of 334 pages, Forever A Man With The Lord: Huggy's Journey of Faith, was an extensive collection of my inspirational poems, songs, thoughts, reflections, stories, and messages. This book, which may be best described as a dictionary of my spiritual journey, was intended to be even more inspirational, along with being a lot more biblical, educational, and insightful. Hopefully, I have accomplished that. In the proofreading of my book, I found myself being even more enlightened concerning certain things, and in being a spiritual person it entails a lifetime of learning and focusing on God and Jesus as they direct our lives in spirit, faith, truth, love, understanding, and so very much more.

RAYMOND SANDERS HUGGINS - My father left us in death as I was at a very young age, however he laid the foundation for the kind of man that I have become and still hope to become. I am sure that he would be proud of many things that I have accomplished and stood by me when things weren't going as planned, along with my many mistakes. Much love, honor, and respect go out to my earthly father that I hope to see again some day in Heaven.

HUGGY